DOWNCAST

Biblical and Medical Hope for Depression

JENNIFER HUANG HARRIS, MD
HAROLD G. KOENIG, MD
JOHN R. PETEET, MD

The Christian Medical & Dental Associations was founded in 1931 and currently serves more than 19,000 members; coordinates a network of Christian healthcare professionals for personal and professional growth. It sponsors student ministries in medical and dental schools; conducts overseas healthcare projects for underserved populations; addresses policies on healthcare, medical ethics and bioethical and human rights issues; distributes educational and inspirational resources; provides missionary healthcare professionals with continuing education resources; and conducts international academic exchange programs.

For more information:

Christian Medical & Dental Associations
P.O. Box 7500
Bristol, TN 37621-7500
888-230-2637
www.cmda.org • main@cmda.org

Editing by Mandi Mooney.
Cover design and interior layout by Jay Huron.

ISBN 978-1-7344968-2-6

Library of Congress Control Number: 2020937940

Printed in the United States of America

Dedication

This book is dedicated to Dr. David B. Biebel, who died on May 15, 2018 at the age of 68. Dave was the first author of the original version of this book (titled *New Light on Depression* and published by Zondervan). He was a minister, award-winning author and editor. Dave was born in Boston, Massachusetts on August 13, 1949. He graduated from Windsor High School in Windsor, Vermont, where he received numerous awards for his athletic abilities in baseball and other sports. After high school, Dave attended and graduated from Gordon College in Hamilton, Massachusetts, with a bachelor of arts degree in 1970 and then a master of theological studies degree in 1973. After his ordination, he pastored two churches: Trinity Evangelical Free Church in Windsor as the associate pastor, and Evangelical Free Church of Carney, Michigan as senior pastor. Dave served as co-director with his father, Warren Biebel, of Singing Hills Christian Conference Center in Plainfield, New Hampshire from 1981 to 1987. During this time, he also obtained a doctor of ministry degree in personal wholeness from Gordon-Conwell Theological Seminary in 1986.

Since 1987, Dave focused on the interface of faith and health, editing two national Christian medical magazines and publishing widely in this area. He edited the Physician magazine for Focus on the Family from 1990 to 1992, followed by the Christian Medical & Dental Associations' flagship journal *Today's Christian Doctor* from 1992 to 2011, before joining the staff of Florida Hospital's Publishing division as Managing Editor in mid-2011. He was a prolific author throughout his life, authoring or co-authoring 20 books, including the Gold Medallion winner *New Light on Depression* and the bestseller *If God Is So Good, Why Do I Hurt So Bad*. His first book, *Jonathan You Left Too Soon*, is considered a classic in the field. Just prior to releasing his last book, *Away in a Manger: The Christmas Story from a Nativity Scene Lamb's Point of View*, he re-released *Making God Visible: How to Help a Heartbroken Friend* as a part of his own publishing endeavor, Healthy Life Press.

Dave founded Healthy Life Press in 2008 to help new authors publish their works, especially those who had something to contribute to the topic of spiritual wholeness. This endeavor involved collaboration with a significant group of authors that brought forth more than 40 new titles that are still available through the Healthy Life Press website (www.healthylifepress.com). Throughout the years of his ministry, Dave was a guest on scores of radio and TV programs nationwide. He authored or collaborated on numerous magazine articles (outdoors and Christian) and several book segments. He spoke in workshops, seminars and conference settings throughout the country on the theme of breaking through a loss to find renewal and joy again. His goal was to help people attain and retain optimal physical, emotional, spiritual and relational health (personal wholeness) so they could love the Lord with their whole heart, soul, mind and strength, as well as their neighbors as themselves.

David also had a vibrant personal life. Dave loved sports, hunting, fishing and golfing, he had a passion for cooking and he was an avid photographer. He enjoyed bowhunting for elk and deer, mushrooming, camping and otherwise roaming the beautiful Rockies with his wife, Ilona, and the company of his beloved Springer Spaniels. He also published articles and photos in a local sports magazine and articles for Prudent Living, Inc. of Windsor. We will dearly miss him, but Dave lives on in his many books, articles and a generation of students and colleagues he inspired and nurtured in their faith (including this author).

Harold G. Koenig, MD
Professor of Psychiatry & Behavioral Sciences
Associate Professor of Medicine
Director, Center for Spirituality, Theology and Health
Duke University Medical Center, Durham, North Carolina
Adjunct Professor, Dept of Medicine, King Abdulaziz University, Jeddah, Saudi Arabia
Adjunct Professor of Public Health, Ningxia Medical University, Yinchuan, P.R. China
Visiting Professor, Shiraz University of Medical Sciences, Shiraz, Iran

This book is also dedicated to my parents, who taught me the value of love and perseverance, and to my husband, who showed me the riches of grace.

– *Jennifer Huang Harris, MD*

Table of Contents

Foreword

In July 2008, my wife Pam and I had just finished 12 years of ministry in Kenya as medical missionaries, and we were returning home to the U.S. It had been an extremely challenging five-year term of service at Tenwek hospital for several reasons. Just six months before returning home, we had faced the need to consider an evacuation during nationwide violence after a disputed presidential election. Pam experienced daily mood swings with frequent tears and much anxiety during our final four months in Kenya. Though I was a physician, I attributed to my wife's emotional lability to the tense days in which we lived. We regularly talked through the stresses we faced as a family and as a missionary community, but I never considered a diagnosis of depression. I am so thankful our mission sending agency immediately sent us to a debriefing and renewal conference in Colorado, where a professional counselor suspected Pam was depressed. He recommended she seek help from a Christian counselor and/or mental health professional near our home in Michigan. His final instruction to me: "Mike, don't talk about Kenya or going back to Kenya until Pam gives you permission to do so." We found help from a caring Christian mental health professional and a physician assistant friend who immediately put Pam on Prozac. It took several months, but slowly she returned to her normal emotional baseline that I had known for nearly 17 years of marriage. She eventually regained the peace and joy she had lost. Eleven months after we left Kenya, she woke up one morning and told me, "Honey, I had a good thought this morning about Tenwek, let's go back." We returned to Kenya after a two-year time of healing and restoration for Pam. Since 2008, her story has given hope and encouragement to several hurting and downcast missionaries and friends around the world.

Oh, how I wish this book had been available to me in 2008! Whether you are a healthcare professional, someone who has suffered from depression, a family member, a pastor, a counselor or you are just personally interested in knowing more about a problem that impacts 7 to 10 percent of Americans each year, this book is for you! Drs. Jennifer Harris, Harold Koenig and John Peteet have given us a wonderful tool for the understanding of depression in its various presentations. They have also done a superb job of presenting different strategies for handling depression and living with depression. Their work combines the best medical science and psychiatric research with sound scriptural truth. They address the common myths about depression and tell us stories of the impact of depression in the lives of several well-known individuals in the history of the church. The final three chapters on the critical roles of faith, hope and love in defeating depression are powerful and filled with truth from God's Word. I believe *Downcast* will become a resource in high demand by healthcare professionals and mental health professionals alike, and it will also be sought out by a general public coming to understand that depression is a whole person disorder. I was especially moved by Dr. Koenig's powerful testimony of transformation, taking him from living on the streets of San Francisco, California to the halls of academic medicine as one of the leading authorities in the world on the critical role of spiritual care to comprehensive, whole person care. Given the COVID-19 pandemic's impact upon our sense of well-being and security in 2020, it is indeed appropriate for CMDA to publish *Downcast* as a treatise with hope for recovery during tenebrous times.

Mike Chupp, MD, FACS
Chief Executive Officer
Christian Medical & Dental Associations

PART I:
UNDERSTANDING
DEPRESSION

CHAPTER 1

INTRODUCTION:
Why Are You Downcast, O My Soul?

My tears have been my food
day and night,
while men say to me all day long,
"Where is your God?"...

Deep calls to deep
in the roar of your waterfalls;
all your waves and breakers
have swept over me...

I say to God my Rock,
"Why have you forgotten me?
Why must I go about mourning,
oppressed by the enemy?"

My bones suffer mortal agony
as my foes taunt me,
saying to me all day long,
"Where is your God?"

*Why are you **downcast**, O my soul?*
Why so disturbed within me?
Put your hope in God,
for I will yet praise him,
my Savior and my God.

—Psalm 42, NIV 1984

Depression asks questions. Of all those who come to our offices seeking psychiatric care, those who struggle with depression often bring the most questions. "Why am I depressed?" "Why can't I get over this?" "How long am I going to feel this way?" The Psalms, too, are full of these questions. *"Why are you **downcast**, O my soul?"* the writer David asks in Psalm 42. *"Why have you forgotten me?"* *"Where is your God?"*

Why am I depressed? That question is not easy to answer because depression is not simple.

At first, the answer individuals give to themselves may seem straightforward: I'm depressed because I don't have a job. I'm depressed because I'm single and alone. I'm depressed because I'm struggling with illness.

But not all those without a job are depressed nor are those who are single. Not all who have financial struggles or are being treated for cancer are depressed. And the opposite may be true. There are those for whom everything seems to be going well with their health, relationships, job, personal life, etc. who find themselves inexplicably mired down in depression. Depression is not so straightforward.

Those who would simplify depression often do so in disservice to those who suffer.

We can be some of the worst culprits in the church. In churches where the dominant tone is often that of celebration, joy and victory, it can be extremely hard to walk in the door feeling like your existence is in a vastly different, discordant minor key. As a church, we may judge those with depression for exhibiting a weakness, a lack of faith or perhaps even evidence of unconfessed sin. And even if the church tries to exhibit more compassion toward the depressed, often the attempts fall flat. There's no need to still be sad, they tell us "Rejoice always" (1 Thessalonians 5:16, ESV). "…God causes all things to work together for the good…" (Romans 8:28, NASB). That may be true, but it does not relieve the deep pain of suffering. Depression may remain immovable, despite attempts to trust God, attempts to pray, attempts to be faithful. So the person retreats, hides their depression from others, pastes a smile on their face at church or perhaps stops going at all. And because even those with depression may believe this is just a faith problem, or perhaps they're not trying hard enough, they do not seek any other help and suffer alone. There is a lot of fear and skepticism, and perhaps shame, about using approaches other than religious ones to address depression.

On the other side, many of those in medicine tend to see depression as a problem with the brain. It's easy to do so. If the only tool one wields is a hammer, one had better hope the problem is a nail. So, when someone walks in the clinic with depression, doctors prescribe an antidepressant because that's all they have time to do. Or doctors may send depressed patients to therapy to examine their negative thought patterns or uncover childhood traumas. Tremendous benefits have been seen with medication and therapy, but an exclusively medical approach is often superficial and may ignore the underlying issues. One might draw the analogy of using Tylenol to reduce a fever, without addressing the underlying disease. Deeper issues are at stake.

There is a sense in which depression sees things rightly about our current existence. In this fallen and broken world, we experience disappointment, loss and pain. We experience suffering caused by others, we experience suffering we've caused ourselves and we experience suffering that comes out of the blue. And when we reflect on the brokenness of this world, our own brokenness, the brokenness of our relationships, and how far they all fall short of what should be, the only appropriate response is grief and sadness. The depression we struggle with itself is part of that brokenness. This brokenness gives rise to questions about God. Is God truly sovereign? Is God good? If He is, then why am I struggling so? Where are you, God?

> *Why are you **downcast**, O my soul?*
> *Why so disturbed within me?*
> *Put your hope in God,*
> *for I will yet praise him,*
> *my Savior and my God.*
> *(Psalm 42:11, NIV 1984)*

The Hebrew word translated as "**downcast**" is *shachach*, meaning to be bowed down, humbled. Depression weighs heavy, and the posture of depression is that of one bowed down and turned in on one's self. Depression is full of brooding, dark rumination, a lack of direction or purpose. Yet what is notable about this Psalm, and most of the Psalms, is that though the Psalmist does not shy away from the pain and despair, he doesn't end there. *"Put your hope in God,"* he exhorts himself, *"for I will yet praise him."* There is an unbending as he looks upward and outward toward God. He has a certainty that at some point, there will be an end to these dark clouds, and he will see the sun.

As Christians, our approach to mental health is different because our end goal, our underlying values and our ultimate hope are different. We seek the help of therapy and medication as mercies provided by God for our minds and bodies but our hope is not in them for our salvation. Ultimately, our hope is in God.

We write this book as fellow humans who struggle with depression ourselves, as family members who have loved ones with depression, as psychiatrists who have seen patients benefit greatly from medication and as believers who are deeply convinced God has something to say to those who suffer from depression. We have written this book because while there are thoughtful books out there about depression from the perspective of faith, or useful volumes about psychological treatment and medication, we have not really found a book that can shed light on the complexity of how these all come together.

This book is for those who struggle with depression and for those with loved ones with depression, as well as for pastors, doctors, clinicians, counselors and those in ministry. This book is a comprehensive guide to understanding what depression is, causes for depression, and strategies for fighting and living with depression. It is also a reference for those looking for Christian guidance on subjects such as medication (Chapter 5), psychotherapy and counseling options (Chapter 6), suicidal thoughts and hospitalization (Chapter 9). In this book, we hope to help you walk by faith through the dark path of depression.

CHAPTER 2

DEFINITIONS:
What is Depression?

Case: Sarah

"By my late 30s," she writes, "I had suffered a series of losses over a period of a few years. After years of struggling with infertility, I had conceived, only to lose my unborn child through miscarriage in the fourth month. The grief was deep and painful, but I was not debilitated by it. In fact, I experienced a newfound strength in the wake of it as my faith sustained me…

"A few years later, to our delight, my husband and I adopted a 9-year-old boy who had known great loss and trauma in his own short life. A few months later I conceived again, this time ending in a ruptured tubal pregnancy that almost took my life. There were new waves of grief, but once again I also felt inner strength and resolve. I felt God's power in very tangible ways and knew God would weave the grief into my life in healing ways.

"Within a short time, we began to experience major upheaval as we tried to help our son forge a new life for himself. We had expected this, given his prior life events, but it still stretched us in every way. I loved being a mom, though I also experienced the discouragement of realizing that all the love in the world for our son could not meet his deepest needs. In his young adolescent years, we watched in pain and the worst kind of helplessness as our son descended into a life of drug abuse. As we struggled to anchor him through this time, one of his birth parents swept back into our lives, which sent our son into a tailspin. At the tender age of 15, he left us to live with this birth parent, dropped out of high school and adopted the chaotic lifestyle of drugs and poverty. This was a new kind of grief and loss, leaving me feeling empty and hollow, dejected and demoralized…

"A year later I was still filled with intense sadness and having some difficulties managing anxiety, but I did not consider myself depressed. I was grieving, and grieving hurts. I was also worrying for my husband, whose grief was deep but beyond my reach to help. I did realize, however, that I had lost a sense of knowing what 'normal' was. I felt I was emotionally limping.

"Then we sold the business we had nurtured together for nearly two decades and took positions at a company in another state, leaving behind our home church, close extended family and lifelong friends. The new job did not turn out to be what I had expected. I found myself in a company embroiled in internal struggle and the upheaval of major changes in philosophy and mission—coming apart at the seams.

"My anxiety level became toxic. I became unable to eat or sleep, fearful of getting out of bed and facing the day. I felt guilty for being so weak and ashamed that I felt like I was falling apart. At work, others perceived me as all together because I hid my fears, but at times I was

unable to stop trembling, my heart pounded and my breathing was labored. By the time
I got home from work, I just wanted to curl up on the sofa with a pillow and blanket and
watch television, hoping for sleep to come. I couldn't rest or relax—all I felt was turmoil and
stress, anxiety and darkness.

"In retrospect I can see the depression clearly, but at the time I was blind to it. All I saw was
that I was weak and filled with worry—and I felt guilty about both. It did not occur to me to
see a medical doctor. I was sure my coping problem was due to my emotional weakness, and
it was a sign of failure. So, I kept trying to talk myself into being stronger and getting myself
through this, while berating myself for not being able to pull out of it.

"All the previous losses in my life resurfaced, and I grieved them again. All my former
support systems—long-term friends, home church, extended family—were many miles away.
Eventually, I concluded that I needed help with the anxiety, while at the same time feeling
too overwhelmed to try to find a counselor. I was certain the problem was all in my head,
and I felt ashamed of that. I simply could not muster the strength and energy to search for a
counselor, and I felt guilty about that as well. I was caught in a negative cycle that I couldn't
seem to break.

"Then I learned I needed surgery, which turned out to be a blessing in disguise. My wise
surgeon recognized my depression and anxiety and sent me to a new primary care physician.
I'll never forget that first visit as 'the light went on' when the doctor asked a series of
questions: How was I sleeping? How was my appetite? How was work going? What was
I doing that I enjoyed? I recognized these as classic questions about depression. How had
I missed this in myself? By the time she finished asking her questions, I already knew the
answer. I was clinically depressed.

"Then she explained that, no matter what had brought on this depression, it had become
a biological problem that needed biological treatment. She recommended medication
immediately.

"I had mixed reactions to taking an antidepressant, though. I did not want to turn to pills just
because I couldn't handle life's problems, and I was afraid of developing a dependency on
them. I had always sought to understand myself and to rise to every challenge with God as
my strength. Would this be a cop-out? Would it be escape instead of healing? Would I only
be masking deeper problems? Shouldn't my faith be enough to sustain me?

Yet, I was desperate, and I knew it. Though fearful of the medication and its implications, I
was more fearful of the darkness inside that was smothering my ability to function."

What Depression Looks Like

Some people see depression as a symptom of our times, a product of our society's pursuit of happiness and the machinations of a pharmaceutical industry trying to create a market for its antidepressant medications. The truth is that depression is as old as humanity, at least since Adam and Eve were driven from their place of perfect peace. In the book of Job, which may be the oldest recorded part of the Bible, the long-suffering Job says, "For sighing comes to me instead of food; my groans pour out like water. What I feared has come upon me; what I dreaded has happened to me. I have no peace, no quietness; I have no rest, but only turmoil" (Job 3:24-26, NIV 1984). Clearly, suffering comes to all, and with it, depression often follows.

What does depression look like? Throughout history, dating at least back from Hippocrates to modern times, across many cultures around the globe, there have been consistent descriptions of depression, though it has gone by other names such as melancholia or acedia. The term "depression" was derived from the Medieval Latin verb *deprimere*, "to press down, depress," and refers to the state of dejection, the state of being pressed down, a sinking of the spirits.[1] The depressed person feels like there are external forces pressing down on him or her, causing them to sink.

If a person is depressed, regardless of cause or severity, he or she will most likely exhibit some of the following patterns of thought or action:

> *Low mood nearly every day.* This might be mild and feel like a persistent gloom, or it might be severe to the extent of experiencing mental pain and anguish. Having a "low mood" might seem obvious, but some people who are depressed might not identify with this particular symptom, thought they may have several of the other symptoms below.

> *Loss of motivation and pleasure.* With depression, a person often loses interest in doing the things they normally would feel pleasure in. Indeed, depression can come with a sense of meaninglessness, so that a person feels they can experience neither pleasure nor joy.

> *Loss of energy, or difficulty with thinking and focus.* Depressed people feel physically exhausted most of the time, perhaps because so much of their energy is devoted to mulling over their problems. Completing routine tasks—paying bills, finishing yard work, doing the laundry, preparing a meal, cleaning the house, even taking care of matters relating to personal hygiene—can seem daunting. Thinking may be difficult, and the depressed person may struggle with indecision. At times, the depressed person might wonder if he or she has attention deficit disorder because of inability to focus.

› *Problems sleeping.* Some people have trouble sleeping (insomnia), while others lie in bed all day and night (hypersomnia). Despite being exhausted by feverish thought and worry, depressed people often have difficulty being able to rest. Often depression makes it hard to fall asleep, or it makes sleep fitful. Often, the worst thoughts may occur late at night when there are no other distractions. Either way, the result over time is physical exhaustion, which can lead to other problems, including difficulty thinking, irritability and medical problems.

› *Change in eating patterns.* This, too, can go either way. Some have little appetite and lose weight, while others constantly eat to fill the void. A perceptive observer may note a significant change in the person's weight over time.

› *New physical ailments.* Headaches, backaches, neck aches, joint pain, fatigue, TMJ (temporomandibular joint) syndrome and gastrointestinal disorders are among the numerous physical symptoms that often accompany, and may disguise, depression. These symptoms are real; their pain is real. Yet until the depression itself is treated, the failure of physical symptoms to respond to medical treatment may mystify and frustrate both patient and physician.

› *Impaired memory and thinking.* Although memories of past failures remain (even if the perception of these may not be accurate), often a depressed person cannot remember events in the recent past or important matters in the present, such as appointments or other commitments, phone numbers, names of people, special events and so forth. In addition, the person's perception may be so warped by depression that he or she consistently adopts the most negative interpretation possible of present events or conversations.

› *Difficulty in relationships.* In times of distress, many people with depression tend to withdraw to what feels like the only safe place—within themselves. Many people fear being a burden on others. Relationships, if they exist at all, are mostly superficial. Intimate relationships—knowing and being known—are threatening, because of fears that if he or she were really known, there would be rejection.

› *Difficulty with sexual intimacy.* Decreased libido is common with depression and may make it difficult to maintain normal sexual relations with one's partner. This may be misread as rejection by the other person and experienced as inadequacy by the depressed person.

› *Anger and irritability.* Anger often accompanies depression. The anger may be full blown, with fits of rage, yelling and screaming, or it may be a low burning frustration, an annoyance at others often over trivial matters. When a person is depressed, anger may be a *cause* or it may be a *result* of depression, and it can be nearly impossible to tell which came first. Depression can deplete a person's physical and mental resources so that he or she does not have extra bandwidth to deal with new challenges, responding instead with frustration. Anger and irritability interfere with one's ability to relate to anyone, whether it's a spouse, family, friends or God.

> ***Feelings of worthlessness, helplessness and hopelessness.*** Depression itself can cause these feelings, whether or not they are objectively true. The guilt or shame felt by depressed people can be immeasurable. It is also often beyond the reach of reason and logic. These feelings of worthlessness, taken to an extreme, may tempt even a believer to consider ending his or her life, not only because the person believes that he or she does not deserve to live, but also to put an end to what they feel is the inconvenience and burden on others.

> ***Fear of losing one's mind.*** The pit of depression can be extremely deep. When it is at its worst, a person may worry that he or she may go "over the edge," stop making rational decisions and hurt someone, including loved ones, spouse, children or even their own self. A depressed person may struggle with recurrent thoughts about death or suicide.

If a person were to see a health professional, such as a primary care physician, psychiatrist, psychologist or psychotherapist, the diagnosis would be based on the definition given in the Diagnostic and Statistical Manual of Mental Disorders (DSM), a standardized description of mental disorders currently in its fifth revision, which incorporates many of the characteristics described above. In order to be diagnosed with "Major Depressive Disorder," the person must have had the symptoms for at least a two-week period, and they must also have an impaired ability to function.

Whether or not someone is considered to have major depression depends on the duration and the number of symptoms from which they suffer. A person with mild depression will have at least two of the symptoms above, with only mild loss of interest in several different aspects of life and generally no significant impact on their day-to-day function. Major depression requires the presence of at least five of the symptoms above for most of the day nearly every day, and those symptoms occur on a continuum of severity, including mild, moderate and severe. A person with severe major depression will exhibit most of the symptoms, have a profound loss of interest and be unable to experience pleasure to a disrupting and paralyzing degree.

There is a lot of variability in what depression may look like, but the underlying definition of depression is a change in mood (sad, empty or irritable) accompanied by changes in physical symptoms (sleeping, eating and movement) and thinking (concentration and decision making).

Subtypes of Depression

A number of subtypes of depression are worth exploring, because they may indicate what kind of treatment is likely to be effective. The most common subtypes are based on whether the depression cycles with periods of high mood, whether it is accompanied by psychotic symptoms or if the depression has a relationship to the time of the year or the birth of a child.

Bipolar Disorder

Bipolar disorder, which used to be called manic depression, is a mood disorder with a strong biological component. This disorder is characterized by cycling between distinct periods of highs (mania or hypomania) followed by periods of lows (depression). In mania or hypomania, a person will experience a period of feeling so full of energy that it feels like being driven by a motor. He or she will experience an elevated mood with decreased need for sleep, increased impulsivity, racing thoughts, increased sense of self-importance and the feeling that he or she can accomplish anything.

In bipolar type I, a person experiences full-blown mania. These symptoms last for at least a week, impair a person's ability to function, are obvious to friends or family and may require hospitalization.

In bipolar type II, a person experiences hypomania. The symptoms occur for at least four days and are less severe and impairing. Usually the person with bipolar type II finds that the episodes of major depression which follow hypomania to be debilitating.

It is extremely important for a doctor to know if the depressed person has ever experienced mania or hypomania because this will significantly affect the treatment. For example, if a person with bipolar disorder sees a doctor during an episode of depression and the doctor prescribes an antidepressant, this may cause the patient to flip into a manic episode or may worsen the frequency of mood switches. Such a manic episode may be so disorganized and disruptive that the person can end up psychotic and in the hospital. Bipolar disorder requires a very different treatment regimen with mood stabilizers or anti-dopaminergic medications.

It is also a strongly biological condition that requires lifelong treatment. If a person believes he or she might have had mania or hypomania, he or she should always inform the doctor, whether or not the doctor remembers to ask.

Psychosis

In some cases, a person with major depression can lose touch with reality and develop psychotic symptoms, such as delusions (often of extreme guilt), hallucinations (hearing voices or seeing images that aren't there) or catatonia (when someone stops talking, eating and moving). These symptoms usually call for immediate hospitalization, since they are often severely disabling and occasionally dangerous.

Correct diagnosis is extremely important in this case, since psychotic symptoms are also present in other psychiatric disorders, such as schizophrenia or schizoaffective disorder. Older adults, especially those with Alzheimer's disease or other dementias, are more likely than younger adults to have psychotic symptoms that accompany their depression. Psychotic symptoms may also be the result of other medical conditions (such as delirium), other medications or recreational drug use.

In any case, when depression is accompanied by psychotic symptoms, antidepressants alone will not be enough. Antipsychotic medication or electroconvulsive treatment must be given in addition to antidepressants for successful treatment. (We will address these further in Part II).

Time of Year

Seasonal Affective Disorder (SAD) is a type of major depression linked to the amount of sunlight the person is exposed to on a daily basis. SAD appears at about the same time each year (usually in the winter), and the symptoms resolve with the change of seasons. It occurs more often in northern latitudes due to reduced intensity of sunlight and shorter length of days. The most common symptoms are lethargy and irritability. SAD can be managed with medication, counseling and light (photo) therapy.

Relationship to the Birth of a Child

Depression that occurs during pregnancy before a baby is born, or in the four weeks after delivery are referred to as "peripartum" depressions. The birth of a child is a beautiful event, which causes huge shifts in a woman's life. Dramatic hormonal changes occur in a woman's body after birth, in additiona to the physical recovery from labor and delivery. A newborn's needs for feeding and sleeping disrupt the mother's sleep and routine. Taking on a new role as a parent often causes anxiety and stresses preexisting relationships. Many women have a normal degree of *postpartum blues* following delivery that do not interfere with functioning. *Postpartum depression* is a major depression that starts after the birth of a child. Most worrisome are when psychotic features occur during depression, sometimes with thoughts of harming oneself or the child. This requires urgent medical help. In general, postpartum depression should be taken seriously as it can endanger the health of both the mother and the baby.

Depression: A Common Experience

Major depression, as defined by the DSM, impairs people's ability to function and carry on normal lives across the world. The World Health Organization estimates that globally, the total number of people with depression exceeded 300 million (4.4 percent of the world's population) in 2015. Depression is ranked by the World Health Organization as the single largest contributor to decreased health, and it accounts for an estimated 800,000 deaths per year.[2]

Within the United States, the statistics are even more sobering. Recent studies estimate that between 7 percent and 10 percent of Americans have experienced an episode of major depression within the last 12 months.[3] The lifetime prevalence of major depressive disorder was estimated to be 20.6 percent, meaning that one out of every five people experience depression sometime during their life. In particular, women, young adults and individuals with low incomes (considered to be $19,999 or less) had increased rates of depression.[4]

Clearly, depression is a growing and significant problem.

Is Depression a Disease?

Despite these facts, numerous people, particularly Christians, struggle with the connotations associated with the term "depression." They might agree that they have suffered from the experience described above, but they may disagree that they have been suffering from a medical illness or "disease."

Consider Sarah's words: "*I did not want to turn to pills just because I couldn't handle life's problems, and I was afraid of developing a dependency on them. I had always sought to understand myself and to rise to every challenge with God as my strength. Would this be a cop-out? Would it be escape instead of healing? Would I only be masking deeper problems? Shouldn't my faith be enough to sustain me?*"

Is Sarah struggling with a disease? Or is she just experiencing difficulty with "rising to every challenge?" Is calling her struggle a physical condition a "cop-out?" Does this mean that she is turning to antidepressants instead of turning to God?

These are good questions, and they are questions we will continue to address throughout this book. The first step toward an answer lies in the important distinction between normal sadness and clinical depression.

First consider, what is meant by the word "disease?" The root meaning of the word disease is "dis" (lack of/absence of) and "ease" (comfort/freedom from care). The 1998 Federal Drug Administration (FDA) definition of disease aligns with this: "any deviation from, impairment of, or interruption of the normal structure or function of any part, organ, or system (or combination thereof) of the body that is manifested by a characteristic set of one or more signs or symptoms, including laboratory or clinical measurements that are characteristic of a disease." Conditions such as the flu or cancer fall neatly under this definition.

But what about depression? The DSM definition of depression implies that the *normal structure or function* of the person is to not be depressed. But if the effects of sin in this world include brokenness, if the effect of sin on our bodies is brokenness and if the effect of sin on our relationships is brokenness, how could we not be depressed? One could argue that the opposite is true—if we were to take a hard look at our current condition, *without faith, depression should be the normal response.* The only proper response to brokenness in this world is mourning and weeping. The response of existentialists and nihilists should come as no surprise. But as believers, we do not walk as those without hope (Revelation 21); instead, we look towards the redemption of this world.

Is depression a disease? If you were to step inside the psychiatric floor of a hospital, you might see someone with severe depression who is so immobilized by their despair that they lie in bed, mute, unmoving and catatonic. If you were to follow the progress of this patient for several weeks, you might witness the dramatic recovery to normality after receiving medication and electroconvulsive therapy, where he or she is talking again, is smiling again and is animated. Such examples of severe depression make it clear that there are cases where depression is a disease. This person is not functioning normally, even with the understanding that grief and sadness are part of normal human functions. The grief and sadness have usurped a person's ability to function as a human being who can eat, drink, relate to other people and go on living.

It is important to distinguish normal sadness from clinical depression, which are unfortunately lumped together in the DSM definition. Allan Horowitz and Jerome Wakefield make this critique in *The Loss of Sadness,* where they argue that symptoms alone are inadequate to determine if someone is experiencing clinical depression.[5] Rather, context is crucial. Is the person having an abnormal reaction to their circumstances due to a biological dysfunction, or is it normal sadness brought on by external circumstances? There is no clear way to make a distinction between these under the current DSM classification system.

Normal sadness is strongly tied to the situation, which may often involve loss. The appropriate response is to offer support. On the other hand, sadness "without cause" would be classified as clinical depression, and it often will have no apparent cause or will be out of proportion to the situation. Yet these two conditions may both manifest in the same way.

Is depression a disease? Yes, but it must be teased apart from normal sadness. Context is important. In many ways, depression might be best understood as a symptom that prompts a search for causes, in the same way that a fever indicates an underlying illness. To give Tylenol to a child with a fever, and pronounced the child cured when the fever temporarily fades, is to possibly miss something important and vital.

But in practice, the distinction between normal sadness and clinical depression may be difficult to make. Clinical depression often arises from normal sadness on a continuum. And many of the strategies that are helpful in clinical depression are also helpful in normal sadness, although understanding the causes can direct the treatment more effectively. We explore the myriad causes for depression in the next chapter.

Endnotes

1. Online Etymology Dictionary. https://www.etymonline.com/word/depress?ref=etymonline_crossreference

2. Depression and Other Common Mental Disorders: Global Health Estimates. Geneva: World Health Organization; 2017. Licence: CC BY-NC-SA 3.0 IGO.

3. 2017 National Survey on Drug Use and Health (NSDUH) in the United States, 2012-2013 National Epidemiologic Survey on Alcohol and Related Conditions III in the US

4. Hasin DS, Sarvet AL, Meyers JL, et al. Epidemiology of adult DSM-5 major depressive disorder and its specifiers in the United States [published online February 14, 2018]. JAMA Psychiatry. doi:10.1001/jamapsychiatry.2017.4602

5. Allan Horowitz and Jerome Wakefield. *The Loss of Sadness: How Psychiatry Transformed Normal Sorrow into Depressive Disorder*, Oxford University Press USA - OSO, 2007. ProQuest Ebook Central, http://ebookcentral.proquest.com/lib/harvard-ebooks/detail.action?docID=415907. Created from harvard-ebooks on 2019-08-29 11:53:42.

CHAPTER 3

CAUSES:
Why Am I Depressed?

"While physics and mathematics may tell us how the universe began, they are not much use in predicting human behavior because there are far too many equations to solve. I'm no better than anyone else at understanding what makes people tick, particularly women."

—Stephen Hawking[1]

"Each heart knows its own bitterness, and no one else can share its joy."

—Proverbs 14:10, NIV

What are People Made of?

When it comes to depression, each discipline has a different paradigm for resolving problems. For example, a member of the clergy may insist that a person's depression is entirely a spiritual matter. This clergyman is less likely to suggest the person seek treatment for his body or mind. Psychotherapists sometimes adopt a similar mentality, insisting that the patients will recover if they can resolve their emotional problems, learn new patterns of thought and muster the will to follow through. A person's faith is unlikely to be considered. Physicians may perceive a patient's depression as primarily physical in nature, specifically, a neurological or brain problem for which modern medicine can provide assistance. Once the right medication has been taken for a long enough period, the patient should be functioning normally again. In cases in which the main professional is a social worker, there will likely be a greater emphasis on addressing the social circumstances of the patient's depression. It is easy for each of these views in isolation to miss the sense of the person as a whole.

Why do these disciplines tend toward such compartmentalization? The cure one brings to address a problem depends on what one believes the cause is. And how one goes about identifying the cause has to do with underlying assumptions about who we are as people.

There is a lot of discussion within philosophical and theological circles about who we are as people, whether we are a mind-body-soul, body-soul or just bodies. These distinctions carry implications for cures. Those who hold that we are just physical bodies, as science and medicine tend toward, will reach for physical cures. On the other hand, those who believe the body is just a temporary container for an eternal soul will tend to downplay the body as a cause and focus on the soul.

Arguments can be made on all sides. However, we believe Scripture emphasizes the unity of the person—mind, body and soul. Consider these two passages:

> "You shall love the Lord your God with all your heart and with all your soul and with all your might. And these words that I command you today shall be on your heart. You shall teach them diligently to your children, and shall talk of them when you sit in your house, and when you walk by the way, and when you lie down, and when you rise. You shall bind them as a sign on your hand, and they shall be as frontlets between your eyes. You shall write them on the doorposts of your house and on your gates"
> (Deuteronomy 6:5-9, ESV).

"Now may the God of peace himself sanctify you completely, and may your whole spirit and soul and body be kept blameless at the coming of our Lord Jesus Christ" (1 Thessalonians 5:23, ESV).

These descriptions are not intended to be anatomy lessons. No consistent distinction or partition of the person is described in Scripture. Rather, the language used emphasizes that we are to love and worship God with all of our being—heart, spirit, mind, strength, soul, body—and at all times—sitting, walking, lying down. The material and immaterial aspects of the person function as an essential whole.[2]

Likewise, depression should be addressed as a whole person disorder. In depression, we consider the person as a unity because it is not possible to parse out whether someone's depression is only spiritual, only biological or only psychological.

We believe treatment of the body, mind, and the soul should occur for every depressed person, without neglecting the patient's social context. The primary implication of this standard of care is that, in order to ensure more complete and effective treatment of each person with depression, the person's pastor, physician, counselor, family and church community must become better allies in the healing process. And in order to do so, they must have a deeper understanding of what depression is and how the various underlying causes of depression might interact.

Causes of Depression

Why am I depressed? Why can't I get over this?

It would be nice if the answer were simple. But human behavior and emotions cannot be simplified into a math equation, and so the causes for depression are multiple and complex. Depression can arise after a severe loss or multiple losses and, therefore, can be linked to circumstances. It may be tied to traumatic events while growing up, it may have spiritual roots or it may be primarily a biological illness that is genetically inherited. Most often these causes overlap, although identifying the apparent primary cause can suggest what kind of treatment might be most effective, how long the depression will last and what the prognosis might be. In addition, the longer depression is ignored, the more difficult it is to treat. Depression that might have originally resulted from a difficult situation may over time begin to shape thought patterns, behavior and lifestyle, and it can subsequently affect a person's body. Or the causality can also work in reverse, where someone with a biological disposition toward depression may develop reinforcing thought patterns and behavior, which lead to poor decisions and difficult situations.

We spend some time exploring potential causes of depression, as they help explain why treating depression can often be difficult and complex. People stigmatize depression when they believe it is simple—when they ascribe a person's depression to sin, psychological factors or faulty biology. Understanding the interplay of causes contributing to depression can foster compassion and underscore the importance of utilizing multiple approaches to treat depression.

Situational Causes

Situational causes usually involve a loss of some sort, whether that be the loss of a relationship, loss of a job, loss of health or loss of a home. Sometimes even apparently positive experiences can also lead to depression. Depression in those cases can seem initially puzzling, but it can often be traced to some resulting loss. For example, it could be the loss of a community that accompanies a move, the loss of identity with a change in job or the loss of autonomy that comes with having a child. Depending upon a person's vulnerability (which is influenced by developmental and biological factors), stressful circumstances can precipitate depression. However, no two people react identically, even to the same stressor.

Sometimes a person may suffer due to the results of his own unwise decisions or sin, and they reap what they have sown (Galatians 6:7). For example, cheating on one's income tax can land a person in jail. Cheating on one's spouse may result in a divorce or other family turmoil. Sometimes a sinful response to difficulties can generate stress that in turn produces depression. For example, a person may be wronged, causing him or her to harbor bitterness and resentment that then leads to depression. Or if a person is injured in an accident, he or she may turn to drugs or alcohol to cope with the physical pain of the injury. This can even lead beyond depression and result in addiction, a broken marriage and job loss.

The Diagnostic and Statistical Manual (DSM, as we discussed in the previous chapter) attempts to define milder depression that occurs primarily as a reaction to circumstances under the diagnosis "adjustment disorder." Adjustment disorder is intended to describe depression that is greater than would be expected given the circumstances, though not meeting the criteria for major depression. Depressive symptoms must occur within three months after the stressful psychological or interpersonal event, but also resolve within six months after the situation has ended. However, there are various reasons why a person's response to their circumstances may be greater than what might be expected.

Social factors play a significant, but often neglected, role in why people experience depression. A person's system of means and values strongly determine whether he or she considers a situation threatening, which is why it is so important to take into consideration a person's religious faith. The person's environment influences their capacity to withstand stress. Factors such as socioeconomic status, education and employment affect a person's ability to provide for their physical needs. The relationship between depression and socioeconomic status is often cyclical: depression leads to reduced income and employment, which leads to poverty and in turn increases the risk of further depression. The quality of a person's relationships can enable them to weather challenges or, conversely, increase their stress. Gender and culture play a role in shaping how a person experiences and expresses depression. Deeper systemic injustices can foster depression, such as racism, discrimination, poor working conditions or housing inequality.

There may be traumatic events, such as hurricanes, earthquakes or mass shootings, that impact entire communities. The suffering may fall not only under the category of depression but also of trauma. All of these aspects of a person's context color their depression in the different hues and shades by which loss is experienced.

Perhaps we should identify depression due to loss by the name it has gone by for centuries: *grief*. Losing something valuable causes emotional pain and subsequently, grief. But ignoring the loss may sometimes cause that pain to fester. We as a culture are overly focused on happiness. Uncomfortable with grief and sadness, we tend to rush people through their pain, avoid it or fumble for the right thing to say.

Well-meaning Christian friends are also prone to quote scripture such as "…in all things God works for the good" (Romans 8:28, NIV 1984) or "God won't give you more than you can handle" (1 Corinthians 10:13, paraphrase).

Why are these words not comforting to the sufferer? Despite their truth, the implication of these words is that because of these truths, the person should stop feeling so bad.[3] What these statements are saying is, God works all things for good, so stop feeling so bad. God won't give you more than you can handle, so stop feeling so overwhelmed. These statements betray an underlying impatience with grief, and rather than providing encouragement, make the sufferer may feel he or she lacks adequate faith.

But there is a role for grief and sorrow when faced with loss. John 11:35, "Jesus wept," is well known as the shortest verse in the Bible, but it contains an important truth.

"Now when Mary came to where Jesus was and saw him, she fell at his feet, saying to him, 'Lord, if you had been here, my brother would not have died.' When Jesus saw her weeping, and the Jews who had come with her also weeping, he was deeply moved in his spirit and greatly troubled. And he said, 'Where have you laid him?' They said to him, 'Lord, come and see.' Jesus wept" (John 11:32-35, ESV).

Why did Jesus weep? He had stated earlier that He had the power to raise the dead, and, in fact, in the subsequent verses He did indeed raise Lazarus from the dead. But he did not tell Mary her grief was misplaced or ask, "Why are you weeping?" Rather, He was moved by her grief. He entered into her suffering. Though He knew this loss was only temporary, He entered into the pain of the moment and grieved as well.

To grieve is not to lose faith. Grief is a biblical emotion. Lamentations is a book of the Bible that is devoted to grief. There are numerous Psalms crying out to God over personal pain, regret over sin or in protest against injustice. Grief has a purpose, and when we avoid entering into suffering, it may actually prolong depression.

As Mark Vroegop states in his wise book *Dark Clouds, Deep Mercy:*

"Lament is how we bring our sorrow to God. Without lament we won't know how to process pain. Silence, bitterness, and even anger can dominate our spiritual lives instead. Without lament we won't know how to help people walking through sorrow. Instead, we'll offer trite solutions, unhelpful comments, or impatient responses…. Lament is how Christians grieve. It is how to help hurting people. Lament is how we learn important truths about God and our world."[4]

We have permission to grieve and not to rush to "get over it." This world is broken, and when a person experiences a loss, they become acutely aware of this reality.

So, what can we do? When depression seems to be primarily situation-based, treatment should often include psychotherapy or counseling, combined with support from a pastor, who can point the sufferer to God in their grief and loss. Finding a community to grieve with, whether it be with loved ones or members of a congregation, can be deeply healing. It can also be helpful to involve a physician and consider use of antidepressants, which have been shown to be helpful in reducing symptoms of both normal grief and more severe disordered grief.[5]

But treatment should not stop there. Situational causes can also serve as a call for action to address the situation causing the suffering. When the situation is influenced by socioeconomic deprivation, housing problems or sociological issues such as racism and injustice, social workers who have training in psychotherapy (licensed independent clinical social workers) can be particularly helpful in finding resources and developing practical solutions. When there is an abusive relationship, the sufferer should take steps to ensure their safety and leave the relationship, which may require seeking help from mental health clinicians or domestic violence hotlines.

Developmental Causes

Recent research suggests that childhood abuse or neglect may be one of the largest contributors to developing depression. In one study, 46 percent of individuals with depression reported childhood maltreatment.[6] Negative events that occur during childhood can have a disproportionately large effect on a person, since childhood and adolescence are critical times for development of the brain, as well as for the development of patterns of relating to people, ideas about self and ideas concerning the world. When developmental causes contribute to the depression, the resulting emotional problems can often be chronic, lasting for years or, in some cases, decades. This type of depression has been referred to as "characterological" (personality-related) depression. Symptoms include a persistent inability to appreciate the positive aspects of life along with an almost obsessive preoccupation with the negative. Current stressors in the depressed person's life may intensify a developmental depression, but they are less significant as a primary cause.

The dominant factor in developmental depression appears to be the experience of emotional deprivation during childhood. This does not necessarily imply that early care providers were abusive or neglectful, but it may mean the needs of the child were so great that care providers could not adequately meet them. For example, an emotionally needy infant may require almost constant attention at a time when the mother may herself be experiencing depression. Similarly, marital stress, job pressures or other significant stressors may limit the parents' ability to meet the needs of the child during this critical period of development. Sometimes these patterns can be passed on from generation to generation. The child who has been neglected or abused may not have a good model for parenting and may be quickly overwhelmed by the demands of a child when he or she becomes a parent. This can be exacerbated if there is a genetic predisposition toward emotional illness.

Numerous research studies have found that negative childhood events result in later health problems. The Centers for Disease Control and Prevention (CDC) and Kaiser Permanente studied more than 17,000 people from 1995 to 1997 to determine the impact of Adverse Childhood Experiences (ACE). These experiences were divided into 10 categories: emotional abuse, physical abuse, sexual abuse, physical neglect, emotional neglect, mental illness of a parent, domestic violence, parental separation or divorce, household substance abuse or having a caregiver with a criminal history.

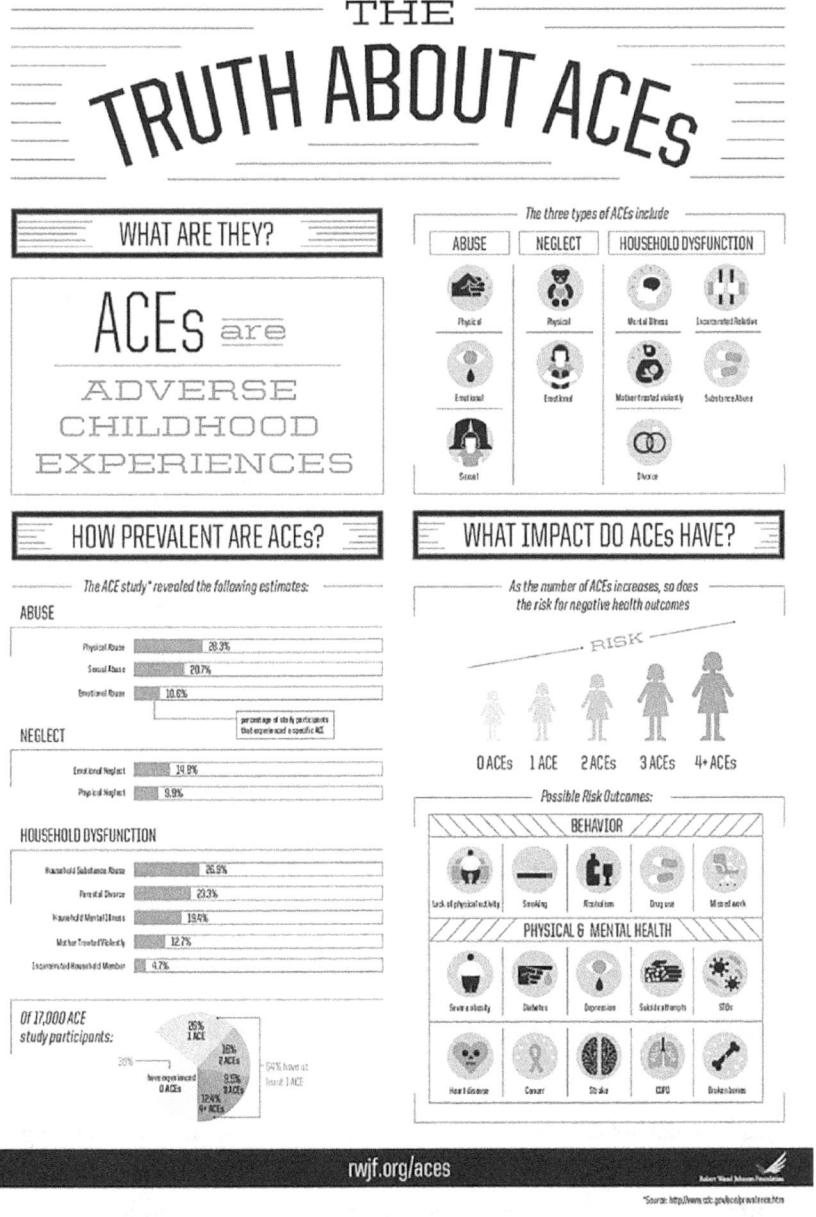

Credit: Robert Wood Johnson Foundation rwjf.org/aces

The study found that many people experience adverse childhood events. Almost two-thirds of participants reported at least one ACE, and more than one in five reported three or more ACEs. Childhood emotional abuse in particular resulted in increased risk for lifetime depressive disorders. The higher the ACE score, the more likely a person was to develop depression, even decades later. Compared to people who had no ACE, people with four or more ACEs had a 4- to 12-fold increased risk for alcoholism, drug abuse, depression and suicide attempts. Notably, these childhood events also impacted physical health in adulthood, including heart disease, cancer, lung disease, skeletal fractures, and liver disease.[7,8]

Nevertheless, adverse childhood events do not necessarily condemn a person to lifelong poor mental or physical health. Positive experiences in early life can protect a child from these negative events. Close relationships are key. Having a loving adult or trusted friend in one's life can decrease the impact of neglect or abuse from parents. In addition, having religious faith and participating in a faith community during childhood may help by promoting forgiveness rather than retaliation, as well as by providing meaning, comfort, hope and social support.[9]

What should we do with the pain and scars from those who have hurt us? We should mourn the broken relationships, lost innocence or parent-child relationships that will never be what they should be. Psychotherapy or counseling is important here for learning new patterns of relating to others. As these early negative experiences can affect one's brain development, treatment with medication can be helpful in situations where counseling is not enough.

Biological Causes

We all exist in human bodies, and the body can be both the cause and the expression of emotions. For example, consider the relationship between anxiety and breathing. If someone has trouble getting enough oxygen, they immediately feel anxious and start gasping for breath. The body's lack of oxygen causes anxiety. This is the body's way of communicating the urgency of obtaining oxygen. On the other hand, if someone experiences an anxiety attack, they can start hyperventilating, along with experiencing a racing heart and sweaty palms. These bodily symptoms are expressions of the person's anxiety. In the same way, depression can be both caused by the body and expressed by the body.

Genetics

For many years, scientists have known that certain forms of depression have a genetic basis, since emotional disorders tend to run in families. In studies of identical twins, about 40 percent to 50 percent of individuals develop depression if their twin has depression. This would suggest that the cause of depression in such cases is about half genetic and half due to environmental factors. If someone has a parent or sibling with major depression, then that person has a significantly increased risk of developing depression.[10]

It is important to note that no gene has been identified that causes depression 100 percent of the time. Thus, genetics can increase the vulnerability to depression, but does not fate that individual to having depression. Situational factors are important. In a spiritual sense, this parallels the fact that although we are all born with (i.e., we inherit) an inclination to sin, God still holds us personally accountable when we give in to temptation. This does not mean, however, that a person is necessarily depressed because they have sinned. Many other factors may be at play.

Chemicals in the Brain

The popular notion that depression is due to a "chemical imbalance" is not quite accurate. This theory first arose because of the discovery that a certain medication given for tuberculosis also made the patients feel less depressed. Scientists soon found that the medication altered the transmission of a neurotransmitter (a brain signaling molecule) in the brain called *serotonin*, and they speculated that depression must be due to a deficiency of serotonin. This led to the hypothesis that depression is due to a "chemical imbalance" of neurotransmitters such as serotonin, norepinephrine or dopamine. The idea of a chemical imbalance is an attractive one since it is easy to grasp, and this idea was heavily marketed by the drug industry. However, while it does seem these neurotransmitters play a role in mood, the idea that depression is a chemical deficiency is overly simplistic. One major flaw with this theory is timing. When a person takes an antidepressant, the increase in neurotransmitter levels in the brain occurs immediately, but it may take weeks before depression improves. In addition, there is no clear standard for what a "normal" level of neurotransmitters is. The brain is not a bath of chemicals, but rather an organ that processes information and uses neurotransmitters to send messages. These neurotransmitter levels vary in different parts of the brain as a way to communicate different messages. It would be just as nonsensical to say the content of a book was wrong because it has a deficiency of vowels. Neurotransmitters like serotonin do play a role in depression, but depression is not as simple as a neurotransmitter deficiency.

Neurocircuitry

More recently, psychiatric research has focused on *neurocircuitry* (the connections between different parts of the brain) as being correlated with depression. The brain encodes information by developing new connections between parts of the brain, and either strengthening or removing these connections, in a process called *neuroplasticity*. Taking this into account, the neuroplasticity hypothesis proposes that inappropriate editing of these brain circuits is what causes depression. Certain areas of the brain have been shown to be different in depressed people: the *hippocampus*, which is involved in learning; the *limbic system*, which is involved in emotion; and the *thalamus*, which processes sensory input. Antidepressants and exercise have been found to increase the release of *neurotrophic factors* (brain growth factors), which increase the formation of new connections between brain cells. This would explain why antidepressants take so long to work, as brain cells take weeks to grow and develop connections. In addition, this explains why the combination of medication and psychotherapy is more beneficial than either treatment alone, since the antidepressants could increase the growth of new neurons and the psychotherapy could help with the editing process by strengthening positive brain connections. Very simply put, medication could be considered fertilizer for the brain and psychotherapy could be considered the gardener who pulls out the weeds and encourages the growth of good things.

Stress Hormones

Another biological pathway contributing to depression involves the stress hormone system. In a normal functioning system, when a person faces a stressor, such as being chased by a lion, the body releases hormones such as cortisol which activate the "fight or flight" system. These hormones increase heart rate, speed up reaction time and sharpen vision, all in an effort to help the person survive. Usually, once the person reaches safety, the body stops the release of these hormones, calms down and returns to its normal resting state. However, in some individuals, the body becomes stuck in "fight or flight" mode even after the lion is long gone. This eventually causes damage to the body and the brain. This theory is particularly relevant when it comes to adverse childhood events. Stress in childhood can sensitize the hormone system and make it over-reactive to stress later in life.

Inflammation

This theory proposes that depression may be caused by the immune system kicking in to fight infection through a process called *inflammation*. This is based on two observations. The first observation is that individuals who are depressed may behave like someone with the flu. They are not hungry, may sleep all the time, isolate themselves from other people and feel tired. All of these sickness behaviors are a result of inflammation. The second observation is that people who struggle with chronic illnesses such as autoimmune diseases often suffer from depression. Sickness behaviors are helpful when a person is sick by preventing the spread of disease and fostering healing. However, they are not as helpful in depression, when there is no infection to fight. Research studies suggest that up to one-third of those with depression show evidence of increased inflammation, even in the absence of medical illness.

For people who are depressed, strategies such as good sleep habits, regular exercise, a good diet and supplements may be helpful, but they are unlikely to cure depression on their own.

Sex Hormones

Fluctuations in sex hormones can have an influence on mood, and some people are more sensitive to this than others. Women have 60 percent to 70 percent higher rates of depression than men. Since this number is consistent across many countries, the difference between genders is most likely due to biology and not to culture. It is likely that hormones cause differences in neurocircuitry, so women tend to internalize stress as depression and anxiety, whereas men channel stress into external behaviors such as violence, aggression or substance abuse.[11,12]

Estrogen plays a key role in mood regulation, and women must adapt to constantly fluctuating hormone levels throughout their lifetimes. Women often experience an increase in depression or irritability a week or two before their period starts. This is called Premenstrual Syndrome when less severe or Premenstrual Dysphoric Disorder when more severe. As we discussed in the previous chapter, pregnancy and delivery cause large fluctuations in hormones and, along with the stress that comes with parenthood, can increase the risk of developing peripartum or postpartum depression. If a woman has had previous depression triggered by hormonal changes, she has increased risk of developing depression during menopause. These mood changes can be treated with antidepressants, hormone therapy and/or utilizing non-medication options such as exercise, a healthy diet and vitamin supplementation.[13] As for testosterone, there is some evidence that low testosterone can contribute to depression in men, but the link does not seem as strong.[14]

Sleep

Sleep is mysterious but vital to the body's functioning, as it is necessary for energy, healing, concentration, learning, metabolism and growth. Sleep is vitally connected to mood. Inadequate sleep can lead to irritability, difficulty focusing and increased negativity, and it can also worsen depression, anxiety and ADHD. Yet, in our culture, we often deprive ourselves of sleep, whether to watch a television show or to squeeze in more work. Sleep is both a gift from God and an act of trust in God: "It is in vain that you rise up early and go late to rest, eating the bread of anxious toil; for he gives to his beloved sleep" (Psalm 127:2, ESV). Getting adequate sleep can lessen the burden of depression. If, despite a person's best efforts to get enough sleep, they are fatigued all the time, then the cause may be an underlying medical issue. If a person wakes up unrefreshed, falls asleep easily even when inappropriate, stops breathing or snores at night, they should be evaluated by a doctor for

What is Excessive Drinking?

There are two types:

> **Heavy drinking** – For men, heavy drinking means having four drinks a day or more than 14 drinks in a week. For women, heavy drinking is more than three drinks a day or more than seven drinks in a week.

> **Binge drinking** – This is a pattern of heavy drinking in a short period that brings the blood alcohol concentration (BAC) to 0.08 g/dL, a level at which a person's functioning is impaired and is legally considered intoxicated in many states. For men, binge drinking is five or more drinks within two hours. For women, binge drinking is four or more drinks within two hours.[16]

CAGE Alcohol Self-Assessment (Ewing 1984)

Answer the following questions with yes or no:

> Have you ever felt that you should cut down on your drinking?

> Have people annoyed you by criticizing your drinking?

> Have you ever felt bad or guilty about your drinking?

> Have you ever had a drink first thing in the morning to calm your nerves or get rid of a hangover?

An answer of yes to two or more questions suggests alcohol abuse. Alcohol use disorder is not a battle that can be won alone. Please seek help from your primary care physician or a mental health clinician.

sleep disorders such as sleep apnea or narcolepsy, which are treatable causes of depression. Of course, depression itself can cause insomnia, which we will address in Chapter 5.

Mood Altering Substances or Medication

Use of alcohol, marijuana, other recreational drugs and medication can affect a person's mood. Alcohol works as a depressant, and though alcohol may seem to relieve the pain of depression while intoxicated, ultimately it can cause or worsen depression. This is certainly true for excessive alcohol use (see sidebar), but it can also occur with more moderate use. The same is true for recreational drugs, whether "uppers" or "downers," and these should be avoided in those seeking healing from depression.

Various medications can also cause depression, which is why it is extremely important for a doctor to review a person's medication list. Some common offenders include isotretinoin (Accutane), beta blockers, corticosteroids, acid reflux medications, hormone medications, antiseizure drugs and benzodiazepines.[15]

Medical Conditions

Certain medical illnesses have a strong correlation with depression. For example, people who have a heart condition, such as a heart attack or recent heart surgery, often experience depression. Depression is common among people who have had strokes or traumatic brain injury. Individuals with autoimmune disorders such as multiple sclerosis or lupus often experience depression as well.

If someone experiences a lot of *new* physical symptoms in addition to depression, it is important to seek medical evaluation to ensure a medical illness is not present. For example, if someone experiences new symptoms such as hair loss, skin rashes, fever, sudden weight loss without change in eating habits, joint or muscle pain, or severe fatigue, they should see a doctor to rule out causes such as vitamin deficiencies, thyroid hormone problems, anemia, infection or autoimmune conditions.

Spiritual Causes

All suffering, whether caused by biology, relationships or situational challenges, has a way of driving a person into conversation with God.

> There may be questions about purpose and meaning: Why am I suffering?

> There may be questions about God's presence and timing: Where are you, God? How long will you abandon me?

> There may be questions about God's character: God, are you truly in control? Are you good? Does God really want my good?

> There may be anger, doubt or fear expressed toward God: God, why have you allowed this to happen? What did I do to deserve this?

> Or crying out to God may have ceased, with the individual believing God is not active or God does not care. Silence itself says something about how a person relates to God.

When suffering, some people are forced to confront their beliefs about who God is, what God's intentions are for their life and what God is doing in the world. In these circumstances, people are often forced to become theologians.

Sin and Guilt

Some cases of depression may be caused primarily by spiritual issues, meaning there are unresolved issues between a person and God. Depression may be due to sin. Not only must a person face the consequences of sinful actions, but the burden of guilt from sin can cause depression. We do urge caution here, however. There is a tendency among Christians to attribute all of a person's depression to sin and to go about looking for the sins in that individual's life to explain why they are depressed. This tendency is short-sighted and often due to sins that may be clouding their own vision (Matthew 7:1-5). Christians recognize that we are all sinners. These sins may be bold faced sins, or they may be seemingly innocuous everyday sins. We may misplace our hope in things such as money, power and popularity, as we make idols of these temporary and fleeting gods that ultimately disappoint. When these idols disappoint, the loss of identity and hope can result in depression.

Consider King David, who, although beloved of God and a great king, committed grievous sins and suffered the consequences. He had an affair with Bathsheba, impregnated her and murdered her husband Uriah in an attempt to cover it up. He faced the repercussions of this sin for the rest of his life. Not only did his child die, but evil would plague his family for generations to come in the form of rape, incest, murder and rebellion. David was well acquainted with suffering due to his sin:

> "There is no soundness in my flesh because of your indignation;
> there is no health in my bones because of my sin.
> For my iniquities have gone over my head;
> like a heavy burden, they are too heavy for me.
> My wounds stink and fester because of my foolishness,
> I am utterly bowed down and prostrate;
> all the day I go about mourning"
> (Psalm 38:3-6, ESV).

David clearly knew the source of his suffering, and he was acutely aware of the weight of his sin. What he had done was a disease he could not cure through any action of his own. But he held onto the promise of grace:

> "Purge me with hyssop, and I shall be clean;
> wash me, and I shall be whiter than snow.
> Let me hear joy and gladness;
> let the bones that you have broken rejoice.
> Hide your face from my sins,
> and blot out all my iniquities.
> Create in me a clean heart, O God, and renew a right spirit within me.
> Cast me not away from your presence,
> and take not your Holy Spirit from me.
> Restore to me the joy of your salvation,
> and uphold me with a willing spirit"
> (Psalm 51:7-12, ESV).

God alone was the one who could cleanse David from the dark stain of sin, could create in him a clean heart and restore to him joy and gladness. This is the gospel, and it is the truth around which our faith revolves. The longer one's bones waste away as a result of concealing sin, the deeper one's depression will become. Relief comes from confessing sin and receiving forgiveness from God.

Depression related to guilt, however, can be bidirectional. While guilt due to sin may cause depression, depression itself may also cause a person to feel guilty without reason. Many depressed people blame themselves for situations beyond their control, even to the extent they may become delusional. Experientially, it makes little difference to the depressed person whether he or she is experiencing guilt due to sin or a delusional guilt due to depression.

Desertion by God

Some people are horrified by their sin, and they believe they are beyond the hope of forgiveness by God. They may imagine God does not love them, has deserted them or is punishing them. They may experience doubts about the reality or security of their faith. They may cease believing in God or believe God's grace does not apply to them. This kind of despair is fraught with uncertainty and a sense of hopelessness and helplessness. If people suffering from these thoughts receive misguided counsel to examine themselves for sin, this will only worsen their despair.

Henri Nouwen, a Yale theologian, described his own depression in these terms:

> "Just when all those around me were assuring me they loved me, cared for me, appreciated me, yes, even admired me, I experienced myself as a useless, unloved, and despicable person… Just when I was being praised for my spiritual insights, I felt devoid of faith. Just when people were thanking me for bringing them closer to God, I felt that God had abandoned me. It was as if the house I had finally found had no floors. The anguish completely paralyzed me. I could no longer sleep. I cried uncontrollably for hours. I could not be reached by consoling words or arguments. I no longer had any interest in other people's problems. I lost all appetite for food and could not appreciate the beauty of music, art, or even nature. All had become darkness. Within me there was one long scream coming from a place I didn't know existed, a place full of demons."[18]

Similar musings of other spiritual thinkers throughout the ages suggest that depression of this type is not uncommon among those who are spiritually sensitive, especially when they view their own sinfulness in the light of God's holiness.

The most effective treatment for depression arising from these sources is to fight these lies with the truth of the gospel. The apostle Paul described his own inner struggles in Romans 7:7-24, but he ended with these words of hope: "What a wretched man I am! Who will rescue me from this body of death? Thanks be to God—through Jesus Christ our Lord!... Therefore, there is now no condemnation for those who are in Christ Jesus" (Romans 7:24 – 8:1, NIV 1984). In Nouwen's case, this grace was incarnated in several close friends who joined him on his unexpected journey to the point where he could once again know the assurance of God's love and forgiveness.

Doubt in God's Goodness and Sovereignty

I (JH) once treated a young man, Tom, for persistent depression. He had struggled with alcoholism and heavy drug use in his teens and twenties, but he had been sober for many years by the time he came to see me. We had tried various antidepressants, and he had seen a string of secular therapists. One day, curious about what motivations in Tom's life were important, I finally asked him how he managed to quit using drugs and alcohol. He said faith had saved him. He had always fought for control over his life, and he never submitted to anyone. For the first time in his life, Tom humbled himself and gave control of his life to God. However, several years later he witnessed several events of senseless suffering. His wife's uncle had died suddenly of cancer, and then a month later his wife's mother died in a car accident. The grief of all this tore their once closely-knit family apart. When he shared this at an Alcoholics Anonymous (AA) meeting, someone there responded, "You shouldn't be depressed. God means this all for good." How could a good God allow this, he wondered? After that, he stopped attending AA, stopped attending church and stopped believing in God.

The response of the person at AA to Tom was unfortunately simplistic. How a good God could allow evil and suffering is a difficult question, one which theologians and philosophers have struggled with for time immemorial. I encouraged him to bring these questions to a pastor and really wrestle with them. When Tom lost his faith in God, he also lost that which gave coherence and purpose to his life.

Individuals may hold a wrong theological assumption, which, when challenged, causes them to question their faith and experience depression. For example, some people believe that if a person is obedient to God, they will not experience suffering. When they experience difficulties in their lives despite their faithfulness, their faith can be shaken (John 16:33). A person may be convinced God has called and chosen him or her for a particular task, and they may be experiencing setbacks or closed doors. Or they may struggle when their church falls apart due to conflict, and they find it hard to hold onto the love and beauty of God when faced with the messy sinfulness of their human brothers and sisters. These are questions that should be brought to a pastor and/or a Christian counselor.

Before leaving this topic, we want to note that *unbelievers can also experience spiritual depression*, where they sense that something is missing or that there is a void at the core of their being. Existential questions—about fear of death, loneliness, meaning—all arise from our inherently spiritual nature and desire to connect with something larger than ourselves.

Ultimately, the hope is this awareness may help that person realize his or her need of God, who created humans to be in relationship with Himself.

Ultimate Causes

What are the causes of our behavior? Situational? Developmental? Biological? Spiritual? Ultimately, despite all of depression's causes—painful situations, tragedies from childhood, the frailty of our minds, the brokenness of our bodies, the sinfulness of our souls—depression's ultimate cause can be traced back to sin and the far-reaching consequences of the fall of humankind. But thankfully, our story does not end there.

Jesus models a different way of diagnosing people's problems; in fact, His ministry combined ministering to people's physical needs with ministering to their souls. Consider Jesus' healing of the paralytic:

> And getting into a boat he crossed over and came to his own city. And behold, some people brought to him a paralytic, lying on a bed. And when Jesus saw their faith, he said to the paralytic, "Take heart, my son; your sins are forgiven." And behold, some of the scribes said to themselves, "This man is blaspheming." But Jesus, knowing their thoughts, said, "Why do you think evil in your hearts? For which is easier, to say, 'Your sins are forgiven,' or to say, 'Rise and walk'? But that you may know that the Son of Man has authority on earth to forgive sins"—he then said to the paralytic—"Rise, pick up your bed and go home." And he rose and went home. When the crowds saw it, they were afraid, and they glorified God, who had given such authority to men" (Matthew 9:1-8, ESV).

What is fascinating about this account was Jesus' diagnosis of the paralytic's needs. We would look at the man and think his primary need was physical: to be healed from his paralysis. His friends probably brought the paralytic to Jesus for physical healing. Jesus, however, looked at this man and saw his fundamental problem, one of spiritual paralysis. Thus, Jesus' first words were, "Take heart, my son; your sins are forgiven." To forgive a man's sins seemed to be both the easier thing to do (there is no visible proof) and the harder thing to do (you need to be God to forgive sins). But Jesus did not end there. He proved He has the authority both in heaven and on earth—both over spiritual matters and physical matters. Jesus proved He is Lord over all creation, all that is spiritual, physical and mental.

Depression is a type of paralysis as well, one with spiritual, physical, situational and mental causes. And, ultimately, Jesus will be the one who fully heals, the one to say to those who are depressed, "Rise and walk."

Endnotes

1. http://content.time.com/time/magazine/article/0,9171,2029483,00.html

2. Charles Barber. "The Brain: A Mindless Obsession." Wilson Quarterly. Washington, D.C.: Winter 2008. Brown, Warren S., Nancey Murphy and H. Newton Malony, Eds. Whatever Happened to the Soul? Minneapolis, MN: Augsburg Fortress, 1998. We could easily get lost in the weeds with this debate of who we are, but we leave the finer points of these arguments to others.

3. Devine, Megan. It's OK that you're not OK. Boulder, CO: Sounds True, 2017.

4. Vroegop, Mark. *Dark Clouds, Deep Mercy. Wheaton, Illinois: Crossway, 2019. p21*

5. *Zissok S, Schuchter SR, Pedrelli P, Sable J, & Deaciuc SC (2001). Bupropion sustained release for bereavement: Results of an open trial. Journal of Clinical Psychiatry, 62, 227-230*

6. Lippard, Elizabeth TC, and Charles B. Nemeroff. "The devastating clinical consequences of child abuse and neglect: increased disease vulnerability and poor treatment response in mood disorders." *American journal of psychiatry* 177.1 (2020): 20-36.

7. Felitti VJ, Anda RF, Nordenberg D, Williamson DF, Spitz AM, Edwards V, Koss, MP, Marks JS. Relationship of childhood abuse and household dysfunction to many of the leading causes of death in adults. The Adverse Childhood Experiences (ACE) Study. Am J Prev Med. 1998 May;14(4):245-58. PubMed PMID: 9635069.

8. Chapman DP, Whitfield CL, Felitti VJ, Dube SR, Edwards VJ, Anda RF. Adverse childhood experiences and the risk of depressive disorders in adulthood. J Affect Disord. 2004 Oct 15;82(2):217-25. PubMed PMID: 15488250.

9. Kathleen Brewer-Smyth & Harold G. Koenig (2014) Could Spirituality and Religion Promote Stress Resilience in Survivors of Childhood Trauma?, Issues in Mental Health Nursing, 35:4, 251-256, DOI: 10.3109/01612840.2013.873101

10. Levinson D. The Genetics of Depression: A Review. Biol Psychiatry 2005 doi:10.1016/j.biopsych.2005.08.024.

11. Albert P. R. (2015). Why is depression more prevalent in women? *Journal of psychiatry & neuroscience: JPN, 40*(4), 219–221. doi:10.1503/jpn.150205

12. Bartels, M., Cacioppo, J. T., van Beijsterveldt, T. C., & Boomsma, D. I. (2013). Exploring the association between well-being and psychopathology in adolescents. *Behavior genetics, 43*(3), 177–190. doi:10.1007/s10519-013-9589-7

13. Soares CN. Depression in peri- and postmenopausal women: prevalence, pathophysiology and pharmacological management. Drugs Aging. 2013. Sep;30(9):677-85. doi: 10.1007/s40266-013-0100-1. Review. PubMed PMID: 23801148

14. Seidman SN, Weiser M. Testosterone and mood in aging men. Psychiatr Clin North Am. 2013

Mar;36(1):177-82. doi: 10.1016/j.psc.2013.01.007. Review. PubMed PMID:23538087

15. Qato DM, Ozenberger K, Olfson M. Prevalence of Prescription Medications With Depression as a Potential Adverse Effect Among Adults in the United States. *JAMA*. 2018;319(22):2289–2298. doi:10.1001/jama.2018.6741

16. https://www.niaaa.nih.gov/alcohol-health/overview-alcohol-consumption/moderate-binge-drinking

17. Henri J. M. Nouwen, *The Inner Voice of Love: A Journey through Anguish to Freedom* (New York: Doubleday/Random House, 1996), xiv – xv.

CHAPTER 4

MYTHS AND MISCONCEPTIONS:
Do Real Christians Get Depressed?

One of the oldest documented stories in the Bible is also a story of depression. It's the story of Job, a blameless and upright man who feared God and turned away from evil. He was prosperous, blessed with many children and great wealth, and he was considered the greatest of all the people of the east. That is, until the day God allowed Satan to smite Job and take away—in brutal succession—his property, his children and his health.

Upon hearing of the devastating loss of his children, Job fell to the ground and worshipped, responding, "…'Naked I came from my mother's womb, and naked shall I return. The Lord gave, and the Lord has taken away; blessed be the name of the Lord'" (Job 1:20-21, ESV). His wife, however, responded bitterly, "…'Do you still hold fast your integrity? Curse God and die.' But he said to her, 'You speak as one of the foolish women would speak. Shall we receive good from God, and shall we not receive evil?'" (Job 2:9-10, ESV).

Job's response was one of faith, and yet he also experienced deep suffering, depression and confusion. He spends the rest of the book crying out to God:

> "And now my soul is poured out within me; days of affliction have taken hold of me… God has cast me into the mire, and I have become like dust and ashes. I cry to you for help and you do not answer me; I stand, and you only look at me. You have turned cruel to me; with the might of your hand you persecute me. You lift me up on the wind; you make me ride on it, and you toss me about in the roar of the storm…But when I hoped for good, evil came, and when I waited for light, darkness came"
> (Job 30: 16-36, ESV).

Since the time of Job, people have struggled with depression, as well as the isolation depression brings. It causes sufferers to withdraw from others and feel that no one understands. Unfortunately, the stigma surrounding depression often reinforces the isolation. Not only do others stigmatize those who are depressed, but depressed individuals often believe these misunderstandings about themselves and suffer shame. This stigma arises from ignorance and misunderstandings about what depression is, the causes of depression and how difficult it can be to fight.

Unfortunately, the church, rather than being a place of healing for those who suffer, can become a place of judgement. In 2014, LifeWay surveyed 1,000 Protestant pastors about mental illness. The study found that 74 percent personally knew one or more people who had been diagnosed with clinical depression, and 23 percent of pastors reported having personally struggled with mental illness themselves. Yet, 49 percent of pastors rarely or never spoke to their church about acute mental illness.[1] In the absence of teaching from the church, many Christians adopt the misconceptions about depression that pervade our culture. And, unfortunately, often when pastors do speak up about depression, it may be to perpetuate the falsehood that "real Christians" do not get depressed.

However, Christians who suffer from depression are far from alone. Examples of Christians who have struggled with depression exist from the oldest biblical records to the modern day. Christians who have suffered depression come from all walks of life, both those who preach from the pulpit and sit in the pews, both those who have much and those who have little by the world's standards. Throughout this chapter, we share several of their stories and confront the myths about depression that serve to exacerbate the suffering.

Stories

Joni Eareckson Tada (Advocate for the Disabled)

As a teenager, Joni Eareckson Tada loved sports. She was voted "best athlete" in her high school and planned to pursue a career as a physical therapist. However, one month after her high school graduation, she was on a rafting trip with friends in the Chesapeake Bay, when she attempted an inward pike dive into water that was much shallower than she realized. In one swift moment, she broke her neck, rendering her instantly paralyzed from the neck down. Initially she kept up a brave front, telling everyone she was confident God would heal her. But as time passed, this new reality—inability to move her arms and legs and an utter dependence on others—became increasingly hard to bear.

> "I was once the 17-year-old who retched at the thought of living life without a working body. I hated my paralysis so much I would drive my power wheelchair into walls, repeatedly banging them until they cracked. Early on, I found dark companions who helped me numb my depression with scotch-and-cola. I just wanted to disappear. I wanted to die," she wrote.

> Initially, she clung onto faith that God would heal her paralysis, and she did everything she could to be healed. She prayed. She read the Bible, searching for clues. As her sister drove her home from the third healing crusade, she kept fuming, *"What kind of Savior, what kind of rescuer or healer, would refuse the prayer of a paralytic? Especially a paralytic who claims Christ as her Savior?* I felt bewildered and utterly lost. One morning I awoke early, looked around my shadowy bedroom, and decided I didn't want to get up. *If I can't be healed, I thought, then I'm just not going to do this. . . I am not going to live this way!* I stayed in bed that day. And the next. And the following week. The despair was

claustrophobic, and I finally whimpered, 'I can't live this way. I'm so lost. God, *show* me how to live.' It was my first plea for help. Next came fresh days when my sister would get me up, plop a Bible on a music stand and park my wheelchair in front of it. With a mouth stick, I would flip this way and that, trying to make sense of it all...."[2]

With the prayer and encouragement of her friends and family and her continued study of Scripture, she began to see that God could use her, even without the use of her arms and legs. Indeed, He used her precisely because she did not have the use of her limbs. Decades later, she has been able to say, "All combined, I began to see there *are* more important things in life than walking and having use of your hands. It sounds incredible, but I really would rather be in this wheelchair knowing Jesus as I do than be on my feet without him."

Joni has since founded an outreach ministry for the disabled, called Joni and Friends. She was appointed under Presidents Ronald Reagan and George H. W. Bush to the National Council on Disability, which wrote the first draft of the American with Disabilities Act. She has also authored many books to help others struggling with disability, suffering and pain. All this happened despite her continuing to face many challenges, including complications of her quadriplegia, chronic pain and recurrent breast cancer. How did she get through all this? She writes,

> "It has everything to do with God and his grace—not just grace over the long haul, but grace in tiny moments, like breathing in and out, like stepping stones leading you from one experience to the next. The beauty of such grace is that it eclipses the suffering until one July morning, you look back and see five decades of God working in a mighty way. Grace softens the edges of past pains, helping to highlight the eternal. What you are left with is peace that's profound, joy that's unshakable, faith that's ironclad."[3]

Abraham Lincoln (Politician)

From childhood, Abraham Lincoln was well acquainted with grief. At the age of three, he lost his infant brother. At the age of nine, he experienced a triple blow—the deaths of his aunt and uncle, and then that of his beloved mother, who had instilled in him a love for God and for learning. When he was only 18, his sister, his only remaining sibling, died while giving birth. By the time Lincoln turned 21, he had developed a variety of physical complaints in addition to a perpetual "look of gloom" arising from the fact that his left eye deviated upward. The doctors told him his illness was hypochondria—physical complaints with no medical basis—and stated they could not do anything about his eye.

MYTHS AND MISCONCEPTIONS: Do Real Christians Get Depressed?

Lincoln's first recorded period of depression occurred during the spring of his 24th year when, after having performed well as captain of the militia during the Black Hawk War, he ran for public office and lost. His friends successfully campaigned for his appointment as the village postmaster. Although the job only lasted a few weeks, it soon led to his being hired as a surveyor's assistant. Finally, he was establishing a career path, which took on special importance since he was planning to marry his childhood love, Ann.

Two years later, however, the hammer fell again when Ann became ill and died of typhus. When Lincoln heard of his sweetheart's death, he became deeply depressed and wandered aimlessly among the hills and backcountry, refusing to eat or sleep. It did not help that he had been taught that death was often the direct act of God to punish the loved ones of the deceased person. Lincoln was eventually nursed back to health by his aunt Polly, who ministered to him physically and mentally until he had gone three weeks without a bout of "the chills."

Within a year, Lincoln was seeing another woman, Mary, yet he still battled what had now become a chronic depression. In many ways, this depression was not a surprise given the strong history in the Lincoln family of "melancholia" as well as bipolar mania. Indeed, one of his family members called the difficult bouts with mental illness the "Lincoln horrors."

A fourth period of depression occurred when Mary, the woman he would eventually wed, broke off their engagement on the day they were to be married, partly due to Lincoln's anxiety over the difference in their backgrounds—he being a poor, backwoods country type with only a single year of formal education, and she being well-educated and from a wealthy respectable family. During this bout with depression, friends kept knives and razors away from Lincoln. Lincoln never carried a pocketknife, fearful of his own suicidal tendencies.

At one point, Lincoln wrote: "I am now the most miserable man living. If what I feel were equally distributed to the whole human family, there would not be one cheerful face on earth. Whether I shall ever be better I cannot tell. I awfully forebode that I shall not. To remain as I am is impossible, I must die or be better, it appears to me."[4]

After Lincoln and Mary were married, they continued to experience further problems and conflicts, both due to their backgrounds as well as their temperaments. However, there were no further depressive episodes for 20 years, partly because Lincoln had successfully won his bid for the presidency and was preoccupied with governmental matters, particularly the escalating civil conflict in the United States.

Amid this national crisis, the couple's young son, William, died from a fever. Depression returned with a vengeance. Though affairs of state demanded Lincoln's attention, the bereaved father became socially distant and often shut himself in a room for hours. During this time, the heartbroken man reconciled himself with God, returning to the faith of his childhood, now with a much different, deeper understanding. Two years later, on April 14, 1865, an assassin's bullet ended the long and painful journey of Abraham Lincoln, whom many consider this country's greatest president.

Harold G. Koenig (Physician)

Dr. Harold Koenig grew up on a 20-acre farm in the country about 10 miles from Lodi, California. His parents valued education, especially since they didn't have any, and they valued religion too. They were willing to sacrifice so he could attend a private Catholic high school. He studied hard through high school and college and eventually got into a medical school in San Francisco.

He shared, "Before starting medical school, I became deeply involved in a relationship more intense than anything I had ever experienced before. However, as suddenly as it had begun, the relationship ended, leaving me with a deep sense of loss and an identity crisis—my first glimpse of despair. As I saw the dream of a future life with her vanish, in its place came a heaviness that seemed to center around the chest area. I could not rid myself of this feeling that seemed so incredibly oppressive and suffocating. At first, I became extremely restless, unable to sit still or just relax. After a time, a sense of inertia began to set in. I began to have doubts about myself. And I wondered whether I had what it took to form a close personal relationship with anyone."

"Another change also took place. The crispness and clarity of the world around me began to fade. I saw the sunset, the blue sky, the wildflowers and the ocean as though through smoked glass. Everything—*everything*—had changed. The wonders of nature no longer elicited emotions of beauty, joy and awe within me; in fact, they elicited nothing—no emotion. That was scary.

"Other things did elicit emotion. When I saw couples walking together, I was stung with a sense of yearning and sadness. I couldn't stand to watch any television programs that would remind me of an intimate and close relationship, which he believed was beyond my grasp forever. I seemed to be experiencing every event in life in terms of loss and failure. Although I had never experienced depressive symptoms like this before, I had always been a sensitive person with many fears and insecurities, and all of them came out that summer."

That fall in medical school the academic challenges were intense, like nothing he had ever experienced before. Suddenly Harold's struggle had many levels as he tried to deal with the despair of finding himself—a 22-year-old with little direction or purpose, trying to become a doctor.

He turned to Eastern spiritual practices. He meditated. He attended classes taught by a Yogi or spiritual master. He immersed himself in the New Age writings of Carlos Castaneda and Alan Watts. This was the 1970s, when drugs and mind expansion were the hip things to do, and he did them. But these things didn't work either. The path Harold was taking didn't seem to lead anywhere, at least not to the place he had hoped or expected. Instead it led to his expulsion from medical school as he became more distracted and neglected his studies, completely preoccupied with his newly found Eastern spirituality, which at least brought temporary relief to the emotional pain.

He eventually ended up on the streets of San Francisco, living under houses and working for food day-to-day. He cut off all relationships with friends and family, focusing on a self-styled spiritual path that he created based on what he had learned from my newfound spiritual masters. This continued for more than six months. He was really lost, and his life was a mess. "It eventually dawned on me that this spiritual path was not working" he said, "and this was when my life started to turn around—though a long, long road still stretched ahead."

J.B. Phillips (Bible Translator)

When J. B. Phillips was a child, his father pushed him hard to succeed. After Phillips entered the ministry, his anxieties about performing well for his earthly father manifested themselves in his feelings about his heavenly Father. Troubled by the concept of a demanding God and facing the pressures of ministry, he quit his job as a curate in a church.

However, over time the young clergyman was able to better understand the root of his problematic relationship with God. "Of all the false gods there is probably no greater nuisance than the 'god of one-hundred percent,'" he wrote. "After all, did not Christ say, 'Be ye perfect?' This one-hundred-percent standard…has taken the joy and spontaneity out of the Christian lives of many who dimly realize that what was meant to be a life of 'perfect freedom' has become an anxious slavery."

Phillips's Letters to *Young Churches,* a translation of New Testament epistles, was published in 1947. Several years later, Phillips gave up his work with his church and for a time devoted his life to writing and speaking. His translation of the entire New Testament was immensely popular, especially in Great Britain and the United States, bringing instant fame and multiple speaking opportunities. It was a heady and dangerous time.

From 1955 to 1961, Phillips followed a hectic speaking schedule across the U.S. and in Great Britain. He was a highly successful radio broadcaster, writer and public speaker. Finally, in 1961 the pressures of the author's touring schedule proved too much for him. After six years of frenetic travel and speaking, he was exhausted, depleted. He became depressed. He wrote:

> "Without any particular warning the springs of creativity were suddenly dried up; the ability to communicate disappeared overnight and it looked as if my career as a writer and translator was over. I know now, but had no idea then, that this was the first inkling of a condition known to the medical and psychiatric world as a depression, a condition that was to be with me for several years. After a few months, during which I was not entirely idle, I found the mental pain more than I felt I could bear and I went as a voluntary patient to a psychiatric clinic...

> "My reason for writing [about this] is that it may help someone else who is depressed and in mental pain. It may help simply to know that one whom the world would regard as successful and whose worldly needs are comfortably met can still enter this particular hell, and have to endure it for quite a long time."[5]

Phillips experienced a reprieve from the depression, and he was persuaded by well-meaning folk to continue his translation work, this time taking on the Old Testament prophets Amos, Hosea, Micah and Isaiah. His work *Four Prophets* was released in 1963. Yet again, in the midst of success he was forced to abruptly leave a book signing when he was overcome by a panic attack.

Hospitalized again, the author attributed his breakdown to the pressure he had been under for years. He was unable to find any written Christian encouragement related to depression because it was "another of those forbidden subjects about which a tactful curtain of silence has for many years been drawn…It would have been of inestimable comfort and encouragement to me in some of my darkest hours if I could have come across even one book written by someone who had experienced and survived the hellish torments of mind which can be produced…[an] almost unendurable sense of terror and alienation."

He wrote, "The hardest thing of all to bear is what I can only describe as a nameless mental pain, which is, as far as I know, beyond the reach of any drug, and which I have tried in vain to describe to anyone…But it is so overwhelming that one can understand the temptation to suicide."

Lottie Moon (Missionary)

Charlotte Diggs "Lottie" Moon stood only four feet three inches tall, and yet she left an impact on overseas missions that was far greater than her height. She came from a wealthy family that valued education, and she was one of the first women in the United States to earn a master's degree. In February 1873, in response to a revival sermon on the text "Lift up your eyes, and look on the fields; for they are white already to harvest," Lottie Moon left her home in Cartersville, Georgia, to serve as a missionary to China. It would be 14 years before she would see her friends and family again.

During her first year in China, most of Lottie Moon's missionary work focused on women and children, which was unusual at that time. She taught Sunday school class and cultivated relationships with well-respected Chinese ladies to teach them the gospel and catechisms. Unlike many of her colleagues, she deeply respected the Chinese people. However, once the initial thrill of being on foreign soil dissipated, homesickness and loneliness pervaded her thoughts, and she struggled throughout her lifetime with bouts of depression and despair. Lottie Moon coped with her loneliness by reading, walking along the shore or the beach, swimming and maintaining flowers in a sort of makeshift garden.

She wrote to some of her American supporters:

> "In your native land, surrounded by those who speak your mother tongue and whom you have known from infancy, you can scarcely have any idea how we in this foreign country look forward to the mail and how a chill, a feeling of despondency, will arise when there is nothing for us. The older missionaries say they are forgotten at home, that hardly anyone cares for them; and they tell us newcomers that it will be so with us in the lapse of time."[6]

During the winter of 1885 to 1886, the missionary felt a sense of depression for which she solicited prayer. "I feel my weakness and inability to accomplish anything without the aid of the Holy Spirit," she wrote. "Make special prayer for the outpouring of the Holy Spirit…that I may be clothed with power from on high by the indwelling of the Spirit in my heart."

After returning to the United States in 1891, the burned-out missionary allowed her sister to nurse her back to health, after suffering from exhaustion and a recurrent headache. "I have been so unmerciful to myself in China," she decided, "that I must call a halt now and take a needed rest." She followed this pattern for the rest of her life, often taking a month-long break from her work during the summer, during which she would relax and read. She wrote many letters to her supporters and the Southern Baptist Convention. It was largely through these efforts that funding for foreign missions grew, and the mission board started sending women as evangelists and instituted practices such as regular furloughs to provide better care for their missionaries.

After the Boxer Rebellion (1900 to 1901), she fell into a severe depression because of the famine she saw all around her in China. She refused to eat because she believed the girls she taught were starving. When friends tried to bring Lottie Moon back to the United States to recover her health, she died on the way, breathing her last breath in Japan.

William Cowper (Poet)

William Cowper, born in 1731, was one of the most popular and widely read poets of his day. However, he suffered from severe depression throughout his lifetime, with numerous suicide attempts and hospitalizations. He recalls an idyllic childhood until age five, when his mother died giving birth to his youngest brother. Of seven children, only he and a younger brother survived past childhood. His father sent him to boarding school, where, as a weak and timid child, he was severely bullied, to the extent that he could identify his tormenters by their shoe buckles.

His family intended for him to pursue a career in law, which he attempted despite having little inclination or ability. Under this pressure, he suffered his first episode of depression at the age of 21, which he describes as follows: "I was struck...with such a dejection of spirits, as none but they who have felt the same can have the least conception of. Day and night I was upon the rack—lying down in horror, and rising up in despair."[7]

Depression was to plague him on and off for the rest of his life. His father died in 1756, leaving little behind. However, his family was well connected and arranged a series of jobs for him. They were also able to procure his appointment to a lucrative clerkship of the Journals in the House of Lords. However, some were skeptical of his suitability for the position and demanded he be examined in a public interrogation. Distraught by the pressure of going through this examination for a job that would provide for him financially, yet certain that he would not be able to meet these requirements, he tried to end his life. The day before the examination he took a cab to the wharf intending to drown himself, but he found the water too low and a porter seated there. He then went home and prepared to take a poison that he had purchased, but he found he was unable to take it and was interrupted by his landlord. He then attempted to hang himself, but the garter broke. He told his laundress about these attempts, who in turn called his uncle who canceled the examination immediately. Cowper was oppressed by overwhelming guilt and wrestled with the thought he had attempted the unpardonable sin—self-murder—by his suicidal actions.

Not long after this, he was visited by his cousin, who began to preach the gospel to him. Cowper described this encounter as follows:

> "He spoke of original sin, and the corruption that is in the world, whereby everyone is a child of wrath. I perceived something like hope dawn in my heart…Next he insisted on the all-atoning efficacy of the blood of Jesus, and his righteousness, for our justification. While I heard this part of his discourse, and the Scripture on which he founded it, my heart began to burn within me; my soul was pierced with a sense of my bitter ingratitude towards so merciful a Savior, *and those tears, which I thought impossible, burst forth freely*… Lastly, he urged the necessity of a lively faith in Jesus Christ; not an assent only of the understanding, but a faith of application…and embracing it as a salvation wrought out for me personally. Here I failed, and deplored my want of such a faith. He told me it was the gift of God, which, he trusted, He would bestow upon me. I could only reply, 'I wish he would,' a very irreverent petition, but a very sincere one, and such as the blessed God, in his due time, was pleased to answer."[8]

This exhortation did not bring immediate healing. The next day he continued to lose his grip on reality, became increasingly incoherent and was hospitalized at a mental asylum for a year and a half. Yet, that healing eventually came. One day, he opened Scripture to Romans 3:25, wherein he received the strength to believe. His despair was transformed into joy.

As Cowper recovered, he lived with the Unwin family and moved with them to Olney. There, they attended the church of curate John Newton, who encouraged him and suggested he contribute to a book of hymns, published as the *Olney Hymns*. Newton authored the words of "Amazing Grace." Cowper would contribute, among other songs, the titles "Oh! For a closer walk with God," "There Is a Fountain," and "God moves in a mysterious way."

Mary Unwin encouraged Cowper to write, and he began publishing poetry, which met with great popular acclaim. Nevertheless, the battle of depression was not over. He continued to experience depression on and off, and he had repeated suicide attempts, even amidst his deepening faith and professional success. He had considered marrying Mary Unwin at one point, but this had to be aborted due to a severe depressive episode. However, when she died in 1796, Cowper sank into a deep depression from which he would never emerge, dying in 1800 from dropsy (tuberculosis). Nevertheless, he left a lasting legacy. With John Newton, he wrote a number of anti-slavery poems that Martin Luther King, Jr. was to quote numerous years later in the American civil rights movement. The enduring power of his hymns lies in both the beauty of the language, as well as his intimate knowledge of clinging onto faith in the face of suffering:

God moves in a mysterious way
His wonders to perform;
He plants his footsteps in the sea,
And rides upon the storm.

Deep in unfathomable mines
Of never failing skill,
He treasures up his bright designs
And works his sovereign will.

Ye fearful saints, fresh courage take,
The clouds ye so much dread
Are big with mercy, and shall break
In blessings on your head.

Judge not the Lord by feeble sense,
But trust him for his grace;
behind a frowning providence
He hides a smiling face.

His purpose will ripen fast,
Unfolding every hour;
the bud may have a bitter taste,
But sweet will be the flower.

Blind unbelief is sure to err,
And scan his work in vain:
God is his own interpreter,
And he will make it plain.

Do Real Christians Get Depressed?

The answer to this question should be clear enough by now. There are many people of deep faith who struggle or have struggled with depression. As these stories illustrate, the journey of depression can take many trajectories. There are some who experience depression in the face of a tragedy, whereas others may experience repeated bouts of depression despite apparent success. For all, the battle against depression resembles how someone might fight against a physical illness such as cancer and its recurrences. Or one might compare depression to the apostle Paul's thorn in the flesh. When Paul beseeched God repeatedly to remove this thorn, God answered, "…'My grace is sufficient for you, for my power is made perfect in weakness.' Therefore I will boast all the more gladly of my weaknesses, so that the power of Christ may rest upon me. For the sake of Christ, then, I am content with weaknesses, insults, hardships, persecutions, and calamities. For when I am weak, then I am strong" (2 Corinthians 12:9-10, ESV). Depression, too, is a weakness in which God's greatness can be magnified.

Myths and Misconceptions

There are many myths and misconceptions related to depression, including its causes and treatments. These often contribute to misunderstandings about people with depression, how to help them or even how to relate to them. We offer here a list of several of the most common and harmful myths.

Myth 1: *Depression is due to a lack of willpower.*
Overcoming depression with willpower was my strategy (HGK). I was determined to find my own way out of the emotional mess I was in. I would listen to no one and rejected the advice of friends and family. I figured I could do it entirely on my own through sheer self-mastery. I would pull myself up by my own bootstraps. It didn't work; it never does, because it can't. John Donne said, "No man is an island, entire of itself."[9] We were created to live in relationship, which includes receiving input and guidance from others, since no one person has complete knowledge from all perspectives on a situation.

Over time I became increasingly isolated, withdrawn into a fantasy world of my own creation. This led to my being expelled from medical school, living on the streets and nearly going insane. It took years of senseless wandering and a string of broken relationships before I was finally rescued by coming to know the Lord. He gave me the power to overcome my problems, a direction for my life and a caring faith community that I allowed to support and guide me. Willpower wasn't enough. The force of my emotional demons was just too strong for me. I needed God and His people to get me straight.

When we choose to align ourselves with God's will, He gives us both the will and the ability to work for His good pleasure (see Philippians 2:12-13). That good pleasure is that ultimately all things in heaven and earth will be brought under the lordship of Jesus Christ (see Ephesians 1:3-10). How our lives witness to His power, including His power over depression, is part of that process. We cannot will ourselves well; we can only willfully entrust ourselves and our needs to Him, asking Him to enable and empower us to live with our depression in a way that will honor Him.

Depression is a difficult battle, and willpower is an important strength to bring to the fight against depression. However, some individuals who pride themselves on their self-sufficiency may find it difficult to acknowledge weakness and their inability to overcome depression solely by willpower. It requires humility to acknowledge depression, humility to seek help and humility to rest on God's will for our lives.

Myth 2: *Depression is due to unconfessed sin. Suffering is punishment from God.*
Job was abandoned by his wife and most of his community after his losses, except for four friends, who were most effective in their encouragement when they tore their clothes and grieved silently with him. Unfortunately, when they finally did speak, their counsel to Job betrayed lack of understanding about the God's role in suffering and the appropriateness of Job's depression, for which they were later rebuked by God.

Job's friends claimed Job was suffering from unconfessed sin and demanded he repent. They suggested that Job's children had died because they must have been sinful and deserved it (Job 8:2-6), and furthermore that Job's suffering was also deserved and in fact he deserved more pain. "For you say, 'My doctrine is pure, and I am clean in God's eyes'...Know then that God exacts of you less than your guilt deserves" (Job 11:4-6, ESV).

Job's friends do make some accurate theological points. The consequence of sin is death (Romans 6:23), and since we all have sinned (Romans 3:23), we all do deserve death. But God, in His mercy, does not give us what we deserve. As Romans 8:1 declares, "There is therefore now no condemnation for those who are in Christ Jesus" (ESV). The only antidote to our sins is the fact that our faith in Christ places us "in Him," and as a result, we are justified before God.

The main problem for depressed believers is their guilt over sins God has already forgiven. Depressed Christians are sometimes so painfully aware of their sins that this is all they can focus on, and they are unable to hear the reassurance of grace. Depression can often produce a feeling of guilt, even without any basis in reality. At times, depression can distort a person's thoughts so much that Christians may even become delusional about their sinfulness. In these cases, depression is not a product of sin. Accusing them of sin may make matters worse.

Myth 3: *Depression is self-inflicted. You're depressed because you want to be depressed.*
Charles Spurgeon, one of the most influential English preachers both in his generation and in ours, struggled with depression throughout his lifetime, and he responds to those who make this accusation:

"One affords himself no pity when in this case, because it seems so unreasonable, and even sinful to be troubled without manifest cause; and yet troubled the man is, even in the very depths of his spirit. If those who laugh at such melancholy did but feel the grief of it for one hour, their laughter would be sobered into compassion."[10]

Spurgeon considered the topic of depression among those in ministry to be so important that he devoted an entire lecture to his seminary students on the topic, emphasizing how difficult it could be to treat:

"Causeless depression is not to be reasoned with, nor can David's harp charm it away by sweet discoursings. As well fight with the mist as with this shapeless, undefinable, yet, all-beclouding hopelessness...Resolution might, perhaps, shake it off, but where are we to find the resolution, when the whole man is unstrung? The physician and the divine may unite their skill in such cases, and both find their hands full, and more than full. The iron bolt which so mysteriously fastens the door of hope and holds our spirits in gloomy prison, needs a heavenly hand to push it back."[11]

As Spurgeon emphasizes, depression benefits from the united skill of both the physician and the minister, but it may still prove difficult to shake off. Depression impairs both resolution and hope. Sufferers must often wait for God's heavenly hand to release them from their prison.

It is possible for people to become accustomed to being depressed or to become so familiar with it that change is threatening. But only rarely is depression a conscious choice. Few people would choose to be depressed, in the same way few would choose suffering or chronic pain.

Myth 4: *Depression is self-pity. If you're depressed, you're just feeling sorry for yourself.*

The underlying accusation here is that a person is responding in grief that is out of proportion to their loss. However, people respond to challenging situations in various ways. What may not amount to much of a loss for one person, may be devastating for another. As we discussed in the previous chapter, this may be due to an individual's values (what gives a person their meaning and identity), previous losses they have experienced in the past or a genetic disposition that renders them more sensitive than others.

Indeed, those who are depressed often have lost hope and meaning that used to give direction and purpose to their lives. As pastor and author Zach Eswine put it, "But now imagine how this rupture of meaning feels to sufferers of depression, when 'the world in our heads' is filled not with 'reasons, plans, love and purpose' but with the loss of reasons, plans, love and purpose. In this state, both the world out there and the one within conspire miserably to deny hope. Both the floor and ceiling vanish. We free-fall with no place to land. When realistic hope quits, so do we."[12]

Along the same vein, somebody may tell the depressed individual, "A lot of people have it worse than you. You have nothing to be depressed about." This information may be given with good intentions. They are attempting to give perspective to the depressed person's suffering or may be trying to encourage a spirit of gratitude rather than complaining. Unfortunately, such advice is usually not helpful. The depressed person is often aware that there are those who suffer more than they do and are ashamed about it.

There are some responses that people give that lack sensitivity and are more difficult for us to have a charitable opinion of. Sometimes, others might tell the depressed person, "In fact, I have it worse than you. Let me tell you all the bad things that have happened to me...and I'm not depressed!" Or perhaps even worse, they might even theorize, "If I were you, I would not be so depressed," which is what Job's friend Eliphaz does (Job 5:8-27). As Job said to his friends, "I have heard many such things; miserable comforters are you all. Shall windy words have an end?" (Job 16:2-3a, ESV).

Myth 5: *Depression is due to lack of faith.*
Christians often erroneously believe that if a person is walking closely with God, he or she should not be depressed. Instead, the person should be confident in God's goodness, experience hope and joy and trust God whatever the circumstances. There is the belief that a spiritually mature person should be stoic, unperturbed to aversive life circumstances and immune to suffering.

If this were true, what should we make of the book of Psalms and Lamentations? What about Jesus weeping over the city of Jerusalem or sweating blood in the Garden of Gethsemane? Rather, we are called to "Rejoice with those who rejoice, weep with those who weep" (Romans 12:15, ESV). Stoicism, the belief that one should be detached from suffering, is not what is modeled to us in Scripture. Rather, this derives from the Stoics of Greek philosophy, whom Paul argued against, and which we encounter in modern times in Buddhist-based mindfulness. The answer is not to love people and love the world less, but the answer is rather to love God more.[13]

Spurgeon offers this critique to those who would judge the depressed as lacking in faith: "There are a great many of you who appear to have a large stock of faith, but it is only because you are in very good health and your business is prospering. If you happened to get a disordered liver, or your business should fail, I should not be surprised if nine parts out of ten of your wonderful faith should evaporate."[14]

Some people judge the depressed from the security of their own comfortable situations. It is easy for a person to have faith when things are going well, because they need not lean on their faith. It is when circumstances become difficult that one's faith is tested, and a person must hold tight in desperation to God's promises (Hebrews 11:1, James 1:2-3)

With respect to the spiritual disciplines, critical observers sometimes conclude that a depressed person's inability to engage in these practices is the cause for his or her depression, when it is actually a result of depression. People who haven't experienced depression cannot imagine how much depression makes it difficult to concentrate, sucks away energy and motivation, draws people into themselves and paralyzes action. For these reasons, depressed Christians have difficulty praying, engaging in Bible study and participating in fellowship at church.

Myth 6: *It's easy to tell when you are depressed.*
Depression is not easy to identify, especially for the person who is depressed. One of the hallmark symptoms of severe depression is that people lose the ability to recognize they have an illness that needs treatment. They believe they are dealing with a reality for which there is no possible change or cure. This sense of helplessness and hopelessness is a lie the vulnerable depressed person easily accepts.

Many people also have difficulty differentiating depression from normal grief or normal mood swings. It is very hard for most people to tell when they have crossed over the line from normal discouragement related to failure, loss or disappointment to a depression that affects their ability to function normally in life. Furthermore, the negative stigma associated with depression makes people feel embarrassed over having this condition, so they deny it to themselves, claiming there is nothing seriously wrong and the sadness will pass with time.

Depression is not easy to identify even for mental professionals who are used to making this diagnosis. Masked depression (depression that is covered up by other behaviors or health conditions) is very common. Depression may be masked by self-medication with drugs or alcohol, self-treatment with gambling or sex, or be manifested by physical symptoms that are misinterpreted as coming from medical causes.

On the other hand, many symptoms that look initially like depression may be due to medical causes, such as weight loss from cancer or other physical illness, reduced emotions due to Parkinson's disease or reduced motivation that often occurs in Alzheimer's disease or dementia. Mental conditions such as personality disorder, anxiety disorder or schizophrenia may also be confused with depression. The question of which came first is more of a challenge with trying to understand depression than the age-old question of which came first, the chicken or the egg.

If diagnosis of depression can be difficult for trained professionals, it is only reasonable this would be much harder for a non-professional. This is why, as the saying goes in medicine, "He who treats himself has a fool for a doctor." If doctors are foolish to treat themselves, their families or even their friends (because they may deny that something is wrong or lack the objectivity another doctor might provide), then surely one should to seek an objective professional opinion when the signs or symptoms of depression appear.

Myth 7: *Depression is due to a chemical imbalance.*

The myth that depression is just a chemical imbalance or deficiency can be a particularly insidious one, as it leads to a different kind of stigma. This particular misconception can lead some people to a feeling of helplessness, as they feel there is nothing they can do, the depression is beyond their control and they are dependent on medication for help. This can lead to further hopelessness if it takes several attempts of trial and error to find effective medication. Belief in this myth can also lead people who are depressed to neglect the other strategies—physical, psychological and spiritual—that often help in the fight against depression.

This myth betrays a misunderstanding of how the brain works. While the neurotransmitters serotonin, norepinephrine and dopamine, among others, have a role to play in depression, the brain does not function simply as a bank of neurotransmitters. Rather, the brain is an intricately designed organ that stores information within its neurocircuitry and is constantly adapting and changing.

A better over-simplification would be to consider depression to be a problem with faulty brain wiring. There are multiple ways that the brain can be wired for depression, which includes genetics, traumatic events, negative thought patterns and spiritual beliefs (see Chapter 3). In the same way, there are several ways to "re-wire" the brain, and these involve not only medication but other strategies as well.

In addition, this myth can lead the church to abdicate involvement in the lives of Christians struggling with depression (and mental illness in general). Church members might see depression as a purely physical issue, a matter for doctors and mental health professionals to handle. In reality, depression is tied to many spiritual issues (as there are with any kind of chronic suffering). The church has a role in encouraging its members to continue to walk by faith and look to God for hope and ultimate redemption, while also pursuing the physical and psychological strategies to heal from depression, which can be considered to be given by God out of common grace.

Myth 8: *Depression is a waste of time.*

One popular Christian book actually states exactly this—that depression is a waste of time. Yet when you take a God's-eye view, you see something quite different. The Scriptures are clear that God is doing something in our lives, remaking us into the image of Christ.

Our culture values productivity and accomplishment, efficiency and effectiveness. But consider the wasteful ways in which people spent their time in the Bible. Surely Moses' 40 years in Midian watching over sheep was a waste of time. And then (poor Moses), he was to spend another 40 years with Israel wandering about in the desert, never even entering the promised land. Surely that was a waste of a man who received Egypt's finest education. And then, above all, consider Jesus. Surely Jesus could have done better than spend 30 years of his life training as a carpenter, and then only three years engaged in active ministry. Likewise, consider the wasteful ways in which Jesus spent those precious three years: blessing children (Matthew 19:14) and dining with outcasts when he could have been influencing movers and shakers or been more productive healing or teaching. God has a vastly different value system.

Many of the examples of the people we gave earlier in the chapter are of those who have done "great" things by the world's standards. But those He considers greatest in His kingdom may be people we never know about.

> "At that time the disciples came to Jesus, saying, 'Who is the greatest in the kingdom of heaven?' And calling to him a child, he put him in the midst of them and said, 'Truly, I say to you, unless you turn and become like children, you will never enter the kingdom of heaven. Whoever humbles himself like this child is the greatest in the kingdom of heaven'" (Matthew 18:1-4, ESV).

Without depression, is it possible a person might have accomplished more in their lives? Possibly. Might they have had more friends, more wealth, a more impressive resume? Maybe. But this is not how God defines greatness. Nothing is wasted in God's economy (Romans 8:28).

Bible translator J. B. Phillips wrote,

> "It seems to me that, for the Christian anyway, the undoubted evil of this form of suffering can be turned into good by learning a deeper trust in the real and living God. It may be that we have relied too much upon the props of true and earthly friends. But in this painful experience we are stripped of our pride and pious imaginings. Temporarily at least we have no one who can understand what we are going through. **We are alone in this bewildering world and our only hope is in God, not probably the God who has satisfied us in past years or the God whom we imagined for our comfort, but the Spirit behind all creation. It is to know more deeply this real true God that we are permitted to go through the pains and humiliations of mental pain.**" (emphasis added by the authors)[15]

Many modern Christians only depend on God to do for them what they cannot do for themselves, and as a result, God is more or less an addendum to their lives. Those who have journeyed with Him into and out of depression know (experientially and not just theoretically) that they can only survive when God is present at every moment, the first and only focus of their faith.

God has a purpose in all that He causes or allows. He is going somewhere in our lives. The question is: Are we willing to go there too—on His terms, not ours, wherever that takes us—even depression?

Endnotes

1. http://lifewayresearch.com/wp-content/uploads/2014/09/Acute-Mental-Illness-and-Christian-Faith-Research-Report-1.pdf

2. https://www.thegospelcoalition.org/article/reflections-on-50th-anniversary-of-my-diving-accident/

3. https://www.thegospelcoalition.org/article/reflections-on-50th-anniversary-of-my-diving-accident/

4. Abraham Lincoln, in his 23 January 1841 letter to John Stuart, Lincoln's first law partner.

5. J. B. Phillips, *The Price of Success* (Wheaton, Ill.: Harold Shaw, 1984), 197-202.

6. Catherine B. Allen, *The New Lottie Moon Story* (Nashville: Broadman, 1980), 100.

7. Memes, John. *The Works of William Cowper: The life of William Cowper. Letters, 1765-1783*. Edinburgh: Fraser & Company, 1835

8. Cowper, William. The Works of William Cowper: His Life, Letters, and Poems. London: Phillips, Sampson, and Company, 1855. Page 474.

9. Donne, John. The Works of John Donne. vol III. Henry Alford, ed. London: John W. Parker, 1839. 574-5.

10. Spurgeon, Charles. *Letters to My Students*. Zondervan, 1954. Page 163.

11. Charles Spurgeon. "The Minister's Fainting Fits." from Lectures to My Students: a selection from addresses delivered to the students of Pastor's College Metropolitan Tabernacle, 1869

12. Eswine, Zach. Spurgeon's Sorrows, p79

13. Keller, Tim, Walking with God Through Pain and Suffering, p44

14. Charles Spurgeon, "Night and Jesus Not There," in MTP, Vol 51 (Ages Digital Library, 1998) p457. From Eswine, Spurgeon's Sorrows, p76

15. J. B. Phillips, *The Price of Success* (Wheaton, Ill.: Harold Shaw, 1984), 205.

PART II:
STRATEGIES

CHAPTER 5

THE BODY

"Or do you not know that your body is a temple of the Holy Spirit within you, whom you have from God? You are not your own, for you were bought with a price. So glorify God in your body."

—1 Corinthians 6:19-20, ESV

Our bodies matter to God. Depression tends to deny that, and it tells people they don't matter, their lives don't matter and their bodies don't matter. But that is depression's lie. God certainly paid for lives and our salvation at great cost to Himself. And as a consequence, we are no longer our own. We belong to God. Moreover, He dwells within every believer. Our bodies are not simply our own to use and abuse. This means we are to be stewards of our bodies and care for them, even when we feel worthless and self-destructive. And this is especially true when it comes to depression. To glorify God with our bodies means to care for our bodies, even as depression seems to drain the body of its vitality.

Regardless of what the cause is for depression (see Chapter 3), depression is experienced in the body. People experience depression as physical symptoms, such as difficulty sleeping, change in appetite, lack of energy, moving slowly, difficulty thinking and a dulling of the senses, while food lacks taste and colors appear less bright. So, it makes sense that one way to fight against depression is also through physical strategies involving the body.

In most books about depression, the only two strategies discussed are medication or psychotherapy. While we spend significant time discussing those two strategies, there are a whole host of others involving things like sleep, diet and exercise that can be helpful; although, for anything more than mild depression, they should probably be combined with therapy (Chapter 6) and/or medication.

Ruts in the Road and Neuroplasticity

The brain is one of the mysteries of creation that we are only just starting to understand through science and medicine. As more knowledge about the mechanisms of the brain is uncovered, researchers are also constantly revising their theories about how it works. As we discussed in Chapter 3, an early theory was that depression was caused by a neurotransmitter deficiency in the brain.

But science has moved ahead to understanding the brain as functioning primarily through connections between neurons, through how the brain gets wired and rewired, in a process called neuroplasticity. The brain is constantly changing and adapting, strengthening the pathways used to make them more efficient and removing the pathways we no longer use.

Why is this important? The way that I (JH) often explain it to patients is that the repeated thoughts of depression or anxiety function like ruts in a road. Repeated thoughts wear those ruts deeper and deeper as we use these particular pathways in the brain over and over. So, it becomes easier and easier to slide down these ruts into depression, and it becomes harder and harder to get out of them and create new pathways.

Fortunately, there are ways to break out of those ruts. One particular growth factor to remember is Brain Derived Neurotrophic Factor (BDNF), a protein in the brain that supports neuron survival, growth and development. One might think of it as fertilizer for the brain. Long-term stress decreases the amount of BDNF in the brain and causes shrinkage of the hippocampus, the area in the brain associated with learning and memory. People with chronic depression have atrophy of the hippocampus and the areas of the brain related to motivation and emotion. Fortunately, increasing BDNF in the brain can stimulate re-growth and development in the brain. BDNF can be increased by several strategies, including sleep, exercise, diet, medication, ECT, learning and psychotherapy.[1]

BDNF helps people break out of those ruts in the road, but it also requires positive lifestyle changes in order to establish better, healthier pathways. This paradigm is important to keep in mind during this and the following chapters. Incorporating as many of these strategies as possible increases a person's chances of healing.

Sleep and Rest

Sleep and mood are closely intertwined. Consider what you felt like when you were sleep deprived: perhaps you were more irritable; experienced decreased energy, poor concentration; and had difficulty enjoying things. Sleep deprivation can cause depression.

Is sleep deprivation self-inflicted? If a person's schedule is so busy that they are not allowing themselves time to rest, then sleep needs to be prioritized so they can handle all the tasks the day throws at them. Psalm 127:2 says, "It is in vain that you rise up early and go late to rest, eating the bread of anxious toil; for he gives to his beloved sleep" (ESV).

We need to examine what is driving us to be so busy. Oftentimes there is an underlying fear. Is it fear of not having enough? Is it fear of missing out on some achievement, experience or social event? Is it overcommitment due to fear of saying no and disappointing others? God never intended for our lives to be all about work. Even God, when He had finished with the creation, entered the "Sabbath rest." Our worth does not lie in what we do, but who we are. We can rest in Christ's work on the cross for our salvation. Practically, this means the rest of sleep, as well as considering what it might mean for you personally to remember the Sabbath.

Take time to enjoy activities with friends, take vacations with loved ones and regularly get away from all stress for a period of time. One will not be able to totally eliminate stress—no one can—but a person can learn to manage it proactively instead of feeling like he or she is at its mercy. This management of time, energy and resources may seem difficult, especially if one feels victimized by life in one way or another. Taking time to set goals, however, can give a new sense of mastery over any situation with all its problems.

One possibility is to consider attending retreat centers operated by different Christian groups, which will allow a person to spend a long weekend in the mountains or somewhere in nature where he or she can focus on reflection, scriptural study, prayer and fellowship. These times can be enormously refreshing. One may think that one can't afford the luxury of such a retreat, but the truth may be that one cannot afford not to go.

Two recommended books on this subject are *Margin* and *The Overload Syndrome* by Richard A. Swenson, MD.

Megan, who had struggled with depression for nearly a decade, found that her entire perspective on life changed during a weeklong retreat at a Christian center in the Appalachian Mountains. She was taking antidepressants and seeing a counselor, but she had done so for years with only partial relief of her symptoms. At the retreat, far away from the stresses of her work and family life, something inside of her suddenly clicked during one of the meditation sessions. She had a spiritual revelation about herself. This was followed almost immediately by a deep sense of peace. That peace continued for many months after returning to the real world. When things got crazy in her life, Megan would recall that experience and find the peace again. She found that attending the retreat two or three times a year (combined with continued therapy and antidepressants) helped to control her depression.

Is difficulty sleeping due to depression? Change in sleep patterns is one of the core symptoms of depression, and a person with depression may experience chronic exhaustion despite allowing themselves adequate sleep time. Seventy-five percent of people with depression experience difficulty sleeping (insomnia), but there are also some, particularly young adults and women, who experience excessive sleeping (hypersomnia). Indeed, sleep disturbance can greatly impair quality of life and increases risk of suicide. If sleep problems continue even after the depression symptoms are gone, a person has a higher chance of experiencing a recurrence of depression.[2]

If someone is having difficulty sleeping, the first step might be to examine his or her sleep habits and implement good sleep hygiene.

Sleep Hygiene

The Bedroom Environment

1. Extraneous noise in the bedroom can disrupt your sleep, so use whatever you need to create a quiet environment. Get earplugs or a white noise generator that produces consistent noise, like a sound machine or a fan. Variable noise like television can disrupt sleep.

2. Limit use of the bed to only sleep or sexual activity, so your mind associates the bed with sleep. Avoid watching TV, eating, answering emails, shopping, studying or doing otherwise stimulating activities in bed.

3. Keep the room cool. The ideal sleep temperature is cool, between 60 and 70 degrees Fahrenheit.

Light Rhythms

Light signals to the body's clock when it's time to sleep and when it's time to wake up.

1. Natural light keeps your internal clock on a healthy sleep-wake cycle. So, let in the light first thing in the morning and try to expose yourself to natural sunlight during the day.

2. Artificial lights can alter your body's internal clock. Turn off or dim overhead lights and lamps in your house 30 to 60 minutes before going to bed. Cell phones, computers and TV screens produce blue light, which interferes with the internal clock. It can be helpful to get a blue light filter for these devices, which may be built into the operating system as a "night light." Software apps, physical screen filters and glasses are available to accomplish this as well.

3. Watching a clock as you try to fall asleep can increase your stress level, making it harder for you to fall back asleep once you've woken. Position the alarm clock so it's hard for you to see it from the bed.

Sleep Practices

1. Keep a consistent sleep schedule. Going to bed and waking up at the same time each day, even on the weekends, sets the body's internal clock to expect sleep at a certain time night after night. Waking up at the same time each day is the best way to set your clock, and even if you did not sleep well the night before, the extra sleep drive will help you consolidate sleep the following night.

2. Nap early, or not at all. Many people make naps a regular part of their day. However, for those who find falling asleep or staying asleep through the night problematic, afternoon napping may be one of the culprits. This is because late-day naps decrease sleep drive. If you must nap, it's better to keep it short (less than 30 minutes) and before 5 p.m.

3. Develop a bedtime routine. Creating a set of habits to run through at night will help your body recognize that it's time to unwind. For instance, 30 to 60 minutes before bedtime, consider reading in bed or taking a warm shower or bath. Avoid stressful, stimulating activities, such as doing work or discussing emotional issues. Physically and psychologically stressful activities can cause the body to secrete the stress hormone cortisol, which is associated with increasing alertness. If you tend to take your problems to bed, try keeping a notepad next to the bed, write them down and then put them aside.

4. Go to sleep when you're truly tired. Struggling to fall sleep just leads to frustration. If you're not asleep after 20 minutes, get out of bed, go to another room and do something relaxing, like reading or listening to music in dim light until you are tired enough to sleep. The same is true if you wake up in the middle of the night and can't get back to sleep in about 20 minutes.

Lifestyle Choices

1. Stay away from stimulants at night. Nicotine and caffeine are chemicals that keep you awake, so drinking tea, coffee, cola, eating chocolate, using pain relievers containing caffeine or using anything containing tobacco or nicotine should be avoided for four to six hours before you plan to sleep.

2. Limit alcohol consumption. Although alcohol may help bring on sleep, after a few hours it acts as a stimulant, increasing the number of awakenings and generally decreasing the quality of sleep later in the night. It is therefore best to limit alcohol consumption to no more than one to two drinks per day, and to avoid drinking within three hours of bedtime.

3. Pay attention to food and drink intake before bed. Feeling hungry or overly full at bedtime means you're less likely to get comfortable sleep. Drinking too much liquid late in the evening could cause you to make multiple trips to the bathroom throughout the night.

4. Exercise can help you fall asleep faster and sleep more soundly—as long as it's done at the right time. Exercise helps with mood, and physical fatigue can help with sleep. However, it also stimulates alertness, so try to finish exercising at least three hours before bed or work out earlier in the day.

If a person still experiences difficulty sleeping after implementing these sleep hygiene practices, he or she should consider a medical evaluation with a primary care doctor or sleep specialist to see if there are other causes for insomnia. Sleep disorders such as sleep apnea, restless legs syndrome, narcolepsy or other medical conditions can all cause difficulty with sleep.

If the problem does seem to be insomnia, the next step would be to implement cognitive behavioral therapy for insomnia (CBT-I), which is a program that addresses the underlying causes of poor sleep. CBT-I usually involves practices such as stimulus control, sleep restriction and relaxation training. CBT-I can be obtained several ways, including by finding a therapist who specializes in CBT-I, through a self-guided book/workbook or by using a smartphone app. Currently, three of the more well-known apps are Shut-I, Sleepio (covered by some employers), and CBT-I Coach (free, developed for veterans).

One can also try options such as sleepy herbal tea, gentle stretching, meditating on Scripture or prayer. One final option to consider is medication, although in general use of these should be short-term only. Even medications that can be purchased over the counter such as melatonin or other sleep aids (which typically contain antihistamines such as diphenhydramine) should be discussed with a physician. A physician can prescribe other more potent sleep medications as well, and a psychiatrist in particular can prescribe one that is best suited to a particular mental condition. For example, sedating antidepressants might be ideally suited for someone with depression, and a sedating mood stabilizer might be helpful for someone with bipolar disorder.

Exercise

Exercise is a powerful and underutilized treatment for depression. An analysis of multiple research studies and randomized controlled trials has shown that exercise is just as effective as medication or psychotherapy in treating mild to moderate depression.[3] Adding exercise to treatment increased the effectiveness of antidepressants.[4] Indeed, in one pilot study, 17 individuals whose depression did not respond to antidepressants were enrolled in a 12-week exercise program while continuing their antidepressants. Of the eight people who completed the study, all had a substantial improvement in depression, and five were able to achieve complete remission from depression.[5] Other research suggests that regular exercise can prevent depression and anxiety from even developing.[6]

How does exercise help with depression? There are both immediate and long-term effects. During high-intensity exercise, endorphins are released in the body that decrease sensitivity to pain and can contribute to a sense of euphoria, such as the "runner's high." For low-intensity exercise sustained over time, growth factors such as BDNF are released in the brain. Thirty minutes of aerobic activity per day can increase BDNF in the brain up to 300 percent, as well as improve focus and increase cognitive function.

What kind of exercise? If someone has not exercised for some time or has other health conditions, it would be wise to talk with one's primary care physician before starting on an exercise program. The current recommendation is 30 to 60 minutes per day of moderate aerobic exercise (to the point where it feels "somewhat hard") for at least three days per week or as many days as possible.[7] Ultimately, the best kind of exercise is whatever someone enjoys and will continue doing. This does not necessarily mean only lifting weights at the gym or running. Other ideas might include a pickup basketball league at the local YMCA, long brisk walks around the neighborhood, hiking, P90X boot camp, yoga, dance class or boxing. For those with joint pain, cycling or swimming may be ideal. Another suggestion is to consider incorporating prayer or listening to music, audiobooks or Scripture during exercise (www.esv.org has a great audio version that can be streamed on a devices). Exercise is often hard to stick to alone, so enlisting a friend or family member to drop by regularly to walk around the block or exercise together may be helpful. Exercising outdoors can have other important benefits, and it has been shown to be more effective for depression than exercising indoors.[8]

Light

People used to spend a lot of time outdoors, and it is only in modern times that people have begun to spend less time in the sunlight and more time indoors working under artificial lighting, commuting in cars or sitting in front of devices such as TVs, computers and phones. The importance of light's effect on mood is apparent in Seasonal Affective Disorder, where the decrease in light exposure during the winter causes some people to develop depression (see Chapter 3). Light exposure can also cause a temporary increase in mood, as those who have spent a day at the beach can attest to, and it partially explains why some people are addicted to tanning salons (not recommended due to the risk for skin cancer).

Light exposure can also release endorphins in the skin, leading to a temporary euphoria.[9] Light exposure sets the body's circadian rhythm, which sets all of the body's rhythms for sleep, growth and healing. Light also promotes the formation of vitamin D in the skin, which plays a role in depression as well.

Increasing exposure to light is a relatively easy, low risk way to help with depression. The most straightforward way is to spend time outside in the sun. The proportion of time spent outside versus indoors is the most important factor for light exposure, and the next important influence is season, which affects the length and intensity of daylight. Exposure to less than one hour of daylight per day seems to be correlated with increased depression.[10]

Another option is artificial light therapy (also known as phototherapy), which can be discussed further with a psychiatrist. People who benefit most from light therapy are those who have "atypical depression," a quite common subtype of depression characterized by oversleeping, overeating and social withdrawal.[11,12] One may also ask their physician to obtain labs to check for vitamin D deficiency, which can be easily treated with Vitamin D supplements.[13]

Diet and the Gut

Recently, there has been a lot of popular interest in the connection between the gut and mood. This makes sense. We have an extensive network of nerves in the gut, so much so it is nicknamed the "second brain."

The gut can influence mood through several pathways. The vagus nerve directly connects the gut with the brain. In addition, we have an entire ecosystem of various species of healthy bacteria (the gut microbiome) that inhabit our gut and help us to digest and extract nutrients from our food. These gut bacteria are one of the key producers of neurotransmitters in the body and are the source of 95 percent of the body's supply of serotonin.

Stress and diet can affect the composition of these bacteria, which in return also regulate the immune and stress hormone system in the body. This is why it is not uncommon, for example, for people with stress or anxiety to experience constipation or diarrhea (as people who struggle with a condition called Irritable Bowel Syndrome are keenly aware of), and why antidepressants often initially cause symptoms such as nausea and diarrhea. It is through all these pathways—directly through nerves by producing neurotransmitters and through its influence on immune and stress hormone systems—that the gut can influence brain function and growth.[14,15]

It makes sense to consider what influence our diet might have on our mood. A few pathways are immediately obvious. Alcohol, marijuana and other mind-altering substances, while they might seem to help in the moment, serve in the long run generally to worsen depression. The same is true of consumption of sugar, refined carbohydrates and processed foods, which can lead to brief improvement in mood but results in spikes and crashes in blood sugar levels, producing further cravings and a feeling of lack of control. It is theorized that sugar and refined carbohydrates cause changes in the gut microbiome, increase inflammation and, with the risk of weight gain, all serve in long run to worsen depression.

Dulling the Pain with Alcohol or Drugs

For men, alcohol may be the substance most widely used to self-medicate for depression. As mentioned earlier, alcoholism is higher among men and depression is lower compared to women. It is possible the two are related—men would usually rather medicate with alcohol than talk about their problems with a psychotherapist or depend on an antidepressant medication to make them feel better.

The following is adapted from an article by David Biebel published in *New Man* magazine:

> Gradually, like many men with broken hearts, I began to fill the hole in my heart with alcohol. But the more booze I poured into this hole, the deeper it got. I struggled with this growing dependency, for I knew that only Jesus could satisfy my soul. But I didn't want to let go of the pain, for doing so would be to surrender: "God, you win."
>
> I knew that beyond the wilderness of confusion and on the other side of the mountains of pain, with their valleys of depression, was joy, which was where God wanted to take me. But for years I insisted that if I was going to go there it would have to be on my own terms.
>
> One day, when I was hiking near the Continental Divide in Colorado, I was struck by the awesome beauty of the golden aspens against the cobalt blue sky, and I began to thank God for making it that way. From this simple beginning, the rest came tumbling out. One by one, I laid down before God the things He brought to mind: my sadness, my bitterness, my career, my family. But when He brought up the bottle, I realized that I couldn't imagine facing a day without it. That's when I knew I was in trouble.
>
> I wish I could say the solution was simple, but anyone who has struggled with "demon rum" knows it doesn't let go without a fight. In fact, the struggle intensified over the next few months. The harder I tried to whip it in my own strength, the more I needed the bottle in order to fight the battle. And the more alcohol I poured into that hole in my heart, the deeper it became.
>
> Finally, on Easter morning I was sitting in church thinking: Either the Resurrection is real, or it's not. If it's not, then none of this matters, and I might as well go live in the mountains as a hermit with my dog and gun and a case of Old Grand-Dad and have some fun before I die, which won't be too long from now because I'll certainly drink myself into oblivion.
>
> But if the Resurrection is true, then the power that raised Jesus from the dead is available to me to live the life and fulfill the mission to which God has called me, part of which requires me to stop trying to fill my void with anything other than Himself.
>
> I wish I could say that I've never even wanted another drink. The fact is, the next month following that Easter day was the hardest month I have ever lived. Every day, nearly every minute, every cell in my body longed for a drink. But gradually, as my brain adjusted to seeing life without a haze, the desire diminished in intensity. Still, day by day, I must remind myself that the only way to fill the emptiness that I sometimes still feel is with a more intimate knowledge of God.

Alcohol itself is a depressant, not just of the mind but of the body too. The net result of using alcohol to dull the pain of depression is that after the alcohol wears off the depression intensifies. Using alcohol to dull the pain is bad enough; combining alcohol with drugs, whether street drugs or prescription drugs (or simply self-medicating with drugs) can be a recipe for disaster.

Medications can be abused as well. The most common abuses occur with stimulants such as amphetamines (such as Adderall), diet pills, anxiolytic medications like benzodiazepines, painkillers (such as Oxycodone, fentanyl) or medications for sleep. Many depressed persons are just trying to survive by taking these medications, which provide rapid temporary relief. But a person may become dependent on these medications, and there is a temptation to continue escalating the dosage due to increased tolerance without dealing with the real source of distress. The net result is that the person's problems are compounded rather than relieved. The current opioid crisis is a good example of where these abuses can be deadly.

It can be hard to make changes in diet when a person is depressed, particularly with atypical depression, which is characterized by increased appetite for carbohydrates in particular. In general, research suggests that people who are on diets high in fruits and vegetables, whole grains, fish, olive oil and low-fat dairy (such as in the Mediterranean Diet) experience improvement in depression, compared to those whose diets are characterized by red meat, refined grains, sweets and high fat dairy.[16,17]

In addition, the proportion of healthy bacteria in the gut can be increased by consuming a *variety* of fruits and vegetables, including fermented foods such as yogurt, kimchi, sauerkraut and kombucha. It is also possible to ingest healthy bacteria in the form of probiotic capsules, although since this is a new field, there is no standardization yet of what dose and strains are best.[18]

There is also some evidence that increasing omega 3 fatty acids, particularly those rich in eicosapentaenoic acid (EPA) and docosahexaenoic acid (DHA) such as in fish oil, can be beneficial in depression if taken in supplements with an approximately 60/40 EPA to DHA ratio. This may be due to a reduction in inflammation.[19,20]

Medication

Forrest Jones facilitates a depression support group sponsored by Lookout Mountain Community Church in Golden, Colorado. Without exception, during the time the group meets—usually weekly for three or four months—fellow pilgrims who started out as strangers become close friends, in part due to Forrest's sensitive leadership. The changes in and between the participants are remarkable in themselves, but perhaps even more remarkable is the fact that as recently as 1999, the facilitator was so depressed he couldn't even get out of bed. Here is his story in his own words:

"In retrospect," Forrest said, "I can see that I've had some symptoms of depression most of my life. But about three years ago three unrelated events happened in succession, and this triggered my first major depression—my mother died, I turned fifty, and I quit a job I loved because I didn't see eye-to-eye with my supervisor.

"Over the next year, I gradually slid into the muck of despair. For the first six months I was barely functional. Then it just seemed that my energy left. I could hardly get out of bed. I felt so alone, worthless, mired in misery and emotional pain. I even prayed to die.

"I sensed that my marriage was suffering, and that just added to my feelings of worthlessness. Finally my wife, Connie, confronted me, saying, 'Something has to change. You can't go on like this. You have to get help.'

"Asking for help was the hardest thing I've ever done, partly due to my pride," Forrest continued. "After all, I've been a Christian forty years. Shouldn't I be able to help myself?

"Providentially, only two days after I decided to ask for help, a depression support group was started in a local church. I'll never forget that first meeting because when I walked in, my primary feeling was that I would rather be anywhere other than there. I didn't want to have to describe my struggles, but it was clear from the outset that the room was occupied by a group of special people, each with his or her own story, most of them a lot like my own. So, maybe I'm not so strange, I thought. From that night on, hope took root in my heart…hope that I might someday experience joy again.

"The other thing that happened that night was equally difficult for me. The topic of antidepressant medication came up again and again. I'd rather be dead than have to take drugs for this, was my thought. 'But the right medication will help you think more clearly,' I heard, 'and this will speed your healing.' 'You'd have to stand on me and shove the pills down my throat,' I said. However, the Lord convicted me that if I really wanted to recover, I had to stop insisting that it be on my own terms.

"My physician started me on an antidepressant, which I took for five or six weeks before telling him that it was helping a little, but my life was still mostly gray. He doubled the dosage, and within days the difference was like night and day. Life was beautiful again, in living color. I was happy to be alive.

"It took a long time and the help of a psychiatrist to settle on the right combination of drugs that would most help me. During this long journey, several things have become clear to me: (1) The Lord can use my struggle to help others. (2) Most people who are afflicted with depression are compassionately sensitized to the suffering of others. (3) With today's advanced medications, there is no reason that anyone should slog sadly along in silence as I did for a year, because there is healing to be had."

How Medications Work

We've named this book *Downcast*, and in a very real way those who are depressed are cast down. Those with depression find it very hard to break out of this—they lose their sense of motivation and meaning, they tend to interpret everything through black tinted lenses and they find it very difficult to learn or try something new.

All these aspects of depression have corresponding findings in the brain. People with depression have reduced levels of BDNF, which results in decreased neuron growth and development. Within the brain, there is atrophy of the hippocampus and prefrontal cortex, which are associated with motivation and learning. In contrast, there is overgrowth of the nucleus accumbens and amygdala, which are associated with fear, emotion and sleep regulation.[21,22]

Because depression can have strong biological roots, medication or other biological therapies may be necessary and can be lifesaving. Just as diabetes often requires insulin and high blood pressure requires antihypertensive medications, depression may require drugs to help break out of the cast of depression.

Understanding how antidepressants work is important. Antidepressants do **not** work, as was once popularly thought, by fixing a chemical imbalance. In our experience, this misconception has led to many fears about taking antidepressants, such as that it will change their personality or that they will become dependent on the medication.

Rather, recent research suggests antidepressants work by two mechanisms. The first is by increasing BDNF in the brain, which enhances neuroplasticity and can counter the atrophy that occurs with depression. This process takes weeks to occur.

Antidepressants work through a second more immediate mechanism by altering the black-tinted lenses by which depressed people experience the world and recall events. Depressed people have a negative bias—they tend to pay attention to and remember only negative information, and they disregard positive information. This bias can be addressed through therapy (which we describe in the next chapter) and can be helped by antidepressants. Several studies have shown that after just one dose of an antidepressant, people are more attentive to faces with positive facial expressions, not just to faces with negative expressions. Although the symptoms of depression do not lift so quickly, what is important is that over time, depressed individuals can learn a new way of perceiving the world and their interactions in it.

The practical takeaway from this is that antidepressants work by helping depressed people learn new ways of perceiving and interacting with the world. In order for antidepressants to be effective, individuals must engage in activities that allow learning to occur. They need to engage in activities such as psychotherapy, exercise and social interaction including attending church, serving others or meaningful work. Antidepressants are not a quick fix, so simply staying at home and taking antidepressants will be insufficient to break out of the cast of depression.

Are Antidepressants Effective?

Clinical research studies spanning nearly 50 years have demonstrated that antidepressant drugs are safe and effective treatments for depression compared to placebos (a sugar pill). Yet many critics of psychiatry raise doubts about the effectiveness of antidepressants. They claim antidepressants are a product of pharmaceutical company marketing and collusion with psychiatrists.

These critics cite several studies to support their claims, one of which we examine here. In one highly publicized study in 2000, psychiatrist Arif Khan analyzed the results of 52 studies contained in the Food and Drug Administration (FDA)'s database and reported that in only 48 percent of these studies was an antidepressant superior to a placebo.[23] Many people in the media interpreted Dr. Khan's results to mean that antidepressants are on average no more effective than a sugar pill and, by implication, that antidepressants really don't work. However, the truth is more complicated than that.

For one thing, not all depression is the same. As we discussed in Chapter 2 on definitions, the DSM diagnosis of major depressive disorder describes a wide range of conditions with multiple possible causes. Consequently, two persons who are considered "depressed" by these studies may have very different underlying biological conditions, some which are less responsive to medication.

Most people who are recruited into depression studies have milder forms of depression. These people typically are not depressed enough to be hospitalized, are generally physically healthy, are functioning well enough to come in for clinic visits and comply with the study medication. They are not suicidal and often do not have other medical problems or substance use disorders. Thus, the research subjects Dr. Khan refers to in his article were relatively highly functioning people with mild to moderate uncomplicated depression. For those with milder forms of depression, it is true that antidepressants offer little benefit over placebo. For those with moderate to severe depression, however, antidepressants are substantially more beneficial.[24,25]

Finally, when people are involved in a clinical trial to test the effects of an antidepressant versus placebo, they receive a significant amount of monitoring, social support and encouragement, regardless of whether subjects are taking active drug or placebo. Therefore, there is a good chance their mild to moderate depression will improve just because of the attention they receive.

Given these considerations, we would conclude (contrary to Dr. Khan) that it is actually impressive that 52 percent of such studies actually show a benefit of the antidepressant over the placebo. This number is consistent with findings from the STAR*D trial, one of the largest studies of antidepressant efficacy for depression ever conducted, which involved a randomized control trial of more than 3,000 subjects. The STAR*D trial found that about 60 percent of people experienced at least 50 percent improvement in depressive symptoms with antidepressants.[26]

Thus, antidepressants do work for many people and can be vital in helping to overcome depression. It may take time, trial and error to find the right medication for a person's particular manifestation of depression.

Who Should Take Medication?

Studies have found that for mild to moderate depression, medications have about the same effectiveness as psychotherapy, and that combining the two is even better.[27] Medication can lift depression to the point where a person can at least work with a therapist in changing their thoughts, behaviors or attitudes. For Christians, antidepressants may help to break the paralysis that prevents a person from engaging in spiritual disciplines or participating in fellowship. Antidepressants can help people to function so they can better handle the stressors in their lives. These drugs can truly be lifesaving, and for some depressed persons with a strong biological contribution to their depression, they are necessary and unavoidable.

In general, people with depression should seriously consider taking antidepressants:

> **If they experience a lot of physical symptoms with their depression**, i.e., their depression affects their sleep, appetite and ability to think and focus.

> **If they are unable to make progress in psychotherapy despite hard work for several months.** Adding an antidepressant can help a person engage in psychotherapy and apply the skills they learn.

> **If a person is having trouble functioning because of their depression** and is struggling to fulfill their responsibilities and maintain relationships.

> **If they are experiencing psychotic symptoms,** such as hallucinations or delusions with their depression.

> **If their depression is severe** or they have stopped caring for themselves.

> **If they have thoughts about suicide**, and it becomes urgent to use all means possible to treat the depression.

> **If antidepressants have been helpful in the past**, as there is a good chance they will be helpful in future episodes of depression.

What Antidepressants Can't Do

Unfortunately, antidepressants are not happy pills that permanently and miraculously cure depression. As we have discussed, antidepressants enhance neuroplasticity, the ability of the brain to learn and grow. Therefore, it takes time for antidepressants to work. It usually takes at least four weeks for antidepressants to start to have an effect, and a total of six to eight weeks to exert their full effect. In addition, more than just medication is usually required to achieve complete and lasting remission of symptoms. New patterns of behavior and thinking need to be developed. Antidepressants cannot make up for habitual bad decisions, insensitivity to the needs of others, spiritually wayward behavior, psychosocial stressors or self-defeating thinking. It is crucial to understand and address whatever is at the root of the depression.

Common Questions about Taking Medication

Despite the benefits of medication, many people often refuse to take antidepressants. Here are a few of the common fears.

> **Will it change my personality?**
Antidepressants do not change your values, your interests or who you fundamentally are as a person. But some studies suggest it can affect two particular personality traits: neuroticism and extraversion. Neuroticism is the tendency to interpret everything negatively and to experience emotional instability in response to stress, and it is closely tied to the development of mental disorders such as depression, anxiety and substance use. Extraversion is the state of enjoying human interaction, being social and outgoing. Depression tends to decrease a person's extraversion and cause social withdrawal. Antidepressants can help decrease this tendency towards negativity and increase a person's extraversion.[28]

> **Will it turn me into a zombie?**
Antidepressants decrease the severity of the lows of depression and make it easier to handle challenges. Some people experience this as a decrease in emotional range, as they are not as painfully sad but also do not experience happiness in the same way either. For these patients, decreasing the dose or switching to another antidepressant usually improves these symptoms. But no, these medications never make people into "zombies," if what is meant is an emotionless robot.

> **Will I become addicted to antidepressants?**
Clinically, the word "addiction" is used to describe the behavior of a person who seeks more and more of a substance even when it is detrimental to other important areas of their life, such as their health, relationships, work or other responsibilities. Antidepressants do not give the "high" that is characteristic of drugs people abuse, and so they do not cause addiction. However, antidepressants can cause withdrawal symptoms when stopped suddenly. When someone takes any medication for a long period of time, whether antidepressants for depression or Benadryl for allergies or Advil for headaches, the body adapts to it and therefore will cause side effects if suddenly stopped. For this reason, antidepressants should be tapered off gradually under medical supervision. The presence of withdrawal symptoms, however, does not mean that a person was addicted to the medication.

> **Am I going to be on this medication forever?**
The general recommendation is that if someone has had one uncomplicated episode of mild to moderate depression and recovers, it is worth trying to taper off and stop the medication after nine months.[29] However, if someone has had multiple episodes of depression, or a particularly severe episode of depression, they would likely benefit from staying on an antidepressant to reduce the rate of relapse.

› **Will I have to try lots of different medications? I don't want to be a guinea pig!**
Because each person has such a unique physical makeup, no one can tell ahead of
time what medication, dosage or combination of medications will help to improve an
individual's symptoms. According to the STAR*D trial, about 40 percent of patients
who start a serotonin reuptake inhibitor (SSRI, a type of antidepressant) experience
improvement in depression, and 30 percent achieve complete remission of symptoms. If
the first SSRI fails, about 25 percent who switch to another medication will get better,
or if patients add a new medication to the existing SSRI, about one in three people will
get better.[30] There is hope in the future that with genetic testing we will be better able
to predict which medications are likely to be helpful or intolerable due to side effects.
Unfortunately, we are not yet at that point. For now, treatment with antidepressants
requires patience, both to give them time to work as well as to try various medications if
initially unsuccessful.

Who Should Prescribe Medication?

› **Primary Care Physicians**
For many people, the easiest healthcare professional to turn to would be their primary
care physician (PCP), such as a family doctor or internal medicine doctor, or the medical
specialist a person sees most often, such as an OB/Gyn (obstetrics-gynecologist). The
advantage of this is that these doctors are the easiest to access. Primary care physicians
probably treat more cases of depression today than do psychiatrists, because there are
many more of them. Because health insurers are encouraging medical doctors rather than
refer to psychiatrists to treat depression, this trend is likely to continue to grow.

There is a wide range in how comfortable PCPs may be with treating depression. Some
primary care physicians may have little interest or training in the treatment of depression,
while others have a keen interest and skill in this regard. Some, even if they lack expertise
themselves, may have the ability to call on consult psychiatrists for advice, in a model
of care known as integrative care or collaborative care. It is appropriate to ask a primary
care physician about their interest and expertise in treating depression, and to request a
referral to a psychiatrist if necessary.

The disadvantage of seeking care from a PCP is the risk that a psychiatric condition
such as bipolar disorder or post-traumatic stress disorder may be missed and that it may
take longer to find the effective dose and type of medication. However, for a person
with a straightforward case of depression, with no previous trials of other psychiatric
medication, a primary care doctor can be a good first choice.

⟩ Psychiatrists

Psychiatrists are medical doctors who have completed medical school and four years of specialty training in psychiatry. The advantage of seeking out a psychiatrist is that they should have a full understanding of the various psychiatric diagnosis and their presentations. They will also be well versed in prescribing different types of psychiatric medications and understanding their side effects. In addition, some psychiatrists also provide psychotherapy, and it may be ideal to see someone who can both counsel as well as prescribe medication. However, the disadvantage of seeing a psychiatrist is there may be a long waiting list to see someone who will take insurance; otherwise, it may be quite expensive. In many cases, it might not be a bad idea to ask a PCP if they could start you on an antidepressant while you wait to see a psychiatrist.

Furthermore, it can be really difficult to find a psychiatrist who is also a Christian. One way to locate one is to ask your pastor or a Christian counselor if they can refer you to Christian psychiatrist, or you can search for a psychiatrist in the Christian Health Professional Member Search of Christian Medical & Dental Associations (CMDA) at www.cmda.org.

If a Christian psychiatrist cannot be located, working with a psychiatrist who shares your beliefs is ideal but not crucial. It may be more important to find a psychotherapist/counselor who shares your beliefs, and we will discuss this in the next two chapters. What is important is finding a psychiatrist with good medical training, whom you feel you can communicate with openly, is responsive to your concerns, and respects your faith and its importance in your life. If a psychiatrist is dismissive of your faith or, at worst, sees spiritual beliefs as problematic, it would be wise to find another provider.

⟩ Other Prescribers

Due to the scarcity of psychiatrists, long wait lists and the expense, one might be assigned to see a nurse practitioner who can prescribe medications. Nurse practitioners receive their training on the job, so finding someone with experience who has good supervision from a psychiatrist is important. Just as is true for receiving antidepressant medication from PCPs, it would probably be wise to see a psychiatrist if a person has more complicated psychiatric issues or after multiple failed medication trials.

Some states authorize psychologists (PhDs or PsyDs) to prescribe medication, but this is not an avenue we recommend. Only someone with medical training should prescribe antidepressant medications, since antidepressants can cause problems when administered in certain medical conditions and interact with other medications a person is taking. In addition, depression can sometimes be caused by medical conditions that a medical doctor would need to evaluate the person for.

Straight Talk with Your Doctor

Patients and family members need to know what to expect from their physicians, and physicians need to know that everyone is properly informed. Straight talk about the following issues should help all parties proceed with mutual understanding. Here are some questions to ask:

> **Are we sure the diagnosis is correct?** Many other conditions look like depression but are not. For example, an older adult may be developing dementia, which may appear like depression. Similarly, a younger person may have bipolar disorder and be in the depressed phase. In that case, prescribing an antidepressant may bring on a manic episode and cause a destabilization of the bipolar illness. Depression may be from a side effect or an interaction of medications the patient is already taking. Depression can be confused with fatigue or loss of energy due to an undiagnosed medical condition, which is why each patient thought to have depression should have a full medical workup.

> **Does this depression need an antidepressant?** Many people experience depressed moods that fluctuate from day-to-day but do not last in a sustained manner and are not associated with difficulty sleeping, weight loss or other significant depressive symptoms. These people do not need antidepressant therapy but rather counseling to help them better deal with their day-to-day problems. Similarly, if long-term character or personality factors underlie the depression, then psychotherapy is more likely to help than medication.

> **Is anything more than an antidepressant medication needed?** As we have emphasized, some kind of support, counseling or psychotherapy is also usually necessary, since there are almost always problems coping with life situations underlying or at least contributing to depression.

> **Are there potential medication interactions?** Antidepressants can interact with and interfere with other prescription or over-the-counter medications the person is taking. For example, some antidepressants can interact with cardiac medications, blood thinners or seizure medications.

> **What are the possible side effects?** Patients should ask about what side effects to expect from the antidepressant and how long to expect them. They need to know exactly what to do and whom to call if they start having side effects, as well as which side effects improve with time or should prompt the patient to stop taking the medication immediately.

> **How should the medication be taken?** All antidepressant medication should be started at a low dose and gradually increased. The patient should understand how and when to increase the medication, whether to take the medicine at night or in the morning, and whether to take it with food or on an empty stomach.

> **How long will it be before improvement is seen?** An antidepressant must be taken at the full therapeutic dose for a minimum of six weeks before a conclusion can be reached that the medicine is not working. People need to know that they might feel worse (due to side effects from the medication as their body gets used to it) before they feel better. They should be informed that it is unlikely they will feel better before they have taken the medication for at least two or three weeks.

> **How will changes in the antidepressant's dosage be handled?** People taking antidepressants should call their doctor before they reduce the dose or stop taking it. Sudden dosage reduction or drug discontinuation can result in an unpleasant withdrawal reaction and may contribute to a relapse into depression. For the same reason, patients should also be careful to refill their prescriptions in a timely manner, so they won't run out.

> **When will it be possible to discontinue the medication?** People experiencing their first or second episode of depression should expect to continue taking the antidepressant for at least nine months after they have fully remitted from their depression. Patients who have had three or more episodes of major depression in the past should probably be on lifelong treatment.31 If depression recurs because the medication is discontinued, depressive episodes may become more severe and difficult to control in the future. This is because every episode of recurrent depression may reinforce maladaptive brain circuits.

> **Is the doctor willing to take a team approach to treatment?** Since a combination of treatments is more effective for most people with depression, the doctor should be willing to work with other mental health professionals, family and potentially the person's pastor to achieve optimal physical, emotional and spiritual health.

Factors Involved in Choosing an Antidepressant

Choice of antidepressants is usually influenced by the characteristics of the depression and side effects of the medication. The doctor will often try to match antidepressant side effects to the depressed person's symptoms (for example, insomnia might be treated with an antidepressant that also increases sleepiness).

Sometimes the effectiveness of an antidepressant can be predicted by the response of other blood relatives to the medication. If a depressed person's family member has responded successfully to an antidepressant and had few side effects, this increases the likelihood a depressed person will respond in a similar way, due to the similarity in biological makeup.

Financially, most antidepressant medications are generic and affordable. The newer medications (which tend to be marketed more heavily) are still on patent and are usually much more expensive. In general, it is wise to use a medication that has been proven over time to be safe and effective.

Types of Antidepressants

There are several different classes of antidepressants, and they are grouped by which neurotransmitter the medication affects most: norepinephrine, serotonin, dopamine or their precursors.

The *serotonin reuptake inhibitors (SRIs)* work primarily on serotonin receptors and are the most commonly prescribed medications for depression or anxiety. This category can be subdivided into:

> *Selective serotonin reuptake inhibitors (SSRIs)*, such as fluoxetine (Prozac), sertraline (Zoloft), citalopram (Celexa), escitalopram (Lexapro) and paroxetine (Paxil).

> *Serotonin and norepinephrine reuptake inhibitors (SNRIs)*, such as venlafaxine (Effexor), duloxetine (Cymbalta) and desvenlafaxine (Pristiq).

> *Atypical antidepressants,* such as bupropion (Wellbutrin), mirtazapine (Remeron) and trazodone (Desyrel), have more complicated mechanisms of action and do not only target serotonin.

> *Serotonin modulators and stimulators (SMS)* that have a multimodal action simultaneously modulating one or more serotonin receptors and inhibiting the reuptake of serotonin (e.g., Viibryd or vilazodone, Trintellix or vortioxetine, Fetzima or levomilnacipran), although they are quite expensive and often not covered by insurance.

Tricyclic antidepressants (TCAs), such as nortriptyline, amitriptyline and clomipramine, are an older class of medications, which are still very effective for depression. However, because they tend to have more side effects and can cause cardiac problems in overdose, they are not as commonly used as first-line medications for depression and anxiety. Today, they are more commonly prescribed to prevent conditions such as headaches or irritable bowel syndrome, which are medical problems that are closely intertwined with mental issues.

Monoamine oxidase inhibitors (MAOIs) are a class of medications that inactivate enzymes in the brain that break down neurotransmitter precursors such as tyramine. MAOIs include phenelzine (Nardil) and tranylcypromine (Parnate). These medications are not as commonly used because taking them requires more effort on the person's part, since these drugs may interact with common foods (such as wine and aged cheese) and other drugs, and they may also increase blood pressure to dangerous levels.

Mood Stabilizers

In ancient times, the Greeks and Romans sent the sick to soak in mineral baths, which have since been discovered to have high concentrations of the mineral lithium. Between 1885 and 1895, two Danish brothers discovered that lithium was capable of reducing the recurrence of depression. But it was not until 1949 that lithium became used more widely for the treatment of bipolar disorder.[32] Lithium's popularity grew to the extent that it was even included in the soft drink 7 Up until 1948.

Lithium is one of the few medications that can significantly decrease suicidal thoughts in depressed individuals.[33] Although lithium never proved to be a very good antidepressant on its own for major depressive disorder, it has been found to effectively augment the effects of an antidepressant that is not working very well, particularly if there is a cyclic pattern to depression. For bipolar disorder, lithium is one of the best treatment options. Lithium is helpful during manic or depressed episodes and helps prevent future mood cycles.

Lithium's disadvantage is in its potential side effects, most frequently sluggishness or weight gain. At toxic levels, lithium can cause tremors, and long-term use can damage the kidney and thyroid gland, so regular laboratory monitoring is required. However, these risks are ones many people are willing to accept, as lithium allows those with bipolar disorder to lead relatively normal lives. Lithium does so by preventing recurrent episodes of psychotic mania that disrupt their family and work life, and by preventing severe suicidal depression.

Besides lithium, several other mood stabilizers have emerged over the last 10 years. They have come from a class of drugs called anticonvulsants, which are usually used to prevent seizures in people with epilepsy and have been found to stabilize bipolar mood episodes. These include carbamazepine (Tegretol) or oxcarbazepine (Trileptal), valproic acid (Depakote), gabapentin (Neurontin), lamotrigine (Lamictal) and topiramate (Topamax).

Antipsychotics

When antipsychotics were first developed, they made a huge difference in the lives of people with severe mental illness. Prior to 1954, persons with severe mental illness such as schizophrenia, severe personality disorders or acute mania had to be institutionalized and sometimes physically restrained to keep from harming themselves or assaulting others. Chlorpromazine (Thorazine) and haloperidol (Haldol) were heralded as wonder drugs, enabling those who had previously been confined to psychiatric institutions to live independently in the community and with their families. However, these medications were prescribed at very high doses and were often accompanied by serious side effects, including excessive sedation, muscle stiffness and tremors. After long-term use, patients would sometimes develop repetitive involuntary movements of the face and body (called "tardive dyskinesia").

Since that time, a newer class of medications called "atypical" antipsychotics has largely replaced the older antipsychotics. These drugs include aripiprazole (Abilify), brexipiprazole (Rexulti), cariprazine (Vraylar), clozapine (Clozaril), lurasidone (Latuda), risperidone (Risperdal), olanzapine (Zyprexa), quetiapine (Seroquel) and ziprasidone (Geodon). Although still used primarily in psychotic illnesses such as schizophrenia, these medications are also increasingly used in bipolar disorder, and aripiprazole and quetiapine can be prescribed to augment the effectiveness of antidepressants in major depression. However, although their side effect profile is generally better than the older class of antipsychotics, they still carry risk of side effects, which may include significant weight gain, metabolic problems (increased blood sugar and fats) restlessness or tardive dyskinesia (involuntary repetitive muscle movements).

Benzodiazepines

In the 1960s, benzodiazepines such as chlordiazepoxide (Librium) and diazepam (Valium) were widely marketed to anxious housewives as "Mother's Little Helper" and to stressed out businessmen as "Executive Excedrin," leading to a rapid increase in demand and eventually concerns about over-prescribing and addiction. These drugs and others in their class rapidly relieve the severe anxiety that sometimes accompanies depression. Because of their effectiveness in relieving anxiety, such drugs easily induce dependence and sometimes addiction. They are often abused and sold illegally on the street, which is why they are controlled substances whose prescription is monitored by the federal government. Some short-acting medications such as alprazolam (Xanax) are so difficult to discontinue that a person may need to be hospitalized and carefully monitored as the drug is slowly reduced. Longer-acting medications such as diazepam and clonazepam (Klonopin) are easier to taper off but may build up in the body and result in over-sedation, disequilibrium, memory problems or falls. These risks are significantly increased as a person gets older. About 10 percent to 40 percent of people with long-term benzodiazepine use experience severe withdrawal symptoms when they try to stop them.[34]

As noted above, anxiety often accompanies depression, and anxious depressive thoughts are a manifestation of depression. This sort of anxiety is best treated with antidepressants or counseling/therapy, which promote neuroplasticity and growth, and not with benzodiazepines. Benzodiazepines can actually interfere with a person's ability to learn and engage in therapy. Over time, benzodiazepines can actually make a depression worse because they are central nervous system depressants with an effect similar to that of alcohol.

Despite these dangers, benzodiazepines can be helpful when used sparingly and for the short-term to treat severe anxiety or panic attacks. People who have both severe anxiety and depression are at increased risk of suicide. Therefore, in order to quickly relieve the agitation and distress that may be driving the person toward suicide, benzodiazepines can be prescribed for a brief period in order to gain time for the antidepressant drug to start working, but they should not be used for longer than one month. Benzodiazepines are also often used to help with insomnia, although this practice is not recommended since they can disrupt the quality of sleep and cause fatigue in the long-term.

When an Antidepressant Stops Working

It is not uncommon for antidepressants to stop working after a person has been taking them for several years. This is especially true if there is ongoing environmental stress, internal psychological or spiritual conflict or a continued pattern of poor decisions. It may even occur as a result of unusual stress or disorder in one's spiritual life. In any case, when a medication has lost its effect, physicians can do several things to restore drug effectiveness.

Switching to another antidepressant, either within the same medication class or to a different class, is often effective in regaining effectiveness. For example, if a person has been on an SSRI for several years and it is no longer working, he or she may respond well to an SNRI. Often the person will gain a benefit from the new medication that lasts for months or even years. After some time, he or she could be switched back to the original antidepressant and it might work again.

Sometimes, combinations of drugs may work when either drug alone does not. For example, a SSRI can be used in combination with trazodone (for those with sleep disturbance) or bupropion (for those with sexual side effects or low energy). Antidepressant effectiveness may also be boosted by a strategy called augmentation, in which the doctor may add small doses of lithium, thyroid hormone or an antipsychotic such as aripiprazole (Abilify) to the antidepressant regimen.

In contrast, certain antidepressant drug combinations (such as an MAOI and an SSRI) may have disastrous consequences (hypertensive crisis or serotonin syndrome), so combinations of antidepressants should only be prescribed by physicians familiar with this approach.

Treatment for Bipolar Disorder

Sometimes, other conditions such as bipolar disorder can be misdiagnosed as clinical depression. For people with bipolar disorder, antidepressants may actually worsen their condition and cause suicidal thoughts or worsen the cycling between highs and lows, particularly if prescribed without mood stabilizing medications. Bipolar depression should be treated with a mood stabilizer or antipsychotic, and not with an antidepressant.

Many persons with bipolar disorder have difficulty sticking with their treatment. They will commonly stop their medication when their sense of well-being is restored, which usually results in another cycle of depression and/or mania. The typical behavioral and emotional rollercoaster experienced by a person with bipolar disorder is difficult for the individual and also for his or her family, friends and co-workers, as well as for the medical and other professionals involved.

Interventions for Treatment Resistant Depression

Less than one in 10 depressed people truly have what is called treatment-resistant depression, which is depression that persists regardless of treatment with medications, psychotherapy or both. If someone's depression is not responsive to these treatments, it is worth stepping back and seeing if there is something that has been missed: whether the diagnosis should be reevaluated, or if there are situational factors such as abuse that continue to contribute to depression, or if childhood trauma has been overlooked, or if spiritual factors have not been addressed. If all of these possibilities have been ruled out, additional medical interventions such as electroconvulsive therapy, transcranial magnetic stimulation (TMS) or ketamine may be considered and can help achieve remission.

Case Sarah:

"The first signs of depression started when I was 14 years old, shortly after my father was diagnosed with bone cancer, which left him disabled and periodically bedridden for the next 10 years. Our family was devastated. My mother was a wreck, and my only sibling, a sister three years older than me, distanced herself from the situation. My mother and I became the primary caregivers for my father. I regularly emptied urinals and spit-trays and spoon-fed him when he was in too much pain or too weak from the chemo to lift his arms. It was a whole lot of depressing drama and responsibility for a 14-year-old.

"When I was 15, I started drinking alcohol, smoking cigarettes and then smoking marijuana...Marijuana was like a godsend to me...and provided the feeling that even though life was awful, everything would be okay. Marijuana was my antidepressant. Before long I was getting drunk and high every weekend and eventually smoking marijuana daily. Surprisingly, I was still getting good grades in school, cheerleading, working part-time and helping my mother take care of my father and the house...

"I graduated high school and attended a university about 45 minutes from home—far enough away to not live at home, but close enough to regularly come home to visit my family and care for my father. My D & A (drug and alcohol) use progressed, and I started experimenting with LSD and cocaine. When I was 22 and a senior in college, the D & A use caught up to me. It stopped 'fixing me' as it had before, and I experienced my first major depression. A family doctor put me on Prozac for the depression; however, I continued the D & A use, which caused a psychotic episode with severe paranoia, resulting in my first hospitalization...I withdrew from school because my grades were beginning to suffer. I became estranged from my parents, convinced they were part of a satanic cult because of their involvement in the Masonic order.

"In October 1991 I was hospitalized again in a state of psychosis and depression. After several weeks in the hospital I reconciled with my parents (mostly so I could leave the hospital and live with them) on the condition that I admit I had a problem with D & A, stop using and agree to attend AA (Alcoholics Anonymous) meetings, which I did. My father died three months later. I stayed sober for another four months and then spent the next three years in and out of AA and sobriety, as well as in and out of the psychiatric wards of hospitals. During all this I had a relationship with God and Jesus Christ but regularly fell away and lived in chaos.

"In the summer of 1994 I had been sober for seven months when I decided I did not need my medication any longer. I had been listening to a religious radio station that had a 'Praise in the Night' call-in advice program that aired from midnight to five in the morning. I called in and the minister told me all I needed was God and that I did not need medication, which was exactly what I wanted to hear. I went off the meds and became even more manic, ending up in Florida. After several months I got sober again, regained my sanity, fell into a severe depression and begged my mother to allow me to return home, which she did.

"I was hospitalized for the last time in January 1995 after I had been sober for six months. Hope became a major factor for me during this final hospitalization, when I fell into the deepest pit of depression I had experienced. I had been in the psych ward for over two months, cycled on several types of antidepressants to no avail, and did not feel any less depressed than I did on the day of admission. While doing her rounds, one of the young nurses could see the hopeless state I was in. She said: 'I know you feel totally hopeless right now and that things will never get better. But I want you to know that I, too, went through a severe depression. I was so bad I ended up in Central State Hospital (you had to be really bad to go to Central). But I did get better. I was able to go to school and get my nursing degree, and I am doing really well now. If I could be that sick and recover, so can you.' For the first time I actually had a glimmer of hope that I could come out of the pit of hell called depression.

"Another turning point was while I was still in the hospital and my doctor talked to me about God and quoted Romans 8:31, 'If God is for us, who can be against us?' Up to this time, I had a more difficult time accepting the fact that I needed medication and must faithfully follow my doctor's instructions than I had accepting that I was an addict and could never again use drugs or alcohol. This doctor's profession of faith triggered something within me that allowed me to completely trust him and his judgment, which made me an obedient patient, following all his directives and recommendations. He suggested that ECT might help me.

"Since none of the antidepressants were working, I agreed to a series of ECT treatments, which I now know saved my life. I began attending AA meetings again, even before I was released from the hospital. I also began attending daily church services that were held at the hospital and started reading the Bible regularly, praying and developing my relationship with God. Through it all, I always clung to my relationship with Jesus Christ, and I know that it was because I gave my will and my life to Him that He in turn gave me a new life."

"It has been more than seven years since I was last hospitalized and more than eight since my last manic episode. I have not used alcohol or illicit drugs for over eight years. During the time since my last hospitalization in 1995, I returned to undergraduate school and completed my bachelor's degree, worked for two years in the communications field, then went to Case Western University and graduated with a master's degree. I am now successfully living on my own and am working as the program coordinator of the substance abuse program for an agency in the criminal justice field.

"All of the above is truly a miracle of God and beyond my grandest dreams...After the depths of torment and despair I have experienced, it is a divine blessing to no longer be in a manic state of constant unrest or in the depths of depression when I felt utterly worthless and pathetic, without a bit of hope, constantly wishing to be dead. I now have great joy in the many triumphs God has worked in my life and am thankful that Jesus Christ literally saved me from my torment."

Electroconvulsive Therapy (ECT)

Electroconvulsive therapy (ECT) has the highest response rate and quickest response of any treatment for depression, including antidepressant medication and/or counseling.[35] Among depressed people for whom antidepressant medication has been ineffective, the response rate is 60 to 90 percent.[36] We have seen many cases in which following ECT, a person previously completely disabled by depression may be free from further episodes for months or years.

Research suggests that ECT works through multiple mechanisms: by causing changes in the structure and signaling in the brain, increasing BDNF and other growth factors, and affecting the immune system and gene expression.[37]

ECT was first developed in the 1930s when Italian researchers noticed that depressed patients with epilepsy often experienced improvement in their mood after having a seizure. The seizures were initially induced by chemical means, and electricity was later developed as a more humane way to induce the seizures. After its discovery, ECT became widely used for the treatment of psychiatric disorders, including major depression, psychotic depression, mania and schizophrenia. After the mid-1950s, its use began to drop off as medications were discovered to treat these illnesses.

Before the advent of modern medical technology, ECT induced generalized seizures that made a person's entire body convulse, requiring that patients be strapped down with a bite block placed in their mouths to prevent them from biting their tongues, sometimes resulting in complications such as bone fractures. This was the image presented in the 1975 movie

One Flew Over the Cuckoo's Nest, which turned many people against ECT. As a result, some state legislatures outlawed ECT.

Today, ECT is performed with much more safety and precision. During ECT, an anesthesiologist administers general anesthesia and a muscle block to patients so they do not physically convulse. A small electrical charge is often applied, usually to only one half of the brain (unilateral ECT), the nondominant side, to induce a brief seizure in the brain, although in more severe cases the electrical charge is applied to both halves of the brain (bilateral ECT). The patient sleeps during the procedure and has no memory of the event. Between eight and 12 treatments over a three-week period are usually necessary for significant improvement or remission of depression. Treatments are so safe now that they are often administered to outpatients without hospitalization. People are brought to the ECT treatment center two to three times per week, usually for six to 12 sessions.

Nevertheless, there remain valid concerns about ECT and its side effects. Memory loss is usually the most common concern raised, especially with bilateral ECT. Cognitive impairment from ECT usually lasts a few minutes to days. When memory loss does occur, it usually involves memory of events occurring immediately around the ECT sessions and is often temporary, although it can persist longer in older adults. The administration of ECT today seeks to minimize the risk of memory loss by methods such as brief pulse stimulation and one-sided nondominant hemisphere electrode placement.

The most common side effects that occur with ECT are temporary headaches, muscle aches, nausea and fatigue. There are also rarer side effects such as cardiac arrhythmias, heart attack or strokes for older adults with pre-existing heart disease, or temporary agitation and disorientation following ECT.

There is less stigma against ECT as the technology has improved and the benefits of treatment have been clearly documented. Celebrities such as Carrie Fisher have shared publicly about how life saving ECT has been for them. In the last two decades, there has been a resurgence of interest in ECT as a treatment for people with treatment-resistant depression, those with life-threatening depression (suicidal, severe weight loss, etc.) who cannot wait the time necessary for antidepressant drugs to work and older adults with severe depression (particularly when accompanied by psychotic delusions.) For example, at Duke University Hospital, where Dr. Koenig practices, of the 1,500 ECT treatments done yearly, 70 percent are performed on depressed people over the age of 60. Some remarkable recoveries have been seen in older people whom everyone thought were senile and demented and ready to be admitted permanently to a nursing home. After a series of ECT treatments, some of these people have brightened up, became functional again and were able to return home and live independently.

Transcranial Magnetic Stimulation (TMS)

In some ways, TMS (more specifically, repetitive Transcranial Magnetic Stimulation, rTMS) can be thought of as a lightweight version of ECT. Unlike its cousin ECT, TMS does not require the generation of a seizure to achieve benefits. In TMS, an electromagnet is placed on the scalp, which generates magnetic field pulses roughly the strength of those emitted by an MRI scanner. The magnetic pulses pass through the skull and stimulate the underlying brain tissue. As with ECT, the mechanism of action is unknown, but it is thought the magnetic waves increase the release of growth factors and alter the activity of the molecules in the brain.

TMS has the advantages of not requiring general anesthesia and not carrying the risk of even temporary memory loss. However, the efficacy rate is lower for TMS compared to ECT (38 percent compared to 58 percent in one study), and it requires a substantial time commitment of daily visits lasting about one to two hours for 20 to 30 sessions. Currently, research studies show mixed evidence supporting its use.[38] However, as this treatment carries fewer side effects and less stigma than ECT, there is hope rTMS will eventually become a more viable treatment option.

Vagus Nerve Stimulation (VNS)

VNS involves stimulating the vagus nerve in the neck at regular intervals via a generator (about the size of a tape measure) implanted in the chest. The U.S. Food and Drug Administration (FDA) approved VNS in 1997 for treatment of drug-resistant epilepsy and in 2005 for depressed person who failed at least four medications. The largest study of VNS suggests the improvement in depression occurs slowly. Although there were no significant differences at 12 weeks in that study, by one year 30 percent of patients showed an improvement in symptoms, and many had a decrease in suicidality and number of hospitalizations.[39]

As with all surgical procedures, there are risks and possible complications, in particular damage to the nerves and arteries. Because of this, VNS treatment for depression should be reserved for only the most intractable cases, after nonsurgical treatments such as ECT and rTMS have been tried.

Ketamine

Ketamine is the newest treatment available for treatment resistant depression and is notable for how rapidly it acts. Some studies have found that half of patients experienced improvement in depression within 24 hours of an infusion.[40] However, it is unclear how persistent the benefits are. Most participants experienced a relapse of their depression about two weeks after the sixth ketamine infusion was completed.

Ketamine works on the NMDA receptors that bind to the neurotransmitter glutamate, which activates another pathway involved in neuroplasticity and mood regulation. Ketamine is commonly used in anesthesia for pain relief and sedation, particularly in children. However, it is also abused on the street under the name "Special K" for its dissociative properties, its ability to induce a sense of being detached from the body and, at higher doses, its ability to induce hallucinations.

In 2018, the FDA approved use of a form of ketamine (esketamine) for treatment resistant depression, which is given through intravenous infusion or through a nasal spray (Spravato) twice weekly at an infusion center for up to 12 infusions. Side effects include temporary dissociation and headaches, and hypertension or arrhythmias for those with pre-existing heart problems.[41]

Since it is such a new type of treatment for depression, only time will tell whether this becomes a significant form of treatment. Ketamine is promising for its rapid relief of depression, particularly for those who are severely depressed for whom medication has not been effective. However, since its effects are short lived, it should be combined with other forms of treatment, including therapy and medication, potentially as a way to "jump start" improvement of depression. At the time of publication of this book, this treatment is not currently covered by insurance companies, so it can be quite expensive.

Spiritual Issues Related to Psychiatric Treatment

What does the Bible have to say about the use of medication for depression?

Some Christian counselors and pastors teach that Christians should only use the Bible, faith and the Holy Spirit's power to overcome life's difficulties, including depression. They usually come from one of two camps: (1) they believe depression is only a spiritual problem, or (2) they believe depression is a physical problem but individuals need to have enough faith for physical healing (and likewise do not seek medical help for other physical ailments as well.) With regard to the first camp, we hope we have addressed this issue thoroughly in Chapter 3 on causes, by explaining that what affects us spiritually also affects us psychologically, sociologically and physically, and vice versa. The second camp might be addressed by challenging them to examine their beliefs about how it is that Jesus works in the world. Does Jesus only work through prayer and miracles?

Consider, for example, when Paul included in his letter to Timothy a brief practical suggestion: "No longer drink only water, but use a little wine for the sake of your stomach and your frequent ailments" (1 Timothy 5:23, ESV). It sounds like Timothy struggled with gastrointestinal and other medical problems. Paul's advice to Timothy was not to pray for healing, but to consider taking something medicinal for his health. While we strongly discourage using alcohol to treat medical or psychiatric problems, and Paul strongly discouraged addiction to alcohol (1 Timothy 3:3), few medications were available during that time, so wine was often used as medicine by the Jews and the Greeks. God can work miracles through practical ways, the "common grace" He grants to both believers and unbelievers: "… For he makes his sun rise on the evil and on the good, and sends rain on the just and on the unjust" (Matthew 5:45, ESV). We believe antidepressant medication is one of those means of common grace.

What is God trying to say to you through your depression?

This is the fundamental question to consider while taking antidepressants. We have used the fever metaphor repeatedly, and it is true again here. Depression is like a fever, and while for the minority it may be a purely biological cause, for most others depression is a symptom indicating that something deeper is going on in a person's heart or a situation is making her or him feel deeply unhappy. Antidepressants can "reduce the fever" and give the person time to make the necessary changes in their life.

As C.S. Lewis puts it, "We can ignore even pleasure. But pain insists upon being attended to. God whispers to us in our pleasures, speaks in our conscience, but shouts in our pains: it is his megaphone to rouse a deaf world."[42]

The pain may be so loud that it is difficult to reflect and make changes. As Michael Emlet, a professor of biblical counseling, put it, sometimes medication can "calm the waters of the mind to allow for deep-sea exploration. You can't have a diving expedition if there is a gale on the surface of the water."[43]

Taking antidepressants or other medications is only one step toward healing from depression. The next step is much more difficult, since it requires examining your heart. What is God telling you? What have you been deaf to? What is He shouting at you in your pain?

Are there matters that need closure? Are there issues in your actions or thinking that may be blocking your progress in the Christian life? It may mean that you will need to find someone, a pastor or counselor, who can spend time helping you address the matters you may be avoiding, afraid or ashamed of. It may require someone else's eyes to see the patterns you have been blind to, someone who can help you develop new strategies and behaviors that honor God.

In the end, whatever you decide, the main thing worth taking from your experience with depression is the deeper knowledge that real hope is only found in one place—an ever-deepening relationship with Christ, who understands the depths of our pain and died to heal it all.

Endnotes

1. Perroud N, Salzmann A, Prada P, Nicastro R, Hoeppli ME, Furrer S, Ardu S,Krejci I, Karege F, Malafosse A. Response to psychotherapy in borderline personality disorder and methylation status of the BDNF gene. Transl Psychiatry. 2013 Jan 15;3:e207. https://www.ncbi.nlm.nih.gov/pubmed/23422958

2. Nutt, D., Wilson, S., & Paterson, L. (2008). Sleep disorders as core symptoms of depression. Dialogues in clinical neuroscience, 10(3), 329–336

3. Cooney GM, Dwan K, Greig CA, Lawlor DA, Rimer J, Waugh FR, McMurdo M, Mead GE. Exercise for depression. Cochrane Database of Systematic Reviews 2013, Issue 9. Art.

4. Netz Y. (2017). Is the Comparison between Exercise and Pharmacologic Treatment of Depression in the Clinical Practice Guideline of the American College of Physicians Evidence-Based? *Frontiers in pharmacology, 8*, 257. doi:10.3389/fphar.2017.00257

5. Trivedi MH, Greer TL, Grannemann BD, Chambliss HO, Jordan AN. Exercise as an augmentation strategy for treatment of major depression. J Psychiatr Pract. 2006 Jul;12(4):205-13. PubMed PMID: 16883145

6. Goodwin RD. Association between physical activity and mental disorders among adults in the United States. Prev Med. 2003 Jun;36(6):698-703. PubMed PMID:12744913.

7. Exercise treatment for depression Dunn, Andrea L. et al. American Journal of Preventive Medicine, January 2005. Volume 28, Issue 1, 1 - 8

8. The effects of a multi-modal intervention trial of light, exercise, and vitamins on women's mood. *Brown MA, Goldstein-Shirley J, Robinson J, Casey S, Women Health. 2001; 34(3):93-112.*

9. Fell, G. L., Robinson, K. C., Mao, J., Woolf, C. J., & Fisher, D. E. (2014). Skin ⊠-endorphin mediates addiction to UV light. Cell, 157(7), 1527–1534. doi:10.1016/j.cell.2014.04.032

10. Kripke, Daniel. Brighten Your Life, 2019. ebook: http://www.brightenyourlife.info/

11. Randomized trial of the efficacy of bright-light exposure and aerobic exercise on depressive symptoms and serum lipids. Leppämäki SJ, Partonen TT, Hurme J, Haukka JK, Lönnqvist JK, J Clin Psychiatry. 2002 Apr; 63(4):316-21.

12. Tuunainen A, Kripke DF, Endo T. Light therapy for non⊠seasonal depression. Cochrane Database of Systematic Reviews 2004, Issue 2. Art. No.: CD004050. DOI: 10.1002/14651858. CD004050.pub2.

13. Penckofer S, Kouba J, Byrn M, Estwing Ferrans C. Vitamin D and depression: where is all the sunshine?. Issues Ment Health Nurs. 2010;31(6):385–393. doi:10.3109/01612840903437657

14. Flux MC, Lowry CA. Finding intestinal fortitude: Integrating the microbiome into a holistic view of depression mechanisms, treatment, and resilience. Neurobiol Dis. 2019 Aug 24:104578. doi: 10.1016/j.nbd.2019.104578

15. Foster JA, McVey Neufeld KA. Gut-brain axis: how the microbiome influences anxiety and depression. Trends Neurosci. 2013 May;36(5):305-12. doi:10.1016/j.tins.2013.01.005. Epub 2013 Feb 4. Review. PubMed PMID: 23384445

16. Li Y, Lv MR, Wei YJ, Sun L, Zhang JX, Zhang HG, Li B. Dietary patterns and depression risk: A meta-analysis. Psychiatry Res. 2017 Jul;253:373-382. Doi: 10.1016/j.psychres.2017.04.020. Epub 2017 Apr 11. Review.

17. Molteni R, Barnard RJ, Ying Z, Roberts CK, Gómez-Pinilla F. A high-fat, refined sugar diet reduces hippocampal brain-derived neurotrophic factor, neuronal plasticity, and learning. Neuroscience. 2002;112(4):803-14.

18. Wallace CJK, Milev R. The effects of probiotics on depressive symptoms in humans: a systematic review [published correction appears in Ann Gen Psychiatry. 2017 Mar 7;16:18]. *Ann Gen Psychiatry*. 2017;16:14. Published 2017 Feb 20. doi:10.1186/s12991-017-0138-2

19. Firth J, Teasdale SB, Allott K, Siskind D, Marx W, Cotter J, Veronese N, Schuch F, Smith L, Solmi M, Carvalho AF, Vancampfort D, Berk M, Stubbs B, Sarris J. The efficacy and safety of nutrient supplements in the treatment of mental disorders: a meta-review of meta-analyses of randomized controlled trials. World Psychiatry. 2019 Oct;18(3):308-324.

20. Bloch, M., Hannestad, J. Omega-3 fatty acids for the treatment of depression: systematic review and meta-analysis. *Mol Psychiatry* 17, 1272–1282 (2012)

21. Castrén E. Is mood chemistry? Nat Rev Neurosci. 2005 Mar;6(3):241-6. Review.

22. Reid, I. C., & Stewart, C. A. (2001). How antidepressants work: new perspectives on the pathophysiology of depressive disorder. *The British Journal of Psychiatry, 178*(4), 299-303.

23. A. Khan, R. M. Leventhal, S. R. Khan, W. A. Brown, "Severity of Depression and Response to Antidepressants and Placebo: An Analysis of the Food and Drug Administration Database," *Journal of Clinical Psychopharmacology* 22, no. 1 (2000): 40 – 45.

24. Fournier, J. C., DeRubeis, R. J., Hollon, S. D., Dimidjian, S., Amsterdam, J. D., Shelton, R. C., & Fawcett, J. (2010). Antidepressant drug effects and depression severity: a patient-level meta-analysis. JAMA, 303(1), 47–53. doi:10.1001/jama.2009.1943

25. Vöhringer PA, Ghaemi SN. Solving the antidepressant efficacy question: effect sizes in major depressive disorder. *Clin Ther*. 2011;33(12):B49–B61. doi:10.1016/j.clinthera.2011.11.019

26. Acute and longer-term outcomes in depressed outpatients requiring one or several treatment steps: a STAR*D report. *Rush AJ, Trivedi MH, Wisniewski SR, Nierenberg AA, Stewart JW, Warden D, Niederehe G, Thase ME, Lavori PW, Lebowitz BD, McGrath PJ, Rosenbaum JF, Sackeim HA, Kupfer DJ, Luther J, Fava M. Am J Psychiatry. 2006 Nov; 163(11):1905-17*

27. Dunlop BW, LoParo D, Kinkead B, et al. Benefits of Sequentially Adding Cognitive-Behavioral Therapy or Antidepressant Medication for Adults With Nonremitting Depression. *Am J Psychiatry*. 2019;176(4):275–286. doi:10.1176/appi.ajp.2018.18091075

28. Quilty, Lena C., et al. "Dimensional personality traits and treatment outcome in patients with major depressive disorder." *Journal of Affective Disorders* 108.3 (2008): 241-250.

29. Shelton RC. Steps Following Attainment of Remission: Discontinuation of Antidepressant Therapy. *Prim Care Companion J Clin Psychiatry*. 2001;3(4):168–174. doi:10.4088/pcc.v03n0404

30. Rush AJ, Trivedi MH, Wisniewski SR, et al: Bupropion-SR, sertraline, or venlafaxine-XR after failure of SSRIs for depression. New England Journal of Medicine 354:1231–1242, 2006

31. Shelton RC. Steps Following Attainment of Remission: Discontinuation of Antidepressant Therapy. *Prim Care Companion J Clin Psychiatry*. 2001;3(4):168–174. doi:10.4088/pcc.v03n0404

32. Shorter E. The history of lithium therapy. *Bipolar Disord*. 2009;11 Suppl 2(Suppl 2):4–9

33. Lewitzka U, Severus E, Bauer R, Ritter P, Müller-Oerlinghausen B, Bauer M. The suicide prevention effect of lithium: more than 20 years of evidence-a narrative review. *Int J Bipolar Disord*. 2015;3(1):32. doi:10.1186/s40345-015-0032-2

34. Matheson E, Hainer BL. Insomnia: Pharmacologic Therapy. Am Fam Physician. 2017Jul 1;96(1):29-35. Review

35. Pagnin D, de Queiroz V, Pini S, Cassano GB. Efficacy of ECT in depression: a meta-analytic review. J ECT. 2004 Mar;20(1):13-20. Review

36. Cusin, C., Dougherty, D.D. Somatic therapies for treatment-resistant depression: ECT, TMS, VNS, DBS. Biol Mood Anxiety Disord 2, 14 (2012)

37. Singh A, Kar SK. How Electroconvulsive Therapy Works?: Understanding the Neurobiological Mechanisms. Clin Psychopharmacol Neurosci. 2017;15(3):210–221. doi:10.9758/cpn.2017.15.3.210

38. Cusin, C., Dougherty, D.D. Somatic therapies for treatment-resistant depression: ECT, TMS, VNS, DBS. Biol Mood Anxiety Disord 2, 14 (2012)

39. Rush AJ, Sackeim HA, Marangell LB, George MS, Brannan SK, Davis SM, Lavori P, Howland R, Kling MA, Rittberg B, et al: Effects of 12 months of vagus nerve stimulation in treatment-resistant depression: a naturalistic study. Biol Psychiatry. 2005, 58: 355-363

40. Robert M Berman, Angela Cappiello, Amit Anand, Dan A Oren, George R Heninger, Dennis S Charney, John H Krystal, Antidepressant effects of ketamine in depressed patients, Biological Psychiatry, Volume 47, Issue 4, 2000, Pages 351-354

41. aan het Rot M, Collins KA, Murrough JW, Perez AM, Reich DL, Charney DS, Mathew SJ. Safety and efficacy of repeated-dose intravenous ketamine for treatment-resistant depression. Biol Psychiatry. 2010 Jan 15;67(2):139-45

42. Lewis, CS. "The Problem of Pain, p91

43. Emlet, Micheal. "Listening to Prozac . . .and to the Scriptures: A Primer on Psychoactive Medications." Journal of Biblical Counseling, Vol 26, No. 1

CHAPTER 6

THE MIND

"Whoever trusts in his own mind is a fool, but he who walks in wisdom will be delivered."

—Proverbs 28:26, ESV

The Mind and the Effects of the Fall

When sin entered the world through Adam and Eve, it was not just physical matter and our bodies that became corrupted. Our minds, too, became blinded to knowledge and truth, and became prone to futility, lies and foolishness (Romans 1:18-23). And one place the brokenness of our minds is evident: depression.

Depression distorts people's ability to accurately perceive the world. People with depression tend to have "black-tinted glasses" that only pay attention and remember negative information, filter out the positive and always draw negative conclusions.

Depression speaks lies. Depression tells people, "I'm worthless." "Nobody cares." "I'm a failure." "I'm trapped." "It's my fault." "There's no hope." "God doesn't care." Depression thwarts the ability of the mind to believe truth.

Depression impairs reason. For the severely depressed, their thought process defies logic, often losing their grip on reality.

One of the first steps in treating depression, then, is to be aware of the fallibility of one's own mind and learn to distrust one's depressed thoughts.

Journaling

Journaling can be a helpful practice for those who struggle with depression. For those without someone on whom to unburden themselves, journaling can be a place to be honest and raw without fear of judgement.

Journaling can provide the space for reflection, as depression often arises from hard questions about suffering, self-worth, meaning and purpose. Those with depression often find that their thoughts race in circles, and the act of committing these to paper can allow them to lay down these thoughts. It can also give people perspective on particular issues and help them generate solutions. If a person has difficulty sleeping due to troubling thoughts, writing them down and lifting them up in prayer before bedtime can be helpful.

Journaling can assist us in identifying patterns. Keeping a journal helps us to know ourselves better. We record our hopes, dreams, fears, successes, failures and questions. Keeping a journal helps people see more clearly where they've been, where they are now, and where they are headed.

Journaling can also remind us of God's faithfulness. If we list our specific struggles and make it habitual to lift these up to the Lord in prayer, it gives up the opportunity to see how God answers. Over time a journal's pages may contain more questions than answers. Yet even if we cannot discern the answers to the questions, journaling will help us to see that our personal stories are part of a larger story, woven together by a Storyteller who will one day make sense of it all.

Meditate on What is Good

"Finally, brothers, whatever is true, whatever is honorable, whatever is just, whatever is pure, whatever is lovely, whatever is commendable, if there is any excellence, if there is anything worthy of praise, think about these things" (Philippians 4:8, ESV).

What do we feed our minds? What is our "mental diet?" For those who are depressed, it can be a temptation to surround themselves with people and things that echo their pain and darkness, but these serve only to reinforce the depression. Do we fill our minds with poisonous things?[1]

What kind of company do we keep? Throughout the wisdom literature in Scripture, we are exhorted to be careful about choosing our friends and companions (Proverbs 13:20, Psalm 1). People who frequently complain, are sarcastic or negative and who put others down are likely to breed the same attitude in ourselves.

What do we fantasize about? What comforts do we find ourselves retreating to when we are suffering? Is it food, alcohol, recreational drugs, compulsive spending, gambling or false intimacy? The exhilarating rush of these false comforts can feel like respite from the pain or numbness of depression. But as Proverbs so frequently warns us, the end of all these is death (Proverbs 5-7, Proverbs 20:1).

Transforming the Mind

In Romans 12:2, Paul exhorts his readers: "Do not be conformed to this world, but be transformed by the renewal of your mind, that by testing you may discern what is the will of God, what is good and acceptable and perfect" (ESV).

Our minds are fallen, and they tend toward the ways of the fallen world, yet we are moving toward future glory and renewal. Is psychotherapy a means by which to renew our minds? Psychotherapy, also known as talk therapy, counseling or just "therapy," is the communication between a patient and a therapist using psychological techniques in order to help them with emotional suffering and problems in living. When the depression persists despite attempts to help oneself, it is wise to seek professional help. While the love and support of family and friends is crucial, a psychotherapist or counselor can provide much more effective help.

However, this Scripture in Romans needs to be taken in context of the rest of the passage. The first two verses of Romans 12 are the logical consequence of the entire book, where Paul gives a beautiful exposition of the foundation of our faith. Take a moment to reflect on these verses:

> Depravity: "And since they did not see fit to acknowledge God, God gave them up to a debased mind…They are full of envy, murder, strife, deceit, maliciousness. They are gossips, slanderers, haters of God, insolent, haughty, boastful, inventors of evil, disobedient to parents, foolish, faithless, heartless, ruthless" (Romans 1:28-31, ESV).

> Condemnation: "As it is written, 'There is none righteous, not even one; There is none who understands, There is none who seeks for God'" (Romans 3:10-11, NASB). "For all have sinned and fall short of the glory of God" (Romans 3:23, ESV). "For the wages of sin is death" (Romans 6:23a, ESV).

> Justification by faith: "But God demonstrates His own love toward us, in that while we were yet sinners, Christ died for us" (Romans 5:8, NASB).

> Our identity as children of God: "For you did not receive the spirit of slavery to fall back into fear, but you have received the Spirit of adoption as sons, by whom we cry, 'Abba! Father!'" (Romans 8:15, ESV).

> Our current suffering and our longing for glory: "For I consider that the sufferings of this present time are not worth comparing with the glory that is to be revealed to us…For we know that the whole creation has been groaning together in the pains of childbirth until now. And not only the creation, but we ourselves, who have the firstfruits of the Spirit, groan inwardly as we wait eagerly for adoption as sons, the redemption of our bodies" (Romans 8:18-23, ESV).

> Our victory: "And we know that God causes all things to work together for good to those who love God…and these whom He predestined, He also called; and those whom He called, He also justified; and these whom He justified, He also glorified" (Romans 8:28-30, NASB).

› Our confidence in the love of God: "What then shall we say to these things? If God is for us, who can be against us? He who did not spare his own Son but gave him up for us all, how will he not also with him graciously give us all things? Who shall bring any charge against God's elect? It is God who justifies. Who is to condemn? Christ Jesus is the one who died—more than that, who was raised—who is at the right hand of God, who indeed is interceding for us. Who shall separate us from the love of Christ?…For I am sure that neither death nor life, nor angels nor rulers, nor things present nor things to come, nor powers, nor height nor depth, nor anything else in all creation, will be able to separate us from the love of God in Christ Jesus our Lord" (Romans 8:31-39, ESV).

What comfort and hope there are in these words! And because of all of this, Paul calls on us, "…therefore, brothers, by the mercies of God, to present your bodies as a living sacrifice, holy and acceptable to God, which is your spiritual worship. Do not be conformed to this world, but be transformed by the renewal of your mind, that by testing you may discern what is the will of God, what is good and acceptable and perfect" (Romans 12:1-2, ESV).

These truths are meant to transform our minds, and by that, our lives. When done well, counseling can be a means that God uses to help us see ourselves accurately and to know God more. Given that we are not to have our minds conformed to the patterns of unbelief of the world, Christians should be rightfully careful about what we do with our minds. And that includes seeking help from counselors and psychotherapists. As Paul outlined, our beliefs about the human condition, the nature of suffering, our identity, meaning and hope are fundamentally different from those who are not Christians.

When we seek to change with the help of a counselor, as Christians we need to think critically about what they are proposing about each of these things. Whether explicitly stated or not, each psychotherapist or counselor has their own individual theory about human nature and the best way to help people.[2]

However, psychotherapy is also full of helpful ways of understanding how the mind works. Common grace is at work here too. For milder forms of depression, therapy may be as effective as treatment with antidepressant medication alone or a combination of psychotherapy and antidepressants. Numerous Christians have benefitted from secular psychotherapy and counseling.

Psychotherapy is by no means monolithic, but rather it draws upon many different competing schools of thought and technique. Each of these theories have ideas about what causes depression and how it should be treated, which may be helpful to understand. We now seek to demystify some of the more common types of psychotherapy, present a few hypothetical counseling sessions and provide a brief Christian critique.

PSYCHOTHERAPY THEORIES AND METHODS

Psychoanalysis

Psychoanalysis is where we get the classic stereotype of talk therapy: a person lying on a couch, looking at the ceiling and talking about their dreams, while a bearded psychoanalyst takes notes. Sigmund Freud was the father of psychoanalysis and made a number of key observations. He championed the idea of the *"talking cure"*—that talking could help people with their problems. He also developed the idea of the *unconscious*, which consisted of *instinctual drives*, threatening desires or painful memories that people keep deeply hidden from their own awareness, causing people to behave the way they do. People develop maladaptive *defenses* such as denial or repression to protect themselves from these internal forces.

According to this view, depression (known in his day as melancholia) was aggression turned inward as anger toward oneself. The goal of psychoanalysis is to help the patient uncover unconscious motivations and repressed memories, so the person becomes more aware of how these affect his or her feelings and behavior. Developing insight into one's own behavior is thought to be curative and is supposed to free the individual to act in more intentional ways.[3] The process of psychoanalysis requires several therapy sessions per week and can sometimes take years, which means that it is often limited to those who can financially afford it.

Since Freud, there have been further developments in psychoanalytic theory, many that focus more on relationships, such as the centrality of the mother-child relationship or the relationship between the psychotherapist and client. *Psychodynamic therapy*, or *insight-oriented therapy*, is a simpler, shorter version of psychoanalysis that is accessible to more people.

SESSION

Therapist: *(male psychologist)* Susan, you know in all the times we've talked, you haven't said much about your childhood.

Client: *(Silent. Sullen.)*

Therapist: Did you understand me?

Client: *(Still silent. Finally speaks after another minute of silence.)* Did you need two weeks of vacation to come up with that question?

Therapist: Not necessarily. It had occurred to me earlier. You sound upset even though you knew I'd be gone.

Client: I *am* upset—and rightly so. You left me on my own...just so you could have a good time!

Therapist: Do you recall feeling upset like this when you were a child?

Client: Quite often, actually. I felt like this whenever I thought of my father and how he left us on our own just so he could have a good time and not be bothered with Mom and me anymore. Sometimes I tried to make him come back by hiding and refusing to come out even when Mom looked everywhere for me. I had a secret place.

Therapist: Tell me about that.

Client: It was in a tree trunk on the bank of the stream behind our house. It was hollow on the downhill side, and the hole was big enough for me to climb inside.

Therapist: Weren't you afraid in there?

Client: Not really. I liked it. It was the only place in the world I felt safe. It was dark and sometimes cold, but that's the way I felt most of the time—dark and cold. A squirrel shared that tree with me. He would sit on his branch chattering while I told him how I felt. Sometimes I would take him nuts, apples or whatever.

Therapist: Can you tell *me* how you felt?

Client: Mad. Hurt. Wounded. Empty, like there was a hole in my heart.

Therapist: Were you able to talk about this with anyone...for example, your mother?

Client: Not really, she had enough problems. I never saw her smile after my father left. I wanted to help her, but what could I do? So, we were sad together. Pretty soon she started drinking, and by the time I was a teenager I was stealing some of her whiskey every day, just to keep going. I swore I would never get married, but after she died, I had nobody, and Jack swept me off my feet...and now he's gone, too.

Therapist: So it feels like everybody's abandoned you...and perhaps that nobody would care if you just ceased to exist?

Client: Name one person who would miss me, one person who would even *know* I was gone, much less *care* I was gone.

Therapist: Well, I, for one, would care. And there are a lot of people here who would certainly miss you. But I'm wondering, was that what you were thinking the other night when you overdosed?

Client: It wasn't intentional. I couldn't remember how many pills I had already taken. It was a mistake to add the whiskey, sure. But I just felt so lonely with no one to talk to. And you had been gone so long, and I...

Therapist: You wanted to punish me for going?

Client: I didn't think of it that way. I guess I hoped that when they couldn't find me, it might make you come back. I remember crawling into that dark closet with my pills and my bottle and sitting there in the dark like I used to hide in my tree. But there was no squirrel and...well, I don't actually remember what happened after that.

Therapist: Nancy from the half-way house found you, and after a visit to the ER you ended up here.

Client: But even then, you didn't come back.

Therapist: Dr. Bunaphali was available.

Client: You're the only one who understands.

Therapist: I appreciate that, but overdosing is no way to make this point. We all want to understand and help you. In matters of the heart, there are no real experts, just fellow travelers willing to share your pain.

Psychoanalytic theory provides interesting ways of conceptualizing the human mind and behavior. Ideas such as the unconscious and defense mechanisms have been adopted by other psychotherapies. However, significant limitations have caused psychoanalysis to no longer be the dominant form of psychotherapy. Psychoanalysis lacks strong research evidence, although one study has suggested that psychodynamic therapy was just as effective as other evidence-based therapies.[4] In addition, psychoanalysis' benefits are difficult to assess, since it is focused more on personality change than on measurable goals. For Christians, Freud's ideas about our dark instinctual drives have some common features with biblical ideas about human nature, our sinful desires and the resulting internal conflict (Romans 7). However, there is little consideration of God's grace for our sins and His ability to transform our instinctual desires. Freud considered religion to be an illusion, although there are Christian psychoanalysts who believe Christianity can be reconciled with psychoanalysis.

Behavioral Therapy

Behavioral therapy is based on behaviorism, the theory that people act based on what they are conditioned to do. Behavioral therapy maintains that depression results from self-reinforcing behavior. Certain depressive behaviors (irritability, social withdrawal) tend to push people away and reduce pleasure and positive interactions with others. Other depressive behaviors (appearing sad and tearful) tend to elicit sympathy and caring behaviors from others, which tend to reinforce depressive behaviors. Behavioral therapy attempts to identify behaviors that maintain depression and then reduce or eliminate such behaviors. In behavioral therapy, a person learns to identify depression-generating behaviors, acquire new social skills that will increase positive interactions with others, develop problem-solving skills to increase successful interactions with the environment, and structure time to increase pleasurable activities.

SESSION

Therapist: *(female)* So how was this week, on a scale of one to 10?

Client: *(female executive of a non-profit corporation)* About a two. I couldn't face the board meeting the other night.

Therapist: What's the problem?

Client: Well, they seem to think I should be able to carry on as if happy thoughts and a pinch of pixie dust will make their Tinkerbell fly again. I mean, my husband walked out on me! And I was in Africa at the time, doing their business! It really ticks me off.

Therapist: It sounds like you think the board members are your adversaries.

Client: Well, they're not *all* my adversaries. A few—actually a small majority, two women and one man—are on my side...sympathetic and understanding. They seemed satisfied that I showed up at all.

Therapist: And the others?

Client: The others think I can be replaced—like getting a new wife, I suppose—even though I've taken the organization from nothing to where it is now in just nine years. One of them even made a motion that I keep a record of all my business activities for the next month so they could know how I'm spending my time.

Therapist: Did the motion pass?

Client: No. They tabled it after I clearly said I was not willing to subject my work to that kind of intrusion. I think the guy who made the motion knows I've missed some appointments lately, and donations are down. Or maybe he was ticked off because I arrived late...again.

Therapist: How late?

Client: Not more than an hour. I didn't *plan* to be late. I started getting dressed with plenty of time to spare. But the closer the hour got, the slower I seemed to move. It's like my whole self went into slow motion.

Therapist: Have you considered going early?

Client: That would be like showing up early for a root canal.

Therapist: If you were the first one there, you could greet them one by one as they arrive. There's no way around attending board meetings when you are the organization's CEO. You don't have to like it. But the way you're handling it now is alienating people and making you more depressed. Perhaps if you change your approach, other things will change too.

Client: I could try it. I can't go on like this, that's for sure.

Behavioral therapy is practical and can be particularly helpful in teaching skills such as relaxation training for anxiety or panic disorders. However, for some it can feel superficial, particularly since it usually does not delve into thought processes or the past, and treats people as if they are like automatons, rather than people with hopes, motivations and spiritual beliefs.

Cognitive Therapy

Cognitive therapy proposes that depression results from habits of negative thinking that magnify difficulties and barriers while minimizing positives about oneself, others or situations. These habitual thoughts reflect underlying assumptions about life (such as "the world is a dangerous place"), which may be shaped by early childhood experiences.[5] Cognitive therapy seeks to help by coaching individuals to think in a way that is positive, optimistic and reality based. Studies have shown that people can be trained to think in a positive manner, and this results in a decrease of depression, sadness and suffering. Cognitive therapy attempts to transform false, maladaptive ways of thinking into adaptive, truth-based thinking. These negative patterns of thinking include all-or-none thinking, selective abstraction, overgeneralization, personalization and catastrophic thinking.

All-or-none thinking is a tendency to judge situations as either black or white rather than in shades of gray, which is often a more accurate way to perceive reality. For example, as the result of a single mistake, a person might think: "I am worthless" or "I can't do anything right." At other times, the same person may think: "Everyone loves me" or "I'm brilliant." People who think this way may switch from one extreme to the other as the result of a single failure or a single success. There is an inability to see that oneself, other people and most situations are usually highly complex, with both positive and negative aspects, strengths and weaknesses.

Selective abstraction is a tendency to mentally filter out the positive details of a situation and focus on the negative details. For example, someone who is told by his boss at their performance review that he needs to increase his productivity might think, "I'm awful at my job. They're going to fire me," while ignoring the positive feedback he received, i.e., that he did excellent work and was given a bonus.

Overgeneralization is a tendency to draw broad conclusions based on a single event or limited amount of information, and typically includes words such as "always" or "never." For example, "My friend Alice didn't call me last night. She must not like me anymore." Or after a single failed relationship, a person may conclude, "No one will ever love me again," or "I will never find a compatible partner."

Personalization is a tendency to blame oneself for events that aren't entirely under one's control. For example, if a child misbehaves in public, the mother might think, "I don't know how to parent. I'm a failure as a mother," rather than considering that perhaps the child might be hungry or tired or may be learning how to socialize with other children.

Negative thoughts like these distort reality and often lead to painful emotions, fear and suffering. Cognitive therapy helps people to recognize these thoughts, the relationship of these thoughts to emotions, and teaches clients to replace these thoughts with healthier patterns of thinking. Cognitive therapy usually consists of eight to 20 sessions, and it often involves homework and exercises to complete at home.

SESSION

Therapist: *(male)* How are things going?

Client: *(male)* There was a typo in my quarterly report. I put "your" instead of "you're." But I noticed it too late to correct it. When I gave that report to my boss, I just stood there waiting to be fired.

Therapist: Did he notice it?

Client: Don't know. He didn't mention it…though I saw his lip twitch once while he was reading. The whole time I was in his office, all I could think about was that typo. I was so anxious I couldn't concentrate on what he said about my area's increased sales and that this was remarkable given the current state of the economy. The rest of what he said was drowned out by this voice inside my head telling me how stupid I was not to have proofed the report one more time. When I went home after work, I couldn't eat. When I went to bed, I mulled it over for hours. By the time I fell asleep, I had myself convinced that he was just humoring me and that any day now the pink slip would be on my desk when I got to work. I hardly slept at all. Every night since then has been the same.

Therapist: Suppose you talked back.

Client: To my boss? In situations like that I get so nervous that my main concern is trying not to faint.

Therapist: I meant talk back to the voice inside your head. Not out loud, of course. Nobody but you can hear what it's saying or what you're saying to it.

Client: But it's the truth. I should have proofed that report another time.

Therapist: How many times had you proofed it already?

Client: At least five. Why I didn't see it until it was too late, I'll never know.

Therapist: You could tell your inner voice that you did your best.

Client: But my best wasn't good enough.

Therapist: Now *I'm* hearing your inner voice. Since evidently your best was more than good enough for your boss, let's consider the untruth you just told yourself. How about saying, instead, "I gave it my best effort. That's all anyone can ask or expect of me." Repeat that after me.

Client: But...I don't know if I believe that. I mean, it's not what I expect of myself. I expect myself to get it right.

Therapist: I understand, but I would like to hear you say what I said.

Client: I gave it my best effort. That's all anyone can ask or expect of me.

Therapist: Good. Here's an assignment. At the beginning of each day, say to yourself: "Today I will give it my best shot. That's all anyone can ask or expect of me."

Client: I suppose I can try that.

Therapist: There's a mirror on the wall over there. Just for practice, go over and look yourself in the eye and say, "Today I will give it my best shot. That's all anyone can ask or expect of me." *(After client does this, therapist adds):* In addition, at the *end* of each day I want you to say to yourself, "Today I gave it my best shot. That's all anyone can ask or expect of me." Say these things to yourself every day from now until I see you again, and we'll talk about the next step then.

Cognitive therapy focuses on tangible skills and is goal driven, and the research supports its efficacy in different conditions and populations. It focuses on the present, rather than exploring the past or childhood influences that may have contributed to these negative beliefs. Cognitive therapy is strongly influenced by what the therapist considers to be rational, and there is a risk that therapists may impose their values on patients. On the other hand, it can also offer the opportunity for a Christian psychotherapist to examine how a person's spiritual beliefs about life can influence their thought patterns.[6]

Cognitive-Behavioral Therapy (CBT)

Cognitive therapy is often combined with behavioral therapy in cognitive behavioral therapy (CBT). Its main theory is that thoughts, behaviors and feelings all influence each other. Thinking tends to influence behavior (for example, thinking good thoughts about others promotes positive behavior toward them), and behavior tends to influence thinking (for example, smiling at others promotes positive thoughts about them—and usually positive responses from them), and these thoughts and behaviors feed into feelings, and vice versa. One reason we've covered cognitive therapy and behavioral therapy so extensively here is that CBT is rapidly becoming the psychotherapy of choice for depression and anxiety disorders. It does not dwell on understanding the past, but rather focuses on a person's ability to create change in the present, which can feel empowering for those who are feeling helpless because of their depression.

Mindfulness and Acceptance-based Therapies

In the last 20 years, there has been a wave of interest in more spiritually oriented therapies, in the form of Buddhist-based mindfulness and acceptance-based therapies. These therapies stress the idea of *mindfulness*—focusing awareness on the present moment and observing the feelings that arise without judgement. These therapies usually incorporate meditation and yoga, and they have become influential in popular culture. Therapies that include mindfulness and/or acceptance are the following:

> Dialectical and Behavioral Therapy (DBT) focuses on helping people regulate their intense emotions and is often used for treating borderline personality disorder.

> Mindfulness Based Stress Reduction (MBSR) helps people manage stress with meditation and yoga.

> Mindfulness Based Cognitive Therapy (MBCT) combines mindfulness with cognitive therapy and targets those with depression.

> Mindfulness Self-Compassion (MSC) combines mindfulness with encouraging kindness or compassion to oneself.

> Acceptance and Commitment Therapy (ACT) tries to help people accept their difficult feelings and experiences, rather than change them, and encourages individuals to live according to their values.

One of the key benefits from these therapies is the development of *metacognition*—the ability to step back and become aware of one's own mental state without being caught up in it. Mindfulness also focuses on slowing down and being present, rather than dwelling on the past or worries about the future. To some degree, there are similarities to biblical themes of self-awareness and not being anxious about tomorrow (Matthew 6:25-34). There is also a place for silence and meditation in the Christian tradition, although the focus of Christian meditation is not on oneself but on the Person and Word of God.

However, a fundamental assumption of mindfulness that Christians cannot ignore is its advocacy of detachment as the cure to suffering, which is based on Buddhist teachings of impermanence, that all of existence is transient, including our feelings and selves.

As Solomon writes in Ecclesiastes, trying to find happiness through human undertakings—pleasure, acquisition of material goods, power, knowledge, labor—is ultimately meaningless. This futility usually results in suffering. Buddhism (as well as the ancient Greek philosophy of Stoicism) responds to this dilemma by advocating detaching yourself from all desire and feeling, and thus protect oneself from all suffering. However, the Christian answer is radically different. As Tim Keller states, "The answer to this was not to love things less but to love God more. Only when our greatest love is God, a love that we cannot lose even in death, we can face all things with peace. "[7] Rather than close ourselves off from feeling, we lean into loving God and the love of God. The way we can experience all things (Philippians 4:11-13) and open ourselves up to the possibility of suffering is therefore shaped by the knowledge that nothing can separate from the love of God (Romans 8:38-39).

Humanistic Psychotherapy

Humanistic psychotherapy focuses on people's own innate ability for positive change and helping people achieve their full potential. It includes both existential therapy as well as person-centered therapy.

Existential therapy derives from existential philosophy, which focuses on confronting the fear of death and a person's freedom to create meaning in the face of this certainty to address anxiety and isolation. Existential therapy suggests that events that cause a loss of meaning or value can trigger depression, and depression results from the self-deception that results.

Existential therapy deals with all of the ultimate questions, but offers inadequate solutions, because it places the burden on the person to create their own meaning. The therapist becomes, in many ways, a spiritual guide for the person and, depending on the therapist, can lead the person towards nihilism or stoicism.[8] Ultimately, "The fear of the Lord is the beginning of wisdom," and only through Scripture can we answer the questions that existential therapy raises (Proverbs 9:10, ESV). God's answer to our fear of death is Christ's resurrection, and the purpose He gives is our identity in Christ. Our isolation He answers with His redeeming love.

Person-centered therapy was developed by Carl Rogers, and it theorizes that when a person experiences empathy, lack of judgement and unconditional positive regard from the therapist, he or she can discover an innate capacity for change. The therapy does not stress technique, but rather the therapeutic relationship. Like existential psychiatry, person-centered therapy has an optimistic view of human nature, believing there is an innate drive to self-actualize or reach one's full potential. The therapist does not consider him/herself to be the authority on the person's life, but rather he or she provides reflective listening and empathy, which helps the person to discover their own intrinsic ability to heal.

Roger's chief innovation was in stressing the importance of the characteristics of the therapist in helping the person to change. These characteristics—warmth, empathy, authenticity— have been adopted by many other types of therapy.[9] Roger's concept of unconditional positive regard is suggestive of Christian ideas of God's love (Romans 5:6-8), but a key difference is that God's love is not a blanket approval of who we are. Instead, His love is a transformative love that seeks to make us more into His image. In addition, Scripture has a fundamentally different view of human nature. Though we are redeemed and are sanctified by God, we still experience conflict within our nature, whose tendency is not toward self-actualization but toward sin (Romans 7:21-25).

Interpersonal Psychotherapy (IPT)

Interpersonal therapy proposes that a change in a person's relationships is the cause for depression, e.g., the loss of a loved one, a move, a difficult relationship or a change in role.[10] The therapist explores and seeks to understand the positive and negative aspects of the client's interpersonal functioning. For example, if a person is coping with the death of a loved one, therapy might focus on helping the person establish a new identity as a functioning single individual. Or the focus might be on correcting long-standing destructive patterns of social interaction, by modeling positive relationship patterns between the person and the therapist. Studies have shown that learning new, healthier patterns of relating is often quite successful in relieving depression.

SESSION

Therapist: *(male)* You seem more down than usual today.

Client: *(male nurse)* I can't help it. Someone put a note in my jacket pocket at the hospital last night. It said, "Isn't it time to move on?"

Therapist: What do you think it meant?

Client: Well, I'm quite sure it was from Claudia, the head nurse. And it meant that if I continue letting my sadness spill over in a patient setting, I'm going to be looking for employment elsewhere.

Therapist: Perhaps there's a play on words here and she'd like to see you move on with your life...past your grief. How would you characterize your relationship with Claudia before Ron died?

Client: Fine, as far as I was concerned. She seemed to respect my work and appreciate my sense of humor.

Therapist: So maybe the note wasn't a threat but her way of trying to help you.

Client: Am I supposed to turn off my feelings just because I'm at work? I mean my college roommate—my best friend—just died of AIDS. I haven't even told my parents yet. Claudia is the only person who knows what has me down. You'd think she, of all people, would cut me some slack.

Therapist: It may not seem fair, but people do have expectations of professionals. At work you're in constant contact with sick people, many of whom are discouraged. Ordinarily, I'm sure you wouldn't want to drag them down further, would you?

Client: That's true. I mean, I used to be able to find something cheerful to say. But now, especially if a patient's really sick, all I see is Ronnie.

Therapist: It sounds like you really cared about him.

Client: *(nods)*

Therapist: And if you had been able to provide his care when he was dying, you would have not only have provided him with good nursing care but would have tried to cheer him up too.

Client: *(nods again)*

Therapist: Is it possible, then, that when you see Ronnie in the form of a sick patient, you could care for that person as you would have cared for him...including trying to cheer up the patient? That way you wouldn't be denying your feelings but using them to help someone else.

Client: I suppose I could try.

People are relational beings, and IPT stands out because it considers a person in the context of their relationships, which some other therapies neglect. It is particularly helpful for those whose depression results from a significant life event. IPT is a structured therapy that draws on the ideas of psychodynamic therapy, as well as the techniques of CBT, and shares many similar strengths and weaknesses.

Supportive Therapy

In supportive therapy, the therapist actively encourages, comforts and supports people to help them decrease their emotional distress. It may be *eclectic*, drawing upon techniques from multiple other psychotherapy schools. Generally, this type of therapy does not seek to explore the past or challenge thought patterns, but rather it is more practical and seeks to help people use their strengths to get through their daily lives. Supportive therapy is the preferred mode of therapy for people undergoing significant situational stressors, or for those who have mental instability and are unable to tolerate insight-oriented or cognitive types of therapy. If a therapist does not espouse a particular type of therapy, they generally are providing supportive therapy.

Marital and Family Therapy (MFT)

The relationships in the home are important to consider in depression. First, chronic conflict and negative relationship patterns can contribute to depression. Second, depression can take a heavy toll on marital or family relationships, especially when the depressed person is socially withdrawn, is irritable or lacks initiative. Third, having supportive relationships at home can greatly reduce the suffering from depression. Marital or family therapy (MFT) can be helpful for couples or families who have a member who is depressed. MFT usually involves the couple or the entire family meeting together with the therapist, though the therapist may choose to meet with individual members from time to time.

Marital therapy is particularly important for any depressed person who reports a troubled marriage. It is important to keep in mind that marital therapy is *not* about a therapist taking sides and assigning blame, but rather it is about understanding and addressing the negative relationship patterns that have produced the conflict. The success of marital therapy depends heavily on joint participation and shared responsibility for resolving conflicts. Even when a depressed spouse refuses to participate, the other spouse may benefit from therapy aimed at learning to cope with and support the depressed partner.

When there are children in the home, they usually internalize the pain of their depressed parents and often need support as well. Sometimes the child of a parent with depression will strike out at others or exhibit behavioral problems at school. Other times the impact on a child is subtler, as when he or she becomes withdrawn or depressed. When children are the reported cause of family distress, the therapist can observe interactions between family members and provide insight into what kind of interventions might be helpful.

SESSION

Therapist: *(female social worker)* How are you...both of you?

Judy: Surviving, barely.

Jim: *(who recently lost his job)* More than surviving, with your help, thanks. I've been writing about losing my job. Just scattered thoughts for now, but maybe someday it will become a book.

Therapist: Judy, how do you feel about Jim's writing project?

Judy: *(shrugs)* If he feels he has to do it, then I'm not going to stop him. But I wish he'd concentrate on finding another job. I hate having to tell Heather, that's our 13-year-old, that she can't go to a school function, or whatever, because we just can't afford it.

Jim: Well, maybe this will give her a little better appreciation of how we've sacrificed in the past so she could have everything her little heart desired!

Judy: You have *no idea* how this has affected her. Her friends don't even bother to call anymore; they're sick of hearing she can't go because we can't afford it. Sometimes I hear her crying in her room at night.

Therapist: I'd like to talk with Heather sometime soon, just to get her perspective on this. And after that, perhaps we could all participate in a session just to be sure that everybody understands everybody.

Judy: That would be a good idea.

Jim: I don't see why we have to drag Heather into this, but if you insist…

Therapist: Since your whole family system of relationships is affected by whatever happens, from events to psychological distress, it is best when everyone can participate in the healing process too.

Jim: Okay. But adding Heather's gripes to all the rest won't help me find a new job.

Therapist: How about a progress report?

Jim: Frankly, the job hunting is not going too well. Would you believe that nobody wants to hire an architect with 20 years' experience?

Therapist: I would think expertise like that would be valuable.

Jim: Not in my case. Maybe they're afraid I'd be too set in my ways, or maybe they're afraid they'd have to pay too much even though I haven't made any demands. In fact, I can't even get past the receptionists. Lately I find myself almost paralyzed by fear every time I even think about arranging another interview. So instead, I go back to writing again.

Judy: I keep telling him he should be more assertive. I mean, we're desperate here. We'll be into our retirement funds in another month.

Jim: And I keep telling her that if she's so smart, she should go out and find a job herself. She has *no idea* how it feels to get passed over in favor of some 22-year-old fresh-out-of-school rookie. Knowing I'll get nagged when I walk in the door at home makes me want to stay away as long as possible.

Judy: Yeah. Ask him where he goes. Tell her, Jim. The sports bar. He stops there every day and comes home smelling like a brewery. No wonder he can't get up in the morning. No wonder we don't have enough money to pay the bills or for Heather to go out with her friends.

Jim: It's nowhere near what Judy's implying. I have a beer or two, sure, but mostly I just sit and watch sports on the big-screen TV, talk with my friends and try to forget how it felt to get turned down again.

Therapist: A lot of guys handle their pain this way, Jim. But it can lead to trouble if you let it get out of control.

Jim: It won't. I'll keep trying. It's just hard to get up the courage again, and at least my friends there make me feel like I'm still worth something to someone.

Therapist: I understand, but next time we meet you might bring along a list of places where you've applied between now and then. If you haven't found a job by then, maybe we'll be able to come up with some creative alternatives together. *(turning to Judy)* Judy, Jim mentioned the possibility of you working. Is going to work an option for you?

Judy: Not as far as I'm concerned. I quit college when our first child came, and I never went back. What kind of job could a person like me get in today's market?

Therapist: Jim, do you really want her to work?

Jim: Sure. That would be great. Having a job she liked might help her feel better about herself and take her mind off our situation. Of course, the money wouldn't hurt either.

Judy: I'd rather finish my degree first. It would be a lot easier finding a good position if I had a degree.

Jim: Maybe, maybe not. My degree isn't worth diddly-squat. I should have studied something more practical or more technical.

Therapist: I have some good contacts in town in education and technology. Sometimes you can combine education or retraining with a work experience. I suggest that between this meeting and next you spend some time together establishing some goals—as a couple and personally. Have three columns—one for each of you, one for you together. Start from scratch. Let yourself dream again. Ask yourselves where you'd like to be five years from now in terms of your careers and personal lives. Then brainstorm what would have to happen in order to reach your goals individually and as a couple. We'll discuss these lists next time and use them as a basis for forming a plan. What do you think?

Jim: *(looking at the floor)* Sounds great, but I have to warn you that I feel pretty beat down and worthless right now.

Judy: I think we should do it. Otherwise, we'll end up going in circles forever.

A strength of MFT is that this approach focuses on the family, rather than on the individual, and in doing so is consistent with Scripture's emphasis on the family and our interrelatedness. One approach, called "family systems theory," treats each individual (couple or family) as a part of an interconnected system of relationships. When one is well, all the members are well, and when one member is doing poorly, the reverse is true, an idea consistent with Paul's message about the interdependence of the parts of the members of the body of Christ, the church (1 Corinthians 12:12-16).

It is important to examine the ideal of a healthy family or marriage upheld by the therapist. Scripture's ideals of the marriage covenant, the obligations and sacrificial love of parents and children, husbands and wives for each other, are very distinct from the world's ideals.

Group Psychotherapy

In group therapy, individuals participate in sessions with a group of other people, moderated by the group therapist. Group therapy can utilize a variety of psychotherapeutic techniques described in this chapter. The goal of most group therapy for people with depression is to help them learn new skills and resources to better understand and address the causes of their depression. Members of the group also benefit from relationships with each other, as they learn to support and validate each other, and they may gain helpful insights by listening to others describe their experiences. Thus, group therapy can be helpful for those who struggle with loneliness and isolation. In some types of group therapy, the therapist can also make observations about an individual's patterns of relating to other people. Group therapy is also particularly helpful for people who share a common traumatic experience (such as bereavement, divorce, sexual or physical abuse, caregiver stress, etc.).

Christian Counseling Theories

Case: LezLee Guy

Prior to April 1993, 36-year-old LezLee Guy's felt her life was all that any Christian woman could ask. With a husband, Richard, who loved her, and two children, Rich, 16, and Nicholle, 14, LezLee was expecting them all to live happily ever after. Then, like a hellish nightmare, her husband died from a pulmonary embolism (blood clots in the lungs). Two months later, while LezLee and the children were traveling by car to visit the cemetery on Father's Day, an 81-year-old woman lost control of her car and careened into the Guys' car. Nicholle was killed instantly.

Absolutely devastated and in shock, LezLee reached out for help from a counselor associated with her church. This therapist was usually nondirective, expecting LezLee to carry the conversation week after week even though she had little energy to do so. Once, however, he asked her to pretend that Richard was sitting there with them, which was impossible for LezLee at that time due to her deteriorating condition—clinical depression, post-traumatic stress disorder, panic attacks and an eating disorder as a result of which she would ultimately lose 85 pounds. She was taking at least a dozen prescription pills a day in addition to the sleeping pills she mixed with alcohol. Finally, this therapist convinced her to admit herself to the psychiatric ward of a local hospital, the first of half a dozen hospitals to which she would be admitted over time, twice for the eating disorder and the others due to suicide attempts.

LezLee's second Christian counselor saved her life by calling for help during her last suicide attempt, just before Christmas 1996. "He was awesome as a counselor," LezLee said. "I knew he cared. He would cry with me from time to time. Once after leaving his office, I had a panic attack right outside in the hallway. He came out there and sat down with me—he always met me wherever I was at—until I was able to leave. He used Scripture sometimes, but he never threw it at me. Sometimes he offered advice I didn't like but I needed to hear. He was totally dependable, and I always felt secure with him."

LezLee's third Christian counselor saw her briefly after she moved to Colorado in 1997. But this college professor/counselor felt that another counselor would be better for LezLee, so he referred her to a woman who specialized in "prayer therapy."

This fourth Christian counselor made it clear that prayer was all she did. "She believed that the only way people can be healed is through the Holy Spirit," LezLee said. "So we prayed through the whole session, every time. I should say that she prayed. I couldn't pray then, so the whole thing left me feeling extremely uncomfortable."

LezLee's fifth Christian counselor had lost his wife to cancer several years prior to LezLee's first meeting him. "He is so real," LezLee said. "He understands. He tries to help his clients find purpose and meaning in their experiences."

As LezLee's experience illustrates, there is a wide variation in what Christian counseling looks like.

Some Christian counselors practice in ways that are indistinguishable from a non-Christian counselor, such as her first therapist, whose practice seemed to follow non-directive person-centered therapy. In many ways, she was a counselor who just happened to also be a Christian.

Some Christian counselors only use explicitly "spiritual" techniques, such as Lezlee's fourth counselor, who used one version of "prayer therapy." Another example of this is theophostic prayer, whose aim is to help emotionally wounded people find freedom from traumatic memories through a personal encounter with Christ.

Some Christian counselors are more intentional about incorporating the psychotherapy strategies we discussed earlier under a strongly Christian worldview, such as Lezlee's second and fifth counselors. These counselors often have more explicit views on human nature and more developed theories about the nature of problems and therapy strategies. It is this last category of Christian counseling we would like to help you navigate, particularly since there can be strong opinions and disagreement about how we should go about engaging with secular psychotherapy.

Psychology and Christianity

There are many helpful insights from psychology, but how do we incorporate these as Christians? All psychological theories have fundamental assumptions about the human condition, the nature of suffering, our identity, meaning, hope and our ultimate aim in life. As Paul describes in Romans, our underlying assumptions set us apart from the world. Our fundamental problem is sin, both personal sin and sin from a fallen world, which separates us from God. Our fundamental need is for Christ's atonement for our sins. And our goal is not happiness, nor even relief from suffering, but to live in keeping with who we are: children of God, becoming conformed daily more and more to His image. If we consider secular psychotherapy to be the practical application of philosophy, we can hope for Christian counseling to be the practical application of this theology. What does that look like? We review several major approaches to doing so. For the purposes of our book, these can be summarized as: (1) a levels-of-explanation view; (2) a biblical counseling view; (3) an integration view; and (4) a Christian psychology view.[11] All these views agree in their core beliefs - the authority of Scripture and the importance of the Gospel, but there are several primary differences most relevant to counseling:

1. Source of knowledge about people: Which are valid sources of truth? Scripture, theology, philosophy, personal experience, history and/or research?

1. Critique of psychology: To what degree is the approach more critical or more trusting of contemporary psychology?

1. Allegiance: Is the primary allegiance of the counselors to the church or to the community of scholars and clinicians?

(1) Levels-of-Explanation View

The *Levels-of-Explanation view,* or the *Perspectivalism* view, could be summarized as "everyone should stay in their own lane." This view is based on the philosophy that there are different levels by which to understand a person—the atomic level, the chemical level, the cellular level, the mental level and the spiritual level—and that these should all be studied by their respective sciences—physics, chemistry, biology/neuroscience, psychology and theology. In this view, theology should not comment on psychology, since they are studying fundamentally different phenomena.

This view is more common among academics and researchers. Practically speaking, if a Christian counselor espouses this view, it would mean he or she is unlikely to see much conflict between their psychology and faith, and he or she is therefore not critical of psychological theory. This approach might be helpful when an individual needs help dealing with related medical and psychological problems; for example, a patient with dementia who also struggles with depression, in teasing apart which symptoms might be best helped by what kind of specialist.

Representative People/Organizations
David Myers (Hope College), Everett Worthington (Virginia Commonwealth University), Warren Brown (Fuller Theological Seminary), Malcolm Jeeves (University of St. Andrews)

(2) Biblical Counseling View

In 1970, at a time when churches had adopted psychology without much critique, Jay Adams, professor of practical theology at Westminster Theological Seminary, called on pastors to reject the secular models of counseling and instead counsel based on Scripture, which he taught was alone sufficient for understanding human nature and problems. He proposed that counseling should occur as part of pastoral work, and he encouraged pastors to confront the sin in people's lives. Jay Adams named his approach to counseling *nouthetic counseling.* However, over time, a school of thought known as *biblical counseling* diverged from Adam's nouthetic counseling.[12] Nouthetic counseling has fallen out of favor as some have experienced spiritual harm from it, due to its focus on sin and confrontation and the neglect of context and motivation. Biblical counseling remains committed to Scripture-based categories for understanding and addressing human problems, but it developed its own motivation theory and has become more open to learning from psychology.

Biblical counseling's strengths are in dealing with traditional pastoral counseling problems, such as spiritual problems, existential questions and struggles with sin, guilt and hope. Biblical counseling's weakness may be in dealing with more severe and complex mental illness.

Representative People/Organizations
Jay Adams, Ed Welch, David Powlison, Wayne Mack, Christian Counseling and Education Foundation, Association for Biblical Counselors, Master's Seminary, Southern Seminary

(3) Integrative Counseling View

This view generally places the Bible and psychology on equal footing. The Bible provides the Christian worldview and theology, and psychology provides the science and practice of counseling. According to Stanton Jones, one of the key thinkers, "Our commitment to a biblical view of persons provides a presumptive framework, not a fully constructed system of psychology."[13] This view also tends to be more accepting of psychological theory, although thoughtfulness about the psychology techniques used varies widely among counselors.

This is probably the predominant view among most Christian counselors today, as it is the official approach of many of the large Christian-counseling graduate programs. It utilizes the resources of secular psychology and therefore may be more equipped to deal with severe mental illness. However, this view defines a narrower scope for conceptualizing how Christianity affects counseling.

Representative People/Organizations

Clyde Narramore, Stanton Jones, Gary Collins, Minerth and Meier, Focus on the Family (James Dobson), Fuller Theological Seminary, Rosemead (Biola University), Wheaton College, American Association for Christian Counselors, Christian Association for Psychological Studies

(4) Christian Psychology View

This view seeks to construct its own Christian psychological science based on a biblical framework, with its own distinctly Christian theories, research and practice.[14] It is fundamentally similar to biblical counseling in its questioning of psychology's underlying presuppositions, but it differs in its more academic and research focused agenda.

Representative People/Organizations

Larry Crabb, Eric Johnson, Dan Allender, Tremper Longman III, Society for Christian Psychology

Alternative Resources

If a person is unable to seek counseling due to time or financial constraints, it can be helpful to explore some self-help options.

> *Books:* In the appendix on further reading, we list some self-help books and workbooks, both Christian and secular, that can be helpful. These can also assist as a supplement to in-person counseling.

> *Support Groups:* Some churches offer support groups for those with mental health issues, which can be a great way of connecting with community.

> *Smartphone apps / tele-therapy:* Some therapists are able to provide therapy over video-chat, which can help those who have difficulty with mobility or time constraints. One developing technology is chatbot therapy, which uses artificial intelligence to have a conversation and provide basic therapy. Woebot, for example, is a free chatbot app developed by Stanford researchers that delivers basic CBT.

Does it matter?

Perhaps the distinctions between these approaches seem irrelevant to you, rather like splitting hairs. Even we, the authors of this book, lean toward different approaches among ourselves. And no matter what approach a counselor may claim, the efficacy of a Christian counselor depends on numerous other things, such as their spiritual maturity, wisdom, how much their faith has permeated their own life and their own personal qualities.

Why then is this important?

Having a counselor who can consider both psychological and spiritual issues is critical when a depressed person is struggling with questions on which our faith has clear things to say, such as in existential questions like fear of death, meaning and morality. For example, the issue of guilt has particular significance as a Christian, given our views on sin, responsibility and forgiveness. But psychologically, depression can distort reality and produce guilt not based on actual responsibility. A counselor who can appreciate both these perspectives can best help a Christian navigate the truth that lies between a guilty conscience and the false accusations of depression. It is also important for a counselor to know when to refer to a spiritual authority such as a person's pastor, and vice versa.

In the ideal scenario, a person would be able to find a Christian counselor whose theological beliefs and values match their own. But this is not always the case. There are many places where it is hard to find counselors, much less a Christian counselor. And sometimes the available Christian counselors may have personal characteristics that make them less effective counselors than available secular counselors. A person may have to decide on whether to seek help from a certain type of Christian counselor or from a secular counselor, and awareness of these approaches can help in making that choice.

If a secular therapist is hostile to faith and sees religion as evidence of sickness or weakness, we would encourage a person to seek someone else. However, if a skilled secular therapist is respectful, or even curious about the importance of faith in a person's life, then she or he may be worth considering. When a Christian may have other resources for dealing with their spiritual issues and is seeking help for issues not affected by spiritual values, it may be less critical to seek a counselor who is Christian. Secular psychotherapy has many practical skills to offer, and for those who lie suffering at the side of the road, help should not be refused—even if it comes from a Samaritan.

Who Are the Mental Health Professionals?

Believe it or not, anyone can call himself or herself a "psychotherapist" or a "therapist." No specific credentials are involved; no state licensing is required. Certificates to hang on one's wall may be obtained via the internet. It is essential for anyone seeking counseling to carefully inquire about the counselor's qualifications, credentials and training. Licensure or certification requires that the therapist meet certain state or national requirements.

Licensed Mental Health Counselors (LMHC) or
Licensed Professional Counselors (LPC)

Licensed mental health counselors, particularly those who are members of the American Counseling Association, have completed college or university and an additional year or two of training to obtain a master's degree in counseling from an accredited program (in addition to up to two years of supervision while providing therapy).

Social Workers (Licensed Clinical Social Workers - LCSW)

Social workers also provide counseling. Social workers typically have a college degree plus two years of academic and clinical training culminating in a master's degree in social work (MSW) and require additional clinical training in order to be a licensed clinical social worker (LCSW). Social workers also receive special training in case management and can be particularly helpful to those experiencing a need for social services and community resources.

Marriage and Family Therapists (MFTs)

MFTs have masters or doctorate's level graduate training in marriage and family therapy, followed by two years of supervised clinical experience. Marriage and family therapists are usually licensed, and many MFTs are members of the American Association of Marriage and Family Therapists. They evaluate and treat emotional disorders and other health or behavioral problems within the context of the client's network of primary relationships (sometimes called a "family system").

Pastoral Counselors

Pastoral counselors are ministers who have received additional training in counseling. In order to be certified by the American Association of Pastoral Counselors (AAPC), a pastoral counselor must have obtained an undergraduate degree and a graduate degree at a divinity school or seminary, as well as have earned a master's or doctoral degree in counseling or psychology (and be licensed by the state in which they practice). Post-seminary training must include at least 1,375 hours of supervised clinical experience involving individual, group, marital and family therapy, plus 250 hours of direct approved supervision working in both crisis and long-term situations.

Clergy

While many clergy provide pastoral care (not what is technically called counseling), their certification is often ordination to the ministry in general rather than counseling certification. Most will have completed seminary (three years of study after college). Some, however, will have attended Bible college directly after high school to obtain training for the ministry. The amount of training in counseling at seminaries and Bible colleges is highly variable, often minimal (though this has been slowly changing over the last few decades). As a result, many clergy do not have adequate theoretical or clinical training to recognize or treat major depression. Even when they have adequate training and experience to recognize major depression, our view is they should not attempt to function as the depressed person's only professional caregiver, since all persons with major depression benefit from evaluation and appropriate treatment by mental health professionals.

Paraprofessional or Lay Counselors

Most paraprofessional or lay counselors have pursued some kind of training or certification through a seminary or counseling program, and they may or may not have advanced degrees. Christian counselors who are state licensed will have training similar to that of secular counselors (LPCs). For counselors who are not licensed, the quality of their training may vary widely. Some skilled and capable counselors may not have pursued licensure because of differences in their philosophy of counseling. If you are considering working with a lay counselor, we encourage you to familiarize yourself with their program of training and amount of experience. Research studies suggest that lay counselors are generally as effective as professional counselors for most common problems, but for more severe or unusual mental health issues, someone with more experience and training should be sought.

Psychologists

Most psychologists are mental health professionals who have completed college or university and between three and five years of postgraduate education to obtain a doctorate in psychology (PhD, PsyD or EdD). Many psychologists are members of the American Psychological Association, which helps to set educational and ethical standard for their profession. Training in a PhD program typically involves more research and theory, whereas a PsyD program is usually more clinically focused, and an EdD (doctorate in education) program typically provides training for school psychologists. Psychologists typically complete at least a one-year supervised clinical internship prior to becoming an independent psychotherapist.

Psychiatrists

Psychiatrists are medical doctors (MD or DO) who have completed college, four years of medical school and four years of a psychiatry residency. In order to prescribe medication, they must be licensed by the state and, by passing a written and oral board examination, can become "board-certified" psychiatrists. Psychiatrists may be members of their professional organization, the American Psychiatric Association. Psychiatrists prescribe medication, and some also provide psychotherapy. It may be ideal to see one person who can provide both medication and therapy, though a psychiatrist is not necessarily better trained than other licensed professionals at providing therapy (and visits are often limited in time).

Psychiatric Nurses

Psychiatric nurses are licensed by the state, complete an associate's or baccalaureate degree in general nursing and receive on-the-job training specializing in providing psychiatric services. Those with a master's degree (MSN) or a doctorate in nursing (DNP) can prescribe medication under the supervision of a physician and may also provide psychotherapy.

Working with a Therapist

Engaging in therapy can be difficult.

For one, it can be extremely hard to be vulnerable. For a person who has been ground to dust by months or years of circling the millstone of depression, the thought of being probed and analyzed by an unknown person with unknown methods can evoke strong feelings of anxiety. It can be hard to let light in on your darkest demons and acknowledge thoughts and feelings you have been trying to avoid. It can be hard to take an honest look at yourself in the mirror. But the act of opening up and allowing someone else to share in your burdens often is itself healing.

In addition, you should be aware that therapy is not without its risks. Not everyone has the mental strength to explore past traumas, confront lies they have been telling themselves or take responsibility for their actions. Therapy does not always feel good. Therapy can temporarily make your mood worse before it gets better. In this way, therapy is a kind of "psycho-surgery," as there may need to be wounds inflicted before there is healing. A skilled therapist should be cautious about assessing when a person is ready to reopen old wounds, or if this should be done at all.

Trust is vital in a therapeutic relationship. You should look for a therapist you feel comfortable with and who you feel respected by. Without trust, it is hard to be honest and hard to be vulnerable.

It may take time to get to know a therapist, and we would advise meeting with someone for three or four sessions before assessing if the therapy relationship works. If, after that time, one is still finding it hard to trust the therapist and not getting much benefit from the sessions, it may be worth trying another therapist. The effectiveness of therapy depends in part on the goodness of fit between therapist and client. Therapy is expensive, time consuming and involves a lot of personal effort, so finding the right therapist that you "click" with is important. However, do not give up. With the toll that depression may take on a person's life, it may be more costly in the long run not to engage in therapy.

It is important to be honest with a therapist about your feelings. You need to let your therapist know if you are experiencing dark thoughts, particularly suicidal thoughts. If there is something your therapist said that is bothering you, bring this up in the session. A skilled therapist will be able to use that information to understand you better, and a mature therapist will be able to handle honest feedback. A therapist cannot read your mind, though, and can help only with as much as you reveal.

Good therapy requires work. It can be exhausting, and you may find yourself tired the rest of the day. But anything worth building requires work, and the path to wisdom and maturity is hard won.

Endnotes

1. Daily Hope with Rick Warren, Devotional, September 12, 2018. https://www.crosswalk.com/devotionals/daily-hope-with-rick-warren/fill-your-mind-with-biblical-truth-daily-hope-with-rick-warren-september-12-2018.html. The categories of "poison, junk food and healthy food" are borrowed from "Fill Your Mind with Biblical Truth," a devotional from Rick Warren.

2. Tan, Siang-Yang. Counseling and Psychotherapy, p 7. Baker Publishing Group. Kindle Edition

3. Tan, Siang-Yang. Counseling and Psychotherapy (p. 46). Baker Publishing Group. Kindle Edition.)

4. Shedler J. The efficacy of psychodynamic psychotherapy. Am Psychol. 2010 Feb-Mar;65(2):98-109

5. Tan, Siang-Yang. Counseling and Psychotherapy (p. 255). Baker Publishing Group. Kindle Edition.

6. Tan, Siang-Yang. Counseling and Psychotherapy (p. 273). Baker Publishing Group. Kindle Edition.

7. Keller, Timothy. *Walking With God in Pain and Suffering*. New York: Penguin, 2013. p44

8. Tan, Siang-Yang. Counseling and Psychotherapy (p. 122-124). Baker Publishing Group. Kindle Edition

9. Tan, Siang-Yang. Counseling and Psychotherapy (p. 145). Baker Publishing Group. Kindle Edition

10. Markowitz, John C, and Myrna M Weissman. "Interpersonal psychotherapy: principles and applications." *World psychiatry: official journal of the World Psychiatric Association (WPA)* vol. 3,3 (2004): 136-9.

11. Johnson, Eric., ed. *Psychology and Christianity: Five* Views. Downers Grove , IVP 2010.

12. Powlison, David. *The Biblical Counseling Movement: History and Context*. Greensboro, NC: New Growth Press, 2010

13. Johnson, Eric., ed. *Psychology and Christianity: Five Views*. Downers Grove , IVP 2010.

14. Johnson, Eric., ed. *Psychology and Christianity: Five Views*. Downers Grove , IVP 2010.

CHAPTER 7

THE SPIRIT

How firm a foundation, ye saints of the Lord
Is laid for your faith in His excellent Word
What more can He say than to you He hath said
To you who for refuge to Jesus have fled

Fear not, I am with thee; oh be not dismayed
For I am thy God and will still give thee aid
I'll strengthen thee, help thee, and cause thee to stand
Upheld by My righteous, omnipotent hand

When through the deep waters I call thee to go
The rivers of sorrow shall not overflow
For I will be with thee, thy troubles to bless
And sanctify to thee thy deepest distress

When through fiery trials thy pathways shall lie
My grace all sufficient shall be thy supply
The flame shall not hurt thee; I only design
Thy dross to consume and thy gold to refine

The soul that on Jesus has leaned for repose
I will not, I will not desert to its foes
That soul, though all hell should endeavor to shake
I'll never, no never, no never forsake.

by "K," published in Rippon's Hymns (1787)[1]

Case: "Linda"

My dad was a wonderful man. He was a car salesman, which was a good job back then. He was popular, well-liked, a sportsman. I remember sitting with him in the hunting blinds as a child. But he was depressed. I remember calling the ambulance for him quite a bit for what we thought were heart attacks. I think these were really mental issues, although he thought they were physical ailments. The longest he was hospitalized for was one month.

I remember one Christmas Eve he was walking around the house crying and he kept on saying "I'm going to be okay." Of course, I didn't know what in the world was going on. I woke up on Christmas Day and went into mom's bedroom, and asked, "Where's Dad? Is he gone?" Mom said yes. I asked, "For good?" Mom said, "Yes." He had left because someone told Dad he would be better without us because we were too stressful for him.

There was no room to cry about anything. We just had to keep going—my mom, my sister and me. We saw him once a month for six months, but it was uncomfortable and awkward. We didn't know what to say and what to do, because no one ever explained what happened. Then he moved out of the state when I was in seventh grade, and I never saw him again. I still feel a lot of shame about my parents, my dad, the divorce.

Mom always had her cocktails, her martinis. But she didn't really start to drink heavily until I was in high school. She was a mean drunk. When we would go out to restaurants, she would get drunk and argue with waiters. It was embarrassing. She never directed it at me and my sister, but we always tried to be good.

I started getting depressed in high school. I remember getting up in the morning, not feeling like I could get through the day and wanting to just hide. But I never allowed myself to do this. The depression really became a problem for me in college. I was trying to be happy and go along with the crowd, and that led to lots of drinking because that eased up the momentary depression. But I just felt different from everybody else, like a second-class citizen for having divorced parents.

After college there was partying and drinking—everyone was doing it at that time. When I came home, I was very down, and Mom finally sent me to a therapist. That made me more ashamed and horrified that I was going to turn out like my dad. I hated going to the therapist. When I got a job, the depression improved. As long as I was young and working and dating, I felt like I had my head above water, and it didn't get to me.

I met my husband and figured he was good marriage material, so we got married and had kids. I was pregnant with my second child when I came to Christ through a friend's Bible study. It was the first time I experienced that kind of love, the unconditional love of Christ. It was so overwhelming. It was the first time I felt worthy, and accepted, and loved. And it was never going to leave.

At the time, everything looked like it should have been fine. But one day, I was with a friend and started crying for no reason. She encouraged me to return to therapy, and I've been in therapy since then. I think it's kept me alive. I've seen a couple good therapists and a couple bad therapists. It's somewhere that I can talk about something I feel so ashamed of. I also started taking medication and it worked for a while. There were also many good things that were happening in my life. I was busy raising kids, and happy with marriage and how my life was going. I loved being a mom. I felt competent.

Then the thing I feared most happened. My husband had the affair and then filed for divorce. I felt like my head exploded. The betrayal was the worst part. You have been intimate with someone, depended on them for everything, and believed they depended on you. And then, at the end of it all, is the feeling of being alone. The whole experience was a nightmare. Some people go through divorce, go through the motions of it, and then get back on their feet. But for me, it was devastating.

I counted on my faith for every bit of energy, and Christ literally carried me through. I was so in touch with Christ. I was in the Bible all the time. I was going to Bible study or listening to the preacher on the radio. I thought, things can't get any worse, so I'm going to turn over my life entirely to Christ.

Then things started settling down. I moved into my own house, but it was up to me to start this new life. I didn't know how to do it! I became anxious—what am I going to do with my life? What's the point of all this? I'm trying to take my life back into my own hands, and it's not working. I've developed a slight trust issue with Christ now. He let something really bad happen to me, and I'm having trouble trusting that He won't let something really bad happen to me again. It happened with my dad leaving and my parent's divorce. It happened with my own divorce. I want that sense of safety, of feeling safe in God's hands, but I don't feel safe anymore. I feel on my own again. Sometimes I feel like God is there for everyone else but not for me.

I think my Christian walk is going to be where I find the ultimate healing. When I walk closely with Christ and feel loved by Him, everything feels better. But when I get depressed, I can't feel God's love. I know He's bigger than depression, that He's bigger than divorce. I hang onto the truth that God has a plan, that I'm going to heaven, that my children are going to heaven. I hang onto the truth that God is good. Sometimes I don't feel like it, but I know He is. Deep down, I know He is because He said He is.

How can family and friends be helpful? By understanding that I don't want to be where I am. Understanding that I'm not trying to do it to myself. I feel like a failure, and I need their love more than anything now. I also need grace.

What would I say to someone who's struggling with depression? I would listen and tell them their hope is in Christ, because I still believe that. I would understand their struggle and tell them not to be too hard on themselves. There's a misunderstanding out there that people with depression aren't trying hard enough, not pulling themselves up by their bootstraps. If I could do that, I would have."

Linda has been suffering. There is a lot to unpack in her story. Several things seem to contribute to her depression—a likely genetic predisposition, abandonment by her father, a hard childhood and then a husband's betrayal. She has benefitted from medication and therapy. They have helped, but they have not been the complete answer. What has enabled her to make it so far is leaning hard on Christ and at times being carried by Him through the deep waters of sorrow. At the end of the day, in a person's war against depression, this is where the key battle lies—wrestling with God.

This leads us to this chapter on spiritual strategies. A discussion of strategies to fight depression would be incomplete without discussing how depression impacts our hearts, our hopes and our relationship with God.

We are neither pastors nor theologians, but we have observed spiritual strategies that can be helpful and harmful. In addition, there is wisdom to be mined from the past. While scientific understanding of the body is constantly evolving, there is spiritual wisdom that stands the test of time. There are those who have gone before us, who were well acquainted with suffering and with depression. One is the English pastor and theologian Richard Baxter (1615-1691).

Baxter was a prolific writer whose most famous works are *The Christian Directory and The Reformed Pastor*. In addition to serving as a pastor, he functioned for a time as a self-taught physician when his town was unable to recruit one. He treated many who suffered from melancholy (the name for depression at the time) and gained a reputation as a consultant on spiritual disorders.

Baxter considered depression to be the domain of both the pastor and the physician, since depression kept its sufferers from the worship of God.[2] Baxter's understanding of depression, its causes and its cures was remarkable, as much of his advice is just as valuable and helpful 400 years later. We use the practical directions he gives in his "Advice to Depressed and Anxious Christians" to frame this chapter.

1. *"Avoid all unnecessary solitude and, as much as possible, keep honest, cheerful company…for you, [solitude] is a time of temptation and danger. If Satan tempted Christ himself when he was fasting and alone in a wilderness, how much more will he take this as his opportunity against you?"* [3]

For most Christians, silence and solitude is a useful spiritual discipline for prayer, reflection and self-examination. But for those who are depressed, solitude becomes a way of retreating from interactions with others from whom one already feels disconnected, and that is particularly dangerous. With depression comes the temptation to turn inward and withdraw from the swirl of life, perhaps due to lack of interest, due to irritability, due to fear of burdening others or due to shame. But one should not give into the desire to isolate. With isolation comes the risk of darker thoughts and worsening depression.

We were made to be in relationship (Genesis 2:8), both with God and with each other, and God can use others to minister to the depressed. Do you feel yourself tempted to retreat from people, particularly fellow believers? Avoid spending time alone and instead seek out the company of others. But of course, finding "cheerful company" who are sympathetic to those who are depressed may not be an easy task. Perhaps that role might be filled by friends and family. But in this modern age, when many might be disconnected from family, this is a role which the members of a church can fulfill. Perhaps this might mean attending a prayer group, a Bible study, a community group or a support group for depression. This requires that churches welcome, as Jesus did, those who do not "have it all together."

2. *"Be sure that you keep yourself constantly busy—as far as your strength will allow— in the diligent labors of a lawful calling, and don't waste precious time in idleness. Idleness is the opportunity of the tempter: when you are idle, you invite the Devil to come and annoy you. Then you will have time to listen to him and think about all that he will put into your mind, and then to think those thoughts again!"* [4]

How a person spends their time can greatly affect his or her mood. Work—whether paid or unpaid—is an important aspect of healing from depression. Just as Baxter cautions those with depression to avoid solitude, in the same way he cautions them to avoid idleness.

Both isolation and idleness make one vulnerable to Satan's attack through dark, depressive thoughts.

For numerous people, work can serve as an important source of distraction from depression. In *Darkness Is My Only Companion*, Kathryn Greene-McCreight talks about gardening to keep the pain of depression at bay. "Busyness is an important part of healing for me," she writes, "or at least of staving off the symptoms of depressive disorder."[5]

One can gain from work a sense of productivity and a sense of competence, which themselves can counter the feelings of depression. We explore the topic of work further in Chapter 8.

3. *"Do not trust your own judgement in your depressed and anxious condition, as to either the state of your soul or the choice and conduct of your thoughts or ways. Commit yourself to the judgement and direction of some experienced faithful guide."* [6]

Having good advisors, whether a counselor, pastor, wise friend or family member, is important when one is struggling with depression. Depression can impair one's judgement and contribute to difficulty in making decisions. Avoid making any big life decisions (e.g., quitting a job) when depressed without the counsel of others.

Be aware of pitfalls with depression, as it can make one vulnerable to all sorts of temptations.

› *The temptation to overburden oneself*, either with spiritual duties in trying to reassure oneself of a salvation that is already secure or overworking in order to avoid the pain of depression. (See "Sleep and Rest" in Chapter 5.)

› *The temptation to sin*. Although depression itself is not a sin, it makes one more vulnerable to temptation to sin. The symptoms of hopelessness or irritability, or conversely the inward-focus and lack of motivation that are part of depression, can lead one to lose sight of God's central purpose for our lives, namely, that we love the Lord above all else, and love our neighbor as ourselves (Matthew 22:36-40).

› *The temptation to escapism*, whether through alcohol, drugs, pornography, adultery or other addictive behaviors. (See "Dulling the Pain with Alcohol or Drugs" in Chapter 4 and "False Intimacy" in Chapter 8.)

› *The temptation to seek and embrace quick fixes to depression*. Depression is an extremely complex problem that often involves time and hard work to heal. While this approach can be true of those who only look to medication, it is also true for those who believe depression is primarily a spiritual issue. Desperation for relief may drive a person to pursue almost any avenue of help. Sometimes depressed Christians seek a spiritual experience that will eradicate their symptoms once and for all. Depression is essentially a prolonged trial, and while God may sometimes choose to deliver us out of the trial, He sometimes may allow us to remain in the trial longer than we prefer in order that He might sanctify us. Awareness of the often-lengthy timeframe of depression can better prepare the patient and loved ones to dig in for the long haul.

4. *"Ensure that they are under the care of a prudent and capable Christian pastor, both for confidential counsel and for public preaching. Make sure this minister is skillful in dealing with depressed parishioners, and is himself peaceable and not contentious, error-prone, or fond of eccentric ideas."* [7]

It is important to make sure that those who are depressed are under the care of a pastor. However, not all pastors have had training or experience in dealing with depression, as seminaries typically provide little training for dealing with emotional problems. However, this is changing as there is growing awareness that those struggling with mental illness seek the help of clergy first. In one sense, pastors often serve as frontline mental health workers. It is estimated that, overall, clergy provide more total hours providing pastoral counseling than the total hours provided by all members of the American Psychiatric Association. [8]

The pastor plays a vital role in encouraging the suffering by preaching truth and hope from the pulpit, as well as by one-on-one encouragement. A depressed person should ask their pastor if they would be willing to meet periodically for encouragement, to clear up any spiritual misunderstandings and to pray. Ideally, the pastor would work together with a church member's mental health team, physician and therapist. The depressed person should share contact information between their pastor and their mental health team. However, if a pastor is not comfortable being directly involved in the person's care, it may be particularly important to find a therapist (and perhaps a physician) who is a thoughtful Christian and can provide similar functions.

5. *"Strive for the cure of your disease, and commit yourself to the care of your physician and obey him. Don't be like most depressed persons, who will not believe that medication will do them good, but who think it is only their soul that is troubled."* [9]

"Were the malady, as some fancy, a manifestation of demonic possession, medication might nevertheless provide deliverance...Cure the disorder, and the disordered operations of the Devil cease." [10]

Although Baxter is keenly aware of the spiritual aspects of depression and the importance of considering sin and responsibility, he recognizes that these do not deny the need for medical help. The bodily and the spiritual are intertwined, and sometimes using bodily cures can also help with spiritual troubles. Here the question arises, is depression a work of the devil?

On one level, we can consider all effects of the fall and all physical illnesses to be the work of the devil. The devil can use our physical vulnerabilities as a way to tempt us to sin, just as he did Job and Jesus (Matthew 4:1-11). Therefore, by seeking all means to cure the physical disease, "the disordered operations of the Devil [may] cease."

This needs to be clearly distinguished from demon possession, however. We believe demons exist today as they did in the days of Jesus. However, we also believe too many well-meaning Christians attribute to Satan and his minions more influence than they may actually have in the lives of believers. When a person has been bought by the blood of Jesus, making him or her God's possession (see 1 Corinthians 6:19-20), and when the Spirit of the living God resides in his or her heart, it is impossible to be at the same time possessed by a demon, whether of depression or anything else. Believers who show evidence of a life in Christ, who hate their sin and find comfort in God and His promises, cannot be possessed by demons. Baxter suggests that Satan "exercises 'ownership,' as it were, only in the souls of those whose habits are given over to unbelief and sensuality"[11]. The accusation of demon possession can cause severe harm to one who is depressed and should be made only with extreme caution and clear evidence, as exorcism could otherwise be considered a form of spiritual abuse.

6. *"Don't blame yourself any more than there is cause to do for the effects of your disease...Depression is simply a disease affecting the emotions and imagination...."* [12]

Linda refers to the myth that those who are depressed aren't "trying hard enough, aren't pulling themselves up by their bootstraps" (see Chapter 4). On the contrary, many of those who are depressed, particularly Christians, are overly hard on themselves, and they struggle with guilt and self-blame. They blame themselves for the dark thoughts they struggle with, and they blame themselves for their doubts about God.

Having depression does not absolve one of responsibility. For some, depression and guilt are the conviction of the Holy Spirit of sin in their life. But it is complicated. One should not blame oneself for the involuntary effects of depression.

In the last chapter, we talked about how depression can distort the mind and can cause us to perceive our existence through black-tinted glasses. Likewise, depression can distort our perceptions of spiritual reality. Depression can produce feelings of guilt without cause, and people will often blame themselves for situations beyond their control. Those with depression may add more duties and obligations beyond what is stated in Scripture. They may consider their depression to be evidence of their lack of faith, and they then label this as sin as well.

But Christians might protest, "I should feel guilt, because there is meaning and importance to thoughts" (Psalm 139:23-24; Matthew 15: 17-20). Is having an evil thought itself a sin? The distinction needs to be made between temptation and sin.

Random thoughts are constantly drifting across our minds, and depending on our temperaments, we may experience various desires that make us vulnerable to temptation. However, our responsibility lies in whether we act on those temptations (James 1:14-15). Jesus himself was tempted and did not sin (Hebrews 4:15). There is an old saying: "You cannot keep birds from flying over your head, but you can keep them from building a nest in your hair."

Baxter draws helpful parallels between depression, being delirious with a fever and experiencing a nightmare:

> "It is as expected for a depressed person to be impetuous and tormented with doubts, fears, despairing thoughts, and blasphemous temptations as it is for a man to talk incoherently in a fever when his cognition fails. If you had the hideous thoughts in your dreams that you now have while awake, would you not classify them as unavoidable weaknesses rather than unpardoned sins? Accordingly, your disorder makes your evil thoughts morally equivalent to dreams."[13]

These are examples of when the brain can produce images, thoughts and feelings for which the person is clearly not responsible. Have you ever awoken from a dream feeling guilty? Despite telling yourself the events in the dream did not happen, and that you are not responsible for events that happened in the dream, it can be hard to shake the feeling of guilt. The same is true for depression. Depression can paint nightmares in the mind.

7. *"Determine in yourselves more diligently than ever to overcome an inordinate love of the world. It will put your troubles to a good use if you can, so to speak, follow them up to their origins and learn what you cannot bear to do without, and consequently, what you overvalue...The love of something precedes desire and grief over it. Whatever men love, they delight in possessing, mourn to be without, and desire to get."* [14]

Depression can arise from many sources. But at times depression may be a symptom of misplaced love, lifting the curtain so we can see what is really going on in our hearts. As Baxter put it, what is it that we cannot bear to do without? What is our greatest fear? What is it that we dream of possessing? Is it marriage or children? Is it wealth or material things? Is it love of comfort? Is it status and admiration? Is it popularity? Is it achievement and influence? These things are not bad in and of themselves, and grief is appropriate after a loss. But when our mourning is prolonged, we must wonder if we may be overvaluing them and seeking our joy, our meaning and our salvation in them.

The Christian journey of sanctification is full of this kind of progressive refining of our hearts, because we so easily look for heaven here on earth. The purpose of these losses may be to reorient our hopes to heaven. "Do not lay up for yourselves treasures on earth, where moth and rust destroy and where thieves break in and steal, but lay up for yourselves treasures in heaven, where neither moth nor rust destroys and where thieves do not break in and steal. For where your treasure is, there your heart will be also" (Matthew 6:19-21, ESV).

8. *"Do not engage too long a time in any duty you find yourself unable to bear. When you find yourself incapable of private devotions, don't be too hard on yourselves. Spend the most effort on duties you are best able to tolerate. For most, this will consist of praying out loud in the presence of others, and good conversation."* [15]

    "Determine to spend most of your time thanking and praising God, especially when you pray." [16]

Some Christian who struggle with depression might think the appropriate solution would be to spend more time in private devotions—more time praying, more time reading Scripture, more time confessing sin. On the contrary, however, excessive private devotions can be counterproductive for those with depression, particularly those with a spiritual depression who ruminate on their own sinfulness and the wrath of God and/or doubt their own salvation. Christians should not overburden themselves with guilt over spiritual practices. Rather, depressed Christians should focus on spiritual practices that draw the depressed person outward toward others and upward toward God, such as praying with others, fellowshipping with other believers, sitting under good preaching and worshipping together. Songs and hymns can be a particular source of encouragement for those who feel they do not have the words to pray. In addition to "How Firm a Foundation," favorite hymns of mine (JH) are "It is Well With My Soul," "How Deep the Father's Love For Us," and "He Will Hold Me Fast."

9. *"Focus your meditations outwardly, but be sure you do not examine yourself in detail, and don't waste your thoughts thinking about your thoughts... We need to direct the thoughts of self-perplexing, melancholy persons outwardly. This is so because it is the nature of their disorder to be always accusing themselves... You should rationally bring to mind many thoughts about Christ and grace for each one you list about your sin and misery."* [17]

It is the nature of depression for one to turn in on oneself and focus on one's guilt, one's failures and one's hopelessness. We need to take our own thoughts less seriously, and we need to take God's thoughts more seriously (Isaiah 55:8). Linda stated, "When I'm so depressed, I can't feel God's love." Depression distorts our thoughts and our feelings, and it is an important discipline to be constantly preaching to ourselves the truth. And sometimes, feelings lie.

One helpful strategy can be to write out encouraging Bible verses and keep them in a jar next to the bed as a reminder during low periods, or to post them around the house in the kitchen, in the bathroom, in the entryway or wherever they can be easily seen.

10. *"If Satan tosses in abusive thoughts, and if you are unable to cast them out, make light of them, and take less notice of them. Making a great deal of every thought that enters your mind will keep those thoughts in your mind longer."* [18]

Satan is the Great Deceiver, and depression makes us vulnerable to his lies. What do we do when he whispers these lies to us? Baxter provides useful advice here (which interestingly is similar to strategies in cognitive therapy for dealing with irrational thoughts.)

First, we need to recognize our negative thoughts for what they are—Satan's lies about ourselves and lies about God. Secondly, we need to counter these lies with the truth. It may take a pastor's or Christian counselor's help to identify the lie and the appropriate truth. For example, if the lie is Linda's thought, "God is there for everyone except me," the truth to counter this might be Isaiah 43:1-7:

> *"Fear not, for I have redeemed you;*
> *I have called you by name, you are mine.*
> *When you pass through the waters, I will be with you;*
> *and through the rivers, they shall not overwhelm you;*
> *when you walk through fire you shall not be burned,*
> *and the flame shall not consume you...*

Because you are precious in my eyes,
and honored, and I love you…
everyone who is called by my name,
whom I created for my glory,
whom I formed and made" (ESV).

Another lie someone might struggle with might be that their sin is too great for God's love. The truth to consider here is:

"Come now, let us reason together, says the Lord:
though your sins are like scarlet,
they shall be as white as snow;
though they are red like crimson,
they shall become like wool"
(Isaiah 1:18, ESV).

"If we confess our sins, he is faithful and just to forgive us our sins and to cleanse us from
all unrighteousness"
(1 John 1:9, ESV).

If one is still unable to cast out the thoughts, despite countering the lie with the truth, the next step would be to ignore them, or even (if one is able to) use humor to make light of them. Humor is a powerful tool to take the power from Satan's barbs (see C.S. Lewis' Screwtape Letters, Letter #11 on humor). Come up with a set phrase to brush off Satan's lies, such as "Ha, good one," "I'm not falling for that" or "Oh, it's you again." By taking Satan's accusations less seriously and drawing near to God (James 4:7-8), these thoughts lose their power in our minds.

11. *"Be sure that a theological error is not the root of your distress."* [19]

In many cases, a fundamental theological error is causing distress, and this is where a pastor's help becomes critical.

The question of suffering is a big one in depression, since suffering can lead to depression, and depression itself is suffering. We are fortunate to live in a society that is largely insulated from suffering, compared to other places and times where people have had to grapple with the daily reality of illness, death, poverty or war. As a consequence, we are fearful of any kind of suffering. In fact, our modern culture is so fearful of suffering that many people do not consider a life with suffering to be a life worth living. This may explain in part the recent increase in suicide rate and interest in physician-assisted suicide.

Unfortunately, numerous modern churches fail to prepare Christians for suffering. Sadly, the predominant belief is a theological falsehood, that if someone is a true Christian, he or she will be blessed by God and be protected from suffering. As a consequence, when people encounter suffering—when accident, death or pain befalls them—their faith becomes undone. They believe suffering is evidence that God has broken His promises, that God is not powerful, that God does not care or that God does not exist. I (JH) have had countless depressed patients walk into my office who tell me they used to be Christians until they were afflicted by suffering, after which they walked away from their faith. But atheism does not provide better answers for suffering, only random chance and meaninglessness.

People used to turn to religion for answers to suffering, and the church needs to reclaim its voice on suffering. The themes of suffering are woven throughout Scripture. Our faith is borne on the back of a Savior who suffered and died (Isaiah 53:4-5). Shouldn't our faith have the resources to equip us for suffering?

There are a couple of fundamental theological issues here:

1. *How can God be good and allow evil in the world?*

This is the age-old dilemma of theodicy, which many theologians and pastors have tried to answer. We do not have the space or the expertise to answer, so we refer to others who are much wiser. Ssee Phillip Yancey's *Where Is God When It Hurts?*, Joni Earekson Tada's and Steve Estes' *When God Weeps*, C.S. Lewis' *The Problem of Pain*, and Tim Keller's *Walking with God Through Pain and Suffering*.

2. *What does God intend for our lives?*

When it comes to suffering, it may be helpful to remember that God's goal is not our comfort and happiness, but rather our holiness. Paul talks about his own struggle with a thorn in the flesh and about his pleading with God to remove it from him. God's answer was not to take it away. Rather, God's answer to Paul was to teach him to think differently about his suffering.

"But he said to me, 'My grace is sufficient for you, for my power is made perfect in weakness.' Therefore I will boast all the more gladly of my weaknesses, so that the power of Christ may rest upon me. For the sake of Christ, then, I am content with weaknesses, insults, hardships, persecutions, and calamities. For when I am weak, then I am strong" (2 Corinthians 12:9-10, ESV).

God does not promise us a happily-ever-after while we are here on earth. He actually promises the opposite: "Beloved, do not be surprised at the fiery trial when it comes upon you to test you, as though something strange were happening to you" (1 Peter 4:12-13, ESV). He promises we will experience trials and tribulations. But the suffering is not gratuitous. There is value in suffering. Paul learned to see past his own hardship and pain and to instead focus on Christ's glory. When we share in Christ's suffering, our character is refined, and we become more like him (1 Peter 4:13, James 1:2-4).

3. *Can we trust God?*

This was the question Linda wrestled with after she had been afflicted with evil several times in her life and was anxious about what lay ahead. This echoes the fundamental question of faith people have struggled with throughout Scripture. "Can you really trust God?" Satan asked Adam and Eve, questioning God's goodness in withholding the tree of the knowledge of good and evil from them. "Can we trust God?" Abraham questioned as he and his wife remained barren and without children, and then when he was asked to sacrifice Isaac. "Can we trust God?" the Israelites questioned, when they encountered the towering inhabitants of Canaan and ended up prolonging their years wandering in the desert. "Can we trust God?" the disciples wondered as they cowered in the upper room after Jesus had been crucified.

The question "Can we trust God" has an implied second part, which is useful to consider.

Can I trust God to give me what I want? If we look at Paul and his thorn in the flesh, if we look at Jesus pleading in Gethsemane for the cup of suffering to pass, the answer is no. God is not merely a means for us to get what we want. God is not a genie in a lamp, nor a vending machine. He is much bigger than that, and He is much better than that. His wisdom about what is good and what we need is beyond our own wisdom. "For my thoughts are not your thoughts, neither are your ways my ways, declares the Lord. For as the heavens are higher than the earth, so are my ways higher than your ways and my thoughts than your thoughts" (Isaiah 55:8, ESV).

On the other hand, can we trust God to be good? "Oh, taste and see that the Lord is good! Blessed is the man who takes refuge in him!" declares Psalm 34:8 (ESV).

And as John Newton, the pastor and author of the hymn "Amazing Grace," wrote to his grieving sister, "All shall work together for good; everything is needful that he sends; nothing can be needful that he withholds."[20] Yes, we can trust that God is good.

However, we may not always see how the pain was good. As Hebrews 11 describes, many of these people who trusted God died "…not having received the things promised, but having seen them and greeted them from afar, and having acknowledged that they were strangers and exiles on the earth" (Hebrews 11:13, ESV). These people did not see God fulfill His promises, which is a sobering thought. However, what we see here is that God does ultimately fulfill all His promises, though His timeline may be bigger than our lives.

A child needs to trust the parent who takes him for vaccinations. Though the child may shriek and flail as the vaccine is given, his hope is in knowing that his parents love him and that the pain the parent inflicts is for his good, though he may never understand why. In the same way, we need to be as children as we trust our Heavenly Father by turning over to him what we want and what we think we need.

To those who are weary with trying to orchestrate the details of their lives and live in anxiety about the future, Jesus issues this invitation: "Come to me, all who labor and are heavy laden, and I will give you rest. Take my yoke upon you, and learn from me, for I am gentle and lowly in heart, and you will find rest for your souls. For my yoke is easy, and my burden is light" (Matthew 11:28-30, ESV).

12. *Learn to be honest with God, even with all the difficult feelings—the loneliness, the guilt, the doubt, the fear, the anger, the despair, the suffering.*

This last direction is my own, not from Baxter.

This is a tradition that has been largely lost in the church, though there has been a growing rediscovery of the role of lament to give voice to suffering.[21] In the church, we are comfortable with the feelings of exaltation and praise, worship and love songs to Jesus. But we do not know where to turn with the difficult feelings and the hard questions that aren't so easily massaged into joy.

Are we allowed to complain to God? Are we allowed to be angry at Him? Are we allowed to doubt God's power, His goodness or His presence? God never rebukes those in Scripture who humbly cry out to Him in their suffering. He hears their cry. For how many years did the Israelites cry out to God while they suffered as slaves in Egypt, often feeling like they were crying out into the void? Yet God did hear and would deliver them in His time. "Then the Lord said, 'I have surely seen the affliction of my people who are in Egypt and have heard their cry because of their taskmasters. I know their sufferings, and I have come down to deliver them out of the hand of the Egyptians and to bring them up out of that land to a good and broad land, a land flowing with milk and honey…" (Exodus 3:7-8, ESV).

God hears. And God can handle our doubts and our hard questions. Glenn Pemberton, professor at Abilene Christian University writes in *Hurting with God: Learning to Lament with the Psalms*:

> "Although it may appear counterintuitive, an ability to ask difficult questions of God comes not only from submission but also humility…our pride prevents us from telling anyone the truth about ourselves—that I am not okay, that I am confused, that I am angry, that I feel as if God has abandoned me…

> "The psalmists challenge us to decide how serious we plan to be about our relationship with God. And here, the greatest danger is not our questions but our silence. Silence in the place of difficult questions may come because we fear inappropriate, irreverent speech toward God. But silence may also be due to giving up on a relationship or because we have no real expectations of God. Oftentimes, we never ask God difficult questions because we are never disappointed or confused by God -- and we are never disappointed because we never really expected God to do anything in the first place."[22]

Are we silent? Do we have expectations of God? Do we believe God will hold fast to His promises? Do we believe God is active in our lives? Do we believe God sees our suffering and hears our cries?

"For my thoughts are not your thoughts,
neither are your ways my ways, declares the Lord.

For as the heavens are higher than the earth,
so are my ways higher than your ways
and my thoughts than your thoughts.

'For as the rain and the snow come down from heaven
and do not return there but water the earth,
making it bring forth and sprout,
giving seed to the sower and bread to the eater,
so shall my word be that goes out from my mouth;
it shall not return to me empty,
but it shall accomplish that which I purpose,
and shall succeed in the thing for which I sent it.

'For you shall go out in joy
and be led forth in peace;
the mountains and the hills before you
shall break forth into singing,
and all the trees of the field shall clap their hands.

Instead of the thorn shall come up the cypress;
instead of the brier shall come up the myrtle;
and it shall make a name for the Lord,
an everlasting sign that shall not be cut off."

(Isaiah 55:8-13, ESV)

Other Spiritual Strategies

Fasting

Some Christians have tried prayer and fasting in order to break a depression. Fasting is described in many places in Scripture and has been used in many other religious traditions. Fasting involves forgoing, for a period of time, food or other pleasures as a means of heightening spiritual awareness in order to fulfill a difficult task. Its benefits are gained through prayer, Scripture reading and meditation during the fast. The denial of one's desires can prepare the way for a clearer perception of the presence and will of God. Jesus fasted before embarking on His ministry. The disciples were instructed to fast and pray in order to cast out demons (Matthew 17:21). However, it seems fasting was generally undertaken by those who were strong and not weak to begin with. There is no clear indication in Scripture to fast in order to be healed.

Interestingly, there is some recent scientific evidence that fasting can help in depression, possibly by decreasing inflammation, effects on the brain or effects on sleep.[23,24]

However, fasting should be undertaken carefully. If someone is already losing weight because of depression, fasting may make things worse. We recommend fasting only when weight loss is not an issue, while emphasizing that the physical benefits (such as physical cleansing, weight control or weight loss) of fasting are not the primary goals. If you are under medical treatment for depression, this modality should be employed under the supervision of a physician. You should also seek support from your pastor, elders or Christian counselor in this undertaking.

Where fasting involves denial of food, the one who is fasting should be careful to take in liquids adequate to sustain the body. At the very least, this means eight to 10 glasses of water per day (64 to 80 ounces, about two to two and a half liters). Some recommend juice fasting (fasting except for fruit juices) for anyone taking medication, as the calories can aid in absorption of the medication and decrease side effects from medications. In any case, one's physician should be consulted regarding the advisability of fasting, especially if the patient is taking one or more medications or has other medical conditions.

Group Prayer and Laying On of Hands

The apostle James wrote: "Is anyone among you sick? Let him call for the elders of the church, and let them pray over him, anointing him with oil in the name of the Lord" (James 5:14, ESV). There may be a role for this in depression, just as with any medical illness. In our view, differing religious practices in this regard are more a question of denominational traditions than of biblical command, but the ceremony involved may be helpful to a person suffering with depression.

It is important to bear in mind that group prayer is not "magic." The goal is not to manipulate God into doing anything, including healing someone, since we should never put the Lord our God to the test (see Luke 4:12). Rather, it should be considered a way for the body of Christ to lift up the depressed person together. Also, bear in mind that immediately after James mentions anointing with oil, he speaks of confession of sin and forgiveness, including confessing our sins to one another (corporately) so that we may be healed (James 5:15-16). Some interpret the combination of anointing with oil and confession of sin as a depiction of the union of spiritual and medical treatments. Regardless, there is benefit to having the body of Christ lift up the needs of a member together, and it is possible the Lord can bring healing in this way.

When Should a Pastor Refer a Depressed Church Member to a Mental Health Professional?

1. When the person expresses thoughts about suicide, either explicitly or in more subtle ways (such as hopelessness, worthlessness, feeling there is nothing to live for, making preparations such as giving possessions away or engaging in reckless behavior). Immediate help should be sought, such as going to an emergency room or calling 9-1-1.

2. If he or she is threatening to hurt him/herself or someone else.

3. When a person's thoughts seem fixed and cannot be reasoned with or when there is no progress being made in pastoral care.

4. If a person expresses unhealthy religious beliefs and practices that are beyond what are traditionally held, such as continually being tortured by guilt over sin despite repeated assurance of salvation, bizarre beliefs such as that he or she is the second coming of Christ, etc.

5. If a person has lost grasp on reality, is confused about who or where they are or displays memory problems.

6. If someone suffers from a marked decrease in their ability to function, such as quitting work, not taking care of their children, a decrease in self-grooming or becoming suddenly socially withdrawn.

7. If there are complicating factors that make it hard for the pastor to objectively counsel the church member (e.g., difficulty with boundaries, relationship dynamics, etc.).

More Helpful Resources

American Psychiatry Association - Mental Health Guide for Faith Leaders (www.psychiatry.org/faith)

Caring Clergy Project, from the Interfaith Network for Mental Illness (http://inmi.us/for-clergy/)

National Association for the Mentally Ill – Faithnet (https://www.nami.org/faithnet)

How Pastors Can Collaborate with a Mental Health Team

Pastors can play an important role in working with a church member's physician and therapist toward healing.

1. Pastors often benefit from having long-term relationships with their church members, and their observations can be helpful. They can notify the mental health team if there is a concerning change in a church member's behavior or worry for suicidality. Ideally this is done with the patient's consent, but in emergency circumstances where there is concern for suicide or homicide, the pastor can inform the mental health team even without consent.

2. Pastors can serve as an expert for the mental health team regarding their faith practices and what would be considered normal or abnormal beliefs.

3. Pastors are often more trusted than mental health professionals and can encourage the church member to work with their physician and therapist.

4. Pastors can provide hope and encouragement in a way that mental health professionals may be unable to, e.g., by praying with the church member or by providing reassurance of God's love, encouragement in the face of suffering and reminders about hope.

Endnotes

1. It was through a wise mentor, David Powlison, that I (JH)first came to see the richness of this hymn. For his exposition of this hymn as to how it pertains to suffering, please read *God's Grace in Your Suffering* by David Powlison, Crossway, 2018.

2. Lundy, Michael. And JI Packer. "Depression, Anxiety, and the Christian Life: Practical Wisdom from Richard Baxter. Wheaton, IL: Crossway, 2018, p98

3. Lundy and Baxter, ibid, p88

4. Lundy and Baxter, ibid, p97

5. Greene-McCreight, Kathryn. *Darkness Is My Only Companion*. Grand Rapids, MI: 2006. p132

6. Lundy and Baxter, ibid, p99

7. Lundy and Baxter, ibid, p161

8. A.J. Weaver, "Mental health professionals working with religious leaders". In Koenig, H.G., ed. *Handbook of religion and mental health*. San Diego, CA: Academic Press.)

9. Lundy and Baxter, ibid, p100

10. Lundy and Baxter, ibid, p162

11. Lundy and Baxter, ibid, p120

12. Lundy and Baxter, ibid, p96

13. Lundy and Baxter, ibid, p96

14. Lundy and Baxter, ibid, p134-135

15. Lundy and Baxter, ibid, p87

16. Lundy and Baxter, ibid, p156

17. Lundy and Baxter, ibid, p90-92

18. Lundy and Baxter, Ibid, p94

19. Lundy and Baxter, Ibid, p84

20. John Newton, Letters. p189-90

21. Keller, "Walking with God in Pain and Suffering," p240-242

22. Pemberton, Glenn. *Hurting with God: Learning to Lament with the Psalms*. Abilene, TX: ACU Press, 2012. p172

23. Kiecolt-Glaser JK, Derry HM, Fagundes CP. Inflammation: depression fans the flames and feasts on the heat. Am J Psychiatry. 2015 Nov 1;172(11):1075-91. doi: 10.1176/appi.ajp.2015.15020152. Epub 2015 Sep 11. Review

24. Fond, Guillaume, et al. "Fasting in mood disorders: neurobiology and effectiveness. A review of the literature." Psychiatry research 209.3 (2013): 253-258.

CHAPTER 8

THE ENVIRONMENT

"Love and work are the cornerstones of our humanness."

—Sigmund Freud

"And let us consider how to stir up one another to love and good works, not neglecting to meet together, as is the habit of some, but encouraging one another, and all the more as you see the Day drawing near."

—Hebrews 10:24-25, ESV

"All the lonely people,
Where do they all come from?
All the lonely people,
Where do they all belong?"

—From "Eleanor Rigby" by John Lennon and Paul McCartney

Elizabeth was a striking-looking young woman with short red hair and bright blue eyes who came to me (JH) seeking help for depression and social anxiety. At the age of 35, she felt that her life was going nowhere. Every week she would come in, and we would talk about her frustrations. She felt stuck in her job as an administrative assistant for an abusive boss, but she felt this was all that could be hoped for in a job—her parents had hated their jobs too. She would talk about her loneliness—she came home every night to a tiny studio apartment, and all her friends were busy and married with kids. We would try to understand her sense of inferiority with other people, I would encourage her to apply for other jobs and we would try yet another change in her medications, but nothing helped. And then she stopped coming. When that happens, it's generally one of two things: either the patient has gotten much worse, or they have gotten much better. When she came back to check in three months later, her eyes were sparkling. She had finally applied to a job at an educational non-profit, and they had hired her to start two weeks later, which is why she could no longer make our weekly appointments. She also had met someone, a friend of a friend, with whom she felt she had a real connection. Her evenings and weekends were no longer spent alone.

In my experience, either of those things—meaningful work or a meaningful relationship—can often be more effective than medication or psychotherapy for depression. A colleague and I once joked that if we were to offer a dating service and employment agency at our mental health clinic, that would cure most of our patients. Yet so often discussions about depression neglect people's environments—their relationships, their work, how they live their daily lives—and how these might contribute to their emotional state.

We are not individual islands, sufficient unto ourselves, but we are deeply connected to others. Our environment matters. If you take a plant, no matter how healthy it is, and place it in the desert, it too will wither. So when we talk about strategies to help depression, it is important to develop a meaningful life in which one has a sense of what God is doing not just in you but also through you.

Work is important. People who are out of work are three times more likely to report symptoms of major depression than those who are employed.[1]

Relationships are important. The life event most often associated with the development of depression is losing a parent before the age of 11, and the environmental trigger most often associated with onset of depression is loss of a spouse.[2]

Depression is about loss of meaning, loss of hope and loss of direction. Albert Einstein once said, "Life is like riding a bicycle. To keep your balance you must keep moving." In order to get out of the rut of depression, one must have a direction in which to go. Meaningful work and connection with other people are critical to having a direction to keep one going.

Finding Purpose in Relationship

Our ultimate need is for God, but a one-on-one relationship with God is not sufficient. We need other people as well. After all, even when Adam and God had the perfect fellowship in the Garden of Eden, God created a partner for Adam because it was not good for him to be alone (Genesis 2:18).

We were created for community and to be in relationship. 1 Corinthians 12 talks about all Christians as members of the body of Christ and how much we need one another.

> "For just as the body is one and has many members, and all the members of the body, though many, are one body, so it is with Christ...

> "For the body does not consist of one member but of many. If the foot should say, 'Because I am not a hand, I do not belong to the body,' that would not make it any less a part of the body. And if the ear should say, 'Because I am not an eye, I do not belong to the body,' that would not make it any less a part of the body. If the whole body were an eye, where would be the sense of hearing? If the whole body were an ear, where would be the sense of smell? But as it is, God arranged the members in the body, each one of them, as he chose. If all were a single member, where would the body be? As it is, there are many parts, yet one body.

> "The eye cannot say to the hand, 'I have no need of you,' nor again the head to the feet, 'I have no need of you.' On the contrary, the parts of the body that seem to be weaker are indispensable, and on those parts of the body that we think less honorable we bestow the greater honor, and our unpresentable parts are treated with greater modesty, which our more presentable parts do not require. But God has so composed the body, giving greater honor to the part that lacked it, that there may be no division in the body, but that the members may have the same care for one another. If one member suffers, all suffer together; if one member is honored, all rejoice together" (1 Corinthians 12:12-26, ESV).

Indeed, each of us possesses our own dignity and value as a member of the body. Not only are we each created in God's image, but God has bestowed on each of us particular gifts by which we are meant to serve one another. Many of us seek God's purpose for our lives, but we only find our purpose in relationship with one another. An eye, amazing as it is, is useless on its own, but is vital to the body.

The goal of our modern culture is individual self-actualization. We try to pursue our lives in isolation and use our gifts for our own advancement or our own pleasure (or perhaps we bury those gifts, Matthew 25:14-30). But in the process, we lose the purpose for the lives that God has created us for. It is only in relationship and in service of God that we can truly achieve our potential and find our purpose.

Those who are depressed often have lost a sense of their own worth, the gifts God has given them and the role God has given them to play. Everyone needs people in their lives to turn to, those who can incarnate God's love to them when they cannot feel God's love themselves and remind them of their purpose in the body of Christ.

Loneliness

We are certainly not alone in our loneliness. Studies have suggested that more than 40 percent of middle-aged and older adults experience loneliness, and one survey found that 45 percent of people in the United Kingdom experience loneliness.[3]

Scripture includes numerous examples of loneliness as well. One of the best examples may be the prophet Jeremiah, who spent his life alone (Jeremiah 15:17) and was the author both of Jeremiah and Lamentations. He was called to be God's prophet to Israel, which was in exile in Babylon. God commanded him to never marry or have children (which was very unusual at his time), and He also told him to never join in any festivities, neither weddings nor funerals (Jeremiah 16). Throughout his life, he was surrounded by enemies who tried to silence or kill him. He had very few friends. He was known as the "weeping prophet." And yet, God used Jeremiah to give us His promises:

> "Behold, I will gather them from all the countries to which I drove them in my anger and my wrath and in great indignation. I will bring them back to this place, and I will make them dwell in safety. And they shall be my people, and I will be their God. I will give them one heart and one way, that they may fear me forever, for their own good and the good of their children after them. I will make with them an everlasting covenant, that I will not turn away from doing good to them. And I will put the fear of me in their hearts, that they may not turn from me. I will rejoice in doing them good, and I will plant them in this land in faithfulness, with all my heart and all my soul" (Jeremiah 32:37-41, ESV).

God promises to bring Jeremiah, and all of Israel, home from exile. God promises to gather His people and make them live in safety. God promises to give them a right heart. God promises them belonging. They will be His people, and He will be their God. And He promises that He will delight in doing them good.

We too are a people in exile here on earth, as we await God's gathering of His people to our eternal home. Those who struggle with loneliness are only more acutely aware of our reality as exiles, as people who do not belong. God makes these promises of belonging, a home, and an identity to us just as He does to Israel in Jeremiah.

Loneliness exists when there is a discrepancy between what one wishes for in their social relationships compared with one's actual social relationships.[4] Interestingly, one's sense of feeling alone does not correspond to one's actual number of social interactions, and a person can be content even when alone, or they can feel lonely even if they are married or have numerous friends.

Research suggests the best way to help with loneliness is not by increasing social interaction or social skills, but rather by in addressing negative thought patterns about social interactions.[5] As we have discussed before, those with depression have a negative bias when it comes to interpreting the world around them, and this is true of their social patterns as well. They tend to remember the negative parts of social interactions, and then have negative expectations of others. This tends to be a self-fulfilling prophecy, which feeds into their withdrawal and feelings of loneliness. Cognitive behavioral therapy can be one way to address this.

In addition, an important step to combating loneliness is to seek a deeper relationship with other Christians. When someone is lonely and depressed, their inclination might be to wait for someone to reach out to them. But they should strive for the opposite—to reach out and care for others. What is essential to combat loneliness is not simply having more people support you, but rather taking part in a two-way relationship where there is a sense of mutual help and support.[6] Research shows that those who are involved in faith communities are less lonely and have more potential for meaningful relationships. People of faith are those who share beliefs in the things that matter, who are called to mutually love and care for one another.[7,8]

Substituting False Intimacy for Real Relationships

Stealing a glance at a pornographic magazine. Surfing the internet for sexual images. Finding more excitement outside of marriage than in it. Frequenting chat rooms on the internet to find meaningful relationships. Soliciting a prostitute. What lies behind the struggle of sexual addiction? Dr. Harry W. Schaumburg wrote a book titled False Intimacy, and he has a specialized ministry to those affected by pornography.

"Every person needs and longs for true intimacy," writes Dr. Schaumburg. "But, because of hurt and disillusionment encountered in close relationships, many people seek to fill their relational void through false connections — real or fantasized relationships that appear to provide the relief, acceptance, and fulfillment they long for. Pursuing such connections regardless of the cost to one's reputation, health, security, marriage, and self-respect is characteristic of false intimacy."[9]

Anyone can fall prey to this temptation. Dr. Louis McBurney, who has now seen more than 2,200 full-time Christian workers and spouses in his program at the Marble Retreat in Marble, Colorado,[10] describes a common scenario:

> "What we're seeing more commonly [than adultery] is an addictive, compulsive behavior toward pornography, particularly on the internet, which seems like a safe place to go get some relief of your symptoms. Often, one of the things that goes with depression is an interruption of good sexual function, but in the context of pornography a guy doesn't have the same stress as he gets with his spouse, since he has no one to please but himself.

> "When or if the spouse finds out about it, she needs to realize that this isn't about her [most, but not all with this problem are male]. Most spouses jump to the conclusion that if their husband is looking at naked women it's because he's not satisfied with her and her body. But what is going on has a lot more to do with how he feels about himself and his ability to cope with life, while remaining a potent person.

> "Of course, sexual acting out with other women can be a big problem, too. That typically happens when a fellow is down, depressed, and he feels like everybody who comes through the door of his office heaps more criticism on him. All of a sudden this vivacious person comes in and gives him a lot of affirmation and tells him that she really appreciates him, how wonderful he is, and so forth. This support feels very good, and before long that relationship grows into something that's out of bounds. It doesn't usually begin about sex. It begins about his need for affirmation and acceptance, which just happens to come packaged in a female body."[11]

The only real solution to this temptation is to deal with the underlying issue of depression. Relieving pain via false intimacy only leads to addiction to false intimacy. When this happens, one's problems are only compounded, as the person will have to deal with the addiction first and then the depression that left him or her vulnerable in the first place.

A Radically Different Way of Relating

Within Christian community is the potential for relating to others on a much deeper level, bound together as we are in humble awareness of our own sin and having received the forgiveness of Jesus. We are freed to be honest about who we truly are.

Christian community understands people on a level that secular mental health professionals fail to. As German pastor and theologian Dietrich Bonhoeffer (1906-1945) states in *Life Together*:

> "The most experienced psychologist or observer of human nature knows infinitely less of the human heart than the simplest Christian who lives beneath the Cross of Jesus. The greatest psychological insight, ability, and experience cannot grasp this one thing: what sin is. Worldly wisdom knows what distress and weakness and failure are, but it does not know the godlessness of man. And so it also does not know that man is destroyed only by his sin and can be healed only by forgiveness. Only the Christian knows this. In the presence of a psychiatrist I can only be a sick man; in the presence of a Christian brother I can dare to be a sinner. The psychiatrist must first search my heart and yet he never plumbs its ultimate depth. The Christian brother knows when I come to him: here is a sinner like myself, a godless man who wants to confess and yearns for God's forgiveness. The psychiatrist views me as if there were no God. The brother views me as I am before the judging and merciful God in the Cross of Jesus Christ."[12]

This is a radically different way of understanding another person—as a fellow sinner in need of grace. As Christians, none of us are better than others. Rather, as Pastor D.T. Niles put it, we know ourselves to be just one beggar telling another beggar where to find bread. And that bread is the Bread of Life, Jesus Christ.

It is estimated that 70 percent of people suffer from imposter syndrome, the fear of being discovered to be a fraud.[13] And so it is with sin. We are fearful of being discovered for how sinful, how broken and how not put together we are. People are isolated from each other due to shame over their own sin and the fear that other people would reject us if they were to see who we truly are. This isolation and fear only cause sin to grow in our lives and increase the distance we put between each other. Sin feeds our loneliness.

But the confession of sin to one another, as commanded in James 5:16, reverses this loneliness. What does confession of sin do? It upends our instincts to try and impress one another, to try and prove ourselves worthy of one another's love, by confessing our brokenness and need for God. Sin isolates and separates us from fellowship with God and each other. Confessing sin to one another enables us to draw near to one another, bear one another's burdens and lift them together to the Lord (Galatians 6:2).

In Christian fellowship, we are bound together not by common strength, but rather we are bound together by common weakness, and a common dependence on God's strength.

The practice of confessing sin to each other is not common in many churches today. However, it is arguably one of the practices that makes the Alcoholics Anonymous (AA) model of group support so effective as a place of healing for alcoholics. AA is actually a community of people bound together by common confession of sin. When people enter AA, they introduce themselves as sinners: "Hi, I'm Jane, and I'm an alcoholic." Confessing sin to another person and making amends constitute half of the steps in the 12-step program. For many people, AA is the first place where they encounter honest community. Perhaps there is something here from which our churches can learn.

Community is Hard

But community is hard. Relationships are messy. And, unfortunately, churches are full of sinners. (To be a Christian, after all, you must first acknowledge that you are a sinner). People will sin against each other; they will say and do hurtful things, whether intentionally or unintentionally. This can be particularly hard when it is a fellow brother or sister in the church who has sinned against you. People who have been hurt by others often withdraw from community. Those who are depressed are often among those who have been sinned against. They may be fearful of being hurt by others, or they may struggle with shame.

We don't have all the answers for this. But here are a few things to keep in mind. Conflict plagued the early church too (Galatians 2:11-14, Philippians 1:15, 4:2-3), and most likely we are going to experience more of the same this side of paradise. We're called to pray for each other (James 5:16), to love one another (John 13:34), to bear with one another and to forgive one another (Colossians 3:12-13). We know the other person is a fellow brother and sister, a fellow sinner in need of Christ, and we know God is doing His work in their life as well. In the end, all we can do is to trust that God will love and sanctify His church, blemished, wrinkled and ugly though she may be at this moment, and believe that He knows what He is doing and is working to make her beautiful (Ephesians 5:25-27).

Two helpful books on the topic of shame are *The Soul of Shame: Retelling the Stories We Believe About Ourselves* by Curt Thompson, MD, and *Shame, Interrupted* by Edward Welch.

It is also important to take a quick detour to talk about *abusive relationships*—those relationships where one person uses a pattern of threatening and controlling behavior to cause others to live in fear. This includes behavior with any kind of physical or sexual violence, whether it is laying hands on the other person, throwing things at them or destroying property. This includes behavior that forces others to behave in ways they do not want and seeks to maintain control over another person. If someone who is depressed and anxious is in a relationship like this, no amount of medication or psychotherapy can relieve their emotional state until they are no longer in the abusive relationship and are in a place of safety.

Signs of an Abusive Relationship

(Taken with permission from the Domestic Violence Hotline at https://www.thehotline.org/.)

You may be in an abusive relationship if the other person exhibits many of these behaviors:

> Tells you that you can never do anything right
> Shows extreme jealousy of your friends and time spent away
> Keeps you or discourages you from seeing friends or family members
> Insults, demeans or shames you with put-downs
> Controls every penny spent in the household
> Takes your money or refuses to give you money for necessary expenses
> Looks at you or acts in ways that scare you
> Controls who you see, where you go or what you do
> Prevents you from making your own decisions
> Tells you that you are a bad parent or threatens to harm or take away your children
> Prevents you from working or attending school
> Destroys your property or threatens to hurt or kill your pets
> Intimidates you with guns, knives or other weapons
> Pressures you to have sex when you don't want to or do things sexually you're not comfortable with
> Pressures you to use drugs or alcohol

Unfortunately, historically the church has not always protected the vulnerable. Verses such as Ephesians 5:23-6:9, which exhort wives to submit to their husbands, children to obey their parents and slaves to obey their masters, have been misused to excuse the behavior of abusers. God never intended for our relationships with one another to be based on fear and intimidation, but rather on love and trust. He is a God of justice who stands on the side of the oppressed.

Those who are oppressed can make Psalm 10 their cry:

"Why, O Lord, do you stand far away?
Why do you hide yourself in times of trouble?
In arrogance the wicked hotly pursue the poor;
let them be caught in the schemes that they have devised.
For the wicked boasts of the desires of his soul,
and the one greedy for gain curses and renounces the Lord...

"His mouth is filled with cursing and deceit and oppression;
under his tongue are mischief and iniquity.
He sits in ambush in the villages;
in hiding places he murders the innocent.
His eyes stealthily watch for the helpless;
he lurks in ambush like a lion in his thicket;
he lurks that he may seize the poor;
he seizes the poor when he draws him into his net.
The helpless are crushed, sink down,
and fall by his might.
He says in his heart, 'God has forgotten,
he has hidden his face, he will never see it.'

"Arise, O Lord; O God, lift up your hand;
forget not the afflicted.
Why does the wicked renounce God
and say in his heart, 'You will not call to account'?
But you do see, for you note mischief and vexation,
that you may take it into your hands;
to you the helpless commits himself;
you have been the helper of the fatherless.
Break the arm of the wicked and evildoer;
call his wickedness to account till you find none.

The Lord is king forever and ever;
the nations perish from his land.
O Lord, you hear the desire of the afflicted;
you will strengthen their heart; you will incline your ear
to do justice to the fatherless and the oppressed,
so that man who is of the earth may strike terror no more" (ESV).

This psalm is one of the *imprecatory psalms*, psalms that call for judgment and punishment for the enemies of God. This Psalm calls on God to "break the arm of the wicked" (verse 15). For those who live in terror of their abusers, the appropriate response to their situation is a call for justice.

It is important to seek help, especially when physical violence is involved and there is a threat to life and limb. However, these situations can be dangerous, as there is a risk that if an abuser hears that the abused person is trying to get help, they may increase their violence.

If a person's life is in immediate danger, they should call 911. Otherwise, the Domestic Violence Hotline is a resource that has counselors who can help a person plan for safety and will not pressure or force them to do anything. Their website is https://www.thehotline.org/, and online chat is available 24 hours a day, seven days a week. Their phone number is 1-800-799-SAFE (7233) or 1-800-787-3224 (TTY).

Many hospitals also have domestic violence counselors on staff.

In a marriage relationship, couples and marriage counseling can be an important part of restoring a broken relationship and addressing bad relational patterns (see Chapter 6). However, in the case of abuse, couples counseling is not recommended, but rather individual treatment. The model of marriage counseling considers both people to be responsible for relationship problems. But in the case of abuse, the responsibility for the abusive behavior lies squarely with the abuser, and marriage counseling can often confuse and worsen the issue.

Connecting with Others

1. Reach out to Friends
With the depression comes the tendency to want to withdraw and hide, but it is important to counter this by staying connected with friends. Even when we feel weak, worthless or unimportant, we still have a part to play in God's grand scheme of things. It is wise to seek help from others who will help us recapture the joy we've lost, remind of us the truth and refocus our vision to fulfill our sense of calling.

One can ask a friend to meet together regularly to pray. Or it may be helpful to go for a walk together, ask them to accompany one to church or to doctor's visits, do grocery shopping together, see a movie together or watch a sports game together.

2. Become Involved in a Prayer Group or Community Group

Jane was depressed after a breakup with the man she thought she would marry. As she isolated herself, she became more and more depressed, despite seeing a counselor regularly. One day a friend from church invited her to attend a prayer group that met once a week. The prayer group, comprised of eight people, opened with singing, and then a general prayer was said by the group leader. Each person, as he or she felt comfortable, updated the group on the situations they had prayed for during the previous meeting. If things weren't going so well, participants offered support and more prayer. When prayers were answered, everyone joined in praise and celebration. Toward the end, each person expressed prayer needs for the next week. Within a relatively short time, Jane went from being isolated and heavily weighed down by her problems to being one of the most active and helpful members of the group.

With prayer, one takes the concerns that have been running circles in the mind and lifts them up to God. This act of turning over your requests to God (Philippians 4:6) can give great comfort in our loneliness and remind us of our dependence on Him. Prayer in a group setting also connects us with other believers, draws us out of our own struggles and makes us aware of the burdens of others. In bearing one another's burdens, we find that we are stronger together.

3. Find a Support Group

Other kinds of groups can also be helpful, including groups focused specifically on recovery from depression. Difficult as it may be to start attending such a group, when the group has a good leader and its program is constructive and practical, you may be amazed by how often your issues and concerns are shared by others. One of the benefits of these groups is the potential for mutual support—to be engaged in relationships where each person has the opportunity to care for others. There are also support groups available for other issues, such as medical conditions, caregiver support groups, grief or divorce, which can be important for those who feel these conditions have cut them off from community.

4. Volunteer

Helping those in need can counteract the inward torment of depression. Encouraging and supporting others who are struggling with life's problems can draw us outward. When we love our fellow human beings as a service to God, joy begins to flow back into our lives.

Ann was struggling with self-esteem and guilt issues. Several months of psychotherapy and biblical counseling were not effective. Yet when she decided to volunteer one day per week at Agapé House, a home for wayward and neglected children, her depression began to lift. Soon she was volunteering three days a week and was able to reduce the frequency of her physician visits from once or twice per month to once or twice per year. This activity gave her life a sense of meaning and purpose that helped to counteract her feelings of inadequacy and regret. Rather than using all of her energies to mentally beat herself up, she began to battle the negative forces destroying these young people's lives and invested herself in loving these children.

You might experience similar healing through volunteering. Find volunteer work doing something you enjoy. Volunteering at a nursing home, a soup kitchen, a tutoring center, a children's hospital or even an animal shelter might have a similar effect for you. The volunteer experiences which are most likely to cause the most growth usually involve helping other human beings.

5. Find Other Means of Community
Increase the opportunities to find meaningful relationships. Join a pickup sports team or running group, take a class at the local community college or adult continuing education, join a book club or join another community activity.

Finding Purpose in Meaningful Work

Work to live or live to work. Is either option really desirable? In our modern culture, to spend most of your waking hours engaged in a task that is without meaning or pleasure might seem like a living death. On the other hand, the idea of a life consumed only by working seems to lack balance as well. Others may believe meaning is found while backpacking through Europe or visiting the newest restaurant. What we do know about work is the importance of having a task and a sense of purpose with our lives. In Genesis 1, immediately after creating Adam and Eve, God assigns them a task—to be fruitful and multiply and fill the earth and subdue it (Genesis 1:28) We were made not for rest and relaxation, but we were made to do something on this earth. If we believe God has created each person for a purpose and given them gifts to serve other members of the body of Christ, then we can find our purpose in serving others.

As Tim Keller observes in *Every Good Endeavor: Connecting Your Work to God's Plan for the World*, "Work is so foundational to our makeup that it is one of the few things we can take in significant doses without harm. Indeed, the Bible does not say we should work one day and rest six or that work and rest should be balanced evenly but directs us to the opposite ratio. Leisure and pleasure are great goods, but we can take only so much of them."[14]

By work, we don't necessarily mean paid jobs. Much valuable work is unpaid—caring for young children or ill family members, managing a household, serving in church ministry or volunteering. Without this important source of labor, society would cease to function. By work, we also don't mean only the jobs children dream of doing when they grow up, such as teachers, artists, astronauts, musicians or scientists. There is dignity in all kinds of work, whether it is serving coffee, cleaning bathrooms, answering phone calls or restocking canned goods.

Martin Luther once said, "A cobbler, a smith, a peasant, every man, has the office and function of his calling, and yet all alike are consecrated priests and bishops, and every man should by his office or function be useful and beneficial to the rest."[15]

A cobbler has as much dignity in his work as a priest and is just as useful to others. When Paul talks about the church being many members of one body in 1 Corinthians 12, he actually spends most of time addressing those who believe they are not as important because they are do not have prestigious roles. There is dignity in all work if it is done as unto the Lord. As Colossians 3:23-24 states, "Whatever you do, work heartily, as for the Lord and not for men, knowing that from the Lord you will receive the inheritance as your reward. You are serving the Lord Christ" (ESV).

Work and Depression

Questions involving work can also be a big contributor to depression, as intertwined within work are questions about identity and autonomy. Who am I, and how does work define me? Am I good at my job? Will I be able to support myself and live independently? These questions are characteristic of the transitions of young adulthood, but they can also be present in middle adulthood.

The psychologist Erik Erikson considers work (and relationships) to be an integral part of progressing through each stage of life. During middle adulthood (ages 40 to 65), people ask themselves, "Can I make my life count?" At this point, people start to evaluate their lives so far, wonder if they want to continue in their careers for the rest of their working lives and consider their engagement in their families and the larger community. If a person is dissatisfied with his or her life, it can contribute to a sense of uselessness. And in late adulthood, people look back on their lives and accomplishments and consider whether they met their goals and led a worthy life. If not, they may experience a sense of despair.[16] Those who have not completed the tasks of each life stage, and have not had meaningful experiences in their relationships and work, are vulnerable to depression.[17]

Unemployment increases the risk for depression. A Gallup study from 2014 found that the longer a person is unemployed, the greater their report of depression. Those who are unemployed in the short term (less than 27 weeks) have twice the risk of depression as those who are employed (12.4 percent versus 5.6 percent), and those with long term unemployment (longer than 27 weeks) have three times the risk of depression (18 percent).[18] Of course, it's not clear which is the cause and which is the effect—if being unemployed causes depression, or if depression makes it harder to maintain employment—but it is likely that both are true.

Work can offer several benefits for those who are depressed. Work provides a structured routine, a place to be in the morning and a sense of being needed somewhere. It provides opportunities to interact regularly with others. It offers the opportunity to step away from the inward focus of consuming dark thoughts and engage in serving the needs of others. A sense of productivity also comes from being able to provide for one's self. Mastery of a task can also lend a sense of self-worth.

At a very practical level, however, work is critical for those who are living in constant worry about making their next rent payment or finding money for groceries. It is difficult to heal from depression if one is getting evicted. For those struggling with basic needs, social workers (who are often affiliated with doctors' offices, shelters and other agencies) can help with connecting a person with community resources if needed. Churches also take up funds to help members of their congregations with short-term needs, and they may also be aware of other resources available. In addition, it is helpful to consider what can be done to find work or perhaps better-paying work.

Strategies for Finding Work

1. *"Get Well Jobs"* — Addiction recovery programs often encourage those recovering from addictions to find a "get well job," which is a low stress job with a regular and reasonable hours, flexibility and good working conditions that help ease a person back into the working world. This might be a job such as working at a coffee shop or grocery store, or part-time work. The idea is that a high stress and demanding job could lead to a relapse, and the same principles are helpful for depression as well.

2. *Vocational Rehabilitation* — These programs are useful for those who have had a long season of unemployment, whether due to their emotional state, other illness or caring for others. Vocational rehabilitation programs are generally run by state agencies and help people with emotional problems or other difficulties return to the workforce.

3. *Career Counseling* — For those dissatisfied with their current careers, career counseling can help with choosing, changing or leaving a career and is available at any stage in life. Many colleges or universities offer these services to alumni, or one can also find career counselors in the community.

4. *Vocational Education* — Enrolling in a vocational program or trade school can be a practical way to earn the qualification to switch careers, such as a career as a medical assistant, electrician, auto mechanic or hotel manager.

5. *Temp Agencies* — Temporary work can be a way to re-enter work after a period of unemployment, and it offers more flexibility. Doing temp work allows a person to experience different work situations, can help them gain job skills and can sometimes open the door to a more permanent position.

6. *Volunteering* — This may be an easy way to see if you enjoy work in a particular environment, such as at a hospital, and it can be useful when it comes to developing a résumé indicating interest in a field. But even apart from finding paid work, volunteering is a valuable way of doing work, of identifying abilities and gifts and serving other people with them.

The Curse on Work

Unfortunately, just as everything on earth, work is cursed and bears effects of the fall. In Genesis 3:17-19, after Adam and Eve's disobedience, God proclaims, "…cursed is the ground because of you; in pain you shall eat of it all the days of your life; thorns and thistles it shall bring forth for you; and you shall eat the plants of the field. By the sweat of your face you shall eat bread, till you return to the ground…" (ESV).

The curse is not that people would have to work, but rather that the work would come with hardship and frustration. It would no longer be blessed by the abundant productivity it used to have. One can only wonder what that means for what our work in heaven will be like, without the effects of the fall.

All of us have experienced to some degree the hardship and frustration of work. Work is not easy, and it can be a slog. Many of us dread Monday mornings. It takes commitment just to show up every day at the appointed time, and it takes commitment to stay there and fulfill your responsibilities. aithfulness is hard.

But for some, the thorns and thistles may be choking out the fruit of their labor. Strategies for healing from depression may involve taking a hard look at how one's work environment may be contributing to one's mood.

In the Pixar movie *The Incredibles*, Mr. Incredible is a good illustration of the toll work can take on a person. We witness the superhero Mr. Incredible, going by his civilian identity of Bob Parr, becoming progressively more depressed and losing more and more of his sense of personhood as he is forced to take a job at an insurance company working for a ruthless boss. Although he is good at his job, his work rewards greed rather than serving others, and he feels helpless to initiate a change. As Bob's sense of meaning and identity erode, we see him disengaging from his marriage and family life, neglecting his health and turning to the escapism of illicit vigilante work. A useful term for describing Bob's state is burnout.

Burnout is defined as exhaustion, cynicism and lack of efficiency in response to chronic emotional and interpersonal stressors on the job.[19] As people become exhausted by their work, they may try to distance themselves from their work and the people they are serving. This progresses to treating other people more as objects than as unique individuals possessing dignity and often leads to cynicism about the work they are doing. Eventually, as people stop caring about their work, efficiency and productivity drop. Burnout shares similarities with depression, but burnout is more specific to a job, where depression is present everywhere in a person's life. Burnout, however, can certainly progress to depression.

There are several characteristics of work which can lead to burnout and increase one's risk of developing depression.[20]

1. *Workload* — If a person experiences too many demands, or demands that don't match their abilities, the workload can become overwhelming and lead to exhaustion.

2. *Control* — If a person is not given the decision-making ability or resources in their work environment to fulfill their work responsibilities or are held responsible to produce something they lack the capacity to do, this leads to a sense of futility and frustration. This can be due to lack of support or unclear or inconsistent information from supervisors.

3. *Reward* — This can be a lack of financial reward (salary or benefits) according to their level of work, it can be lack of recognition from others or it can be lack of self-motivated reward, i.e., pride in one's work. Lack of feedback from supervisors can contribute to

this. Everyone needs some kind of feedback telling them they are doing a good job. If there is nothing to motivate doing well in one's job, the result can be lack of efficiency.

4. *Community* — A sense of connection to other people, liking and respecting their co-workers, is important for a sense of belonging and value in one's work. Chronic unresolved conflict is poisonous to one's sense of community.

5. *Fairness* — With our innate sense of justice, unfair treatment, unfair rewards or unfair distribution of work can lead to cynicism.

6. *Values* — This includes doing work that is inconsistent with one's values, such as lying to customers. Or a company may have conflicting values, such as a credit card company that advertises it is helping customers, but whose business strategy is really trying to make the most profit off of them. This erodes passion for one's work.

The opposite of burnout is engagement in one's work, which is characterized by energy, involvement and efficiency. Many of the problems in work can be addressed and improved. If someone does not have enough resources or the job skills to fulfill their work, he or she should talk to their supervisor about obtaining training or getting the resources that could improve this. If there is no sense of reward, ask for feedback or perhaps even a raise. If there is lack of fairness, speak with a supervisor to see if this can be remedied, or perhaps a labor union might advocate on your behalf. Community can be fostered. People can tolerate high workloads if they find value in their work, believe they are doing something important or feel well rewarded for their work.[21] Scripture also speaks to the importance of the idea of reward to get through difficult work. "Whatever you do, work heartily, as for the Lord and not for men, knowing that from the Lord you will receive the inheritance as your reward. You are serving the Lord Christ" (Colossians 3:23-24, ESV).

However, some work environments cannot be improved, and a job change must be considered. If there is a lot of turnover in employees at your job, it is worth examining if there is a deeper problem with the work environment. This might involve poor working conditions, dangerous tasks or inadequate pay and benefits. If supervisors or co-workers are abusive, demeaning or disrespectful, that can take a heavy toll on a person's well-being. And if the company or work itself is immoral, this may be difficult to fix.

When it comes to problems in one's environment, whether it is work, housing or relationships, depression often results from a feeling of helplessness and feeling like one does not have power over one's own life. Taking an active stance to fix problems in our environment, whether that means finding ways to make tasks more efficient, talking with supervisors, getting more training or finding a new job, is a better channel for that frustration.

Work is Not Our Salvation

The opposite problem may be true for some people with depression. At times, people may try to fight depression by *overworking*, particularly for those who find their identity in their work.

When Sam was in the early stages of depression, which was due mostly to difficulties in his marriage, he threw himself into work at his florist shop. As long as he was at work, focused on his business and customers, he felt better. This activity took his mind off the problems he was having with his wife. Instead of dealing directly with his relational problems, he spent longer and longer hours at work, finding excuses to stay late and spending time there on weekends. Eventually, the problems in his marriage worsened and his wife filed for divorce. This is when his depression deepened to the point that he sought professional help.

Workaholism is an addiction for all who use work to shield themselves from experiencing the pain of disappointments or depression. "If the going gets hard, we work harder" is their motto. They wonder how anyone could be critical of such an ethic. While distraction may help to reduce the pain associated with conflict or loss, over the long term, avoiding a problem that needs resolving will only worsen the outcome.

Overworking is common among people who are driven to achieve or to try to please someone—father, mother, spouse, church members, God, self and so on. The problem with workaholism is that over time it has the opposite effect from what was hoped for. Instead of those around us being impressed with our efforts to please them, they may feel neglected, even alienated, because to the degree that we are immersed in work, we are not there for them. In other words, as we focus all our energies on secondary things, what matters most slips past us hour by hour, day by day.

The story of Mary and Martha in Luke 10 can be helpful here. Martha was rushing around, consumed with her preparations, while her sister, Mary, was content to sit at Jesus' feet and learn from Him. When Martha complained, asking Jesus to tell Mary to help with the work, Jesus replied, "Martha, Martha…you are worried and upset about many things, but only one thing is needed. Mary has chosen what is better, and it will not be taken away from her" (Luke 10:41-42, NIV 1984).

There is value in work and value in service such as Martha's. However, we can get so consumed in productivity that our priorities become scrambled. Martha was no longer focused on pleasing the Lord, but rather she was consumed with fulfilling her ideas of what the Lord needed. Mary, on the other hand, maintained the right priorities. Ultimately, only one thing matters, and that is sitting in the presence of the Lord.

With all work, there is ultimately a sense of futility (Ecclesiastes 2:18-26). Our work on earth does not last, and no matter how grand one's accomplishment, it is eventually eclipsed by something else or forgotten over time. Work will not earn our salvation. We do not work to earn our own worth or to make a name for ourselves on earth. What is lasting and immortal is doing our work, whatever it is, in service to the Lord, for He has promised us an eternal reward (Colossians 3:23-24).

Managing Work While Depressed

1. Do your best to show up. It can be a temptation to call in sick, lie in bed all day and withdraw from any social interaction. However, the routine and schedule of showing up for work can be helpful for recovery from depression, as long as the workplace itself is not the source of the depression.

2. If possible, reduce stress at work. Limit taking on additional tasks or responsibilities.

3. Take breaks if possible, such as going for a walk or listening to music.

4. Ask for flexibility. See if you can do work from home or get extended time on deadlines.

5. Consider talking to your supervisor or human resources about your depression. This can be a tricky subject, and you may need to assess whether your work environment is sympathetic to mental conditions such as depression. You may ask for work accommodations under the Americans with Disabilities Act. As long as these accommodations do not create too much hardship for employers, reasonable accommodations may include changes in schedule, time off for doctors or therapy appointments, a quiet working environment or permission to work from home. This usually requires a letter from a doctor. People are also protected from workspace discrimination on the basis of depression under the Americans with Disabilities Act.

Endnotes

1. McGee RE, Thompson NJ. Unemployment and Depression Among Emerging Adults in 12 States, Behavioral Risk Factor Surveillance System, 2010. Prev Chronic Dis 2015;12:140451.

2. Benjamin J. Sadock, Virginia A. Sadock, *Kaplan and Sadock's Synopsis of Psychiatry*. Lippincott Williams & Wilkins, 2011. p535

3. Cacioppo, Stephanie, Grippo, Angela J, London, Sarah, Goossens, Luc, & Cacioppo, John T. (2015). Loneliness: Clinical Import and Interventions. Perspectives on Psychological Science, 10(2), 238-249.)

4. Cacioppo, Stephanie, Grippo, Angela J, London, Sarah, Goossens, Luc, & Cacioppo, John T. (2015). Loneliness: Clinical Import and Interventions. Perspectives on Psychological Science, 10(2), 238-249.

5. Masi, Christopher M., et al. "A meta-analysis of interventions to reduce loneliness." *Personality and Social Psychology Review* 15.3 (2011): 219-266.

6. Cacioppo, J. T., & Patrick, W. *Loneliness: Human nature and the need for social connection*. W W Norton & Co, 2008.

7. Idler, Ellen L., et al. "Looking inside the black box of "attendance at services": New measures for exploring an old dimension in religion and health research." International Journal for the Psychology of Religion 19.1 (2009): 1-20.

8. Rote, Sunshine, Terrence D. Hill, and Christopher G. Ellison. "Religious attendance and loneliness in later life." The Gerontologist 53.1 (2012): 39-50.

9. http://www.stonegateresources.org. Also see Harry Schaumburg, False Intimacy, rev. Ed. (Colorado Springs: NavPress, 1997

10. Contact information for Dr. McBurney: Marble Retreat, 139 Bamrockburn, Marble, Colorado 81623. Telephone (970)963-2499. http://www.marbleretreat.org.

11. Schaumburg, Harry. False Intimacy. Rev. ed. Colorado Springs: NavPress, 1997

12. Bonhoeffer, Dietrich. Life Together, New York, NY: Harper. 1954. p118-119.

13. Sakulku, J. The Impostor Phenomenon. The Journal of Behavioral Science, 2011. 6(1), 75-97.

14. Keller, Timothy. *Every Good Endeavor*. New York: Penguin Books, 2012. p37.

15. Luther, Martin. "Address to the Christian Nobility of the German Nationality," 1520.

16. Erikson, Erik. *The Life Cycle Completed*

17. Malone, Johanna C., et al. "Midlife Eriksonian psychosocial development: Setting the stage for late-life cognitive and emotional health." Developmental psychology 52.3 (2016): 496.

18. https://news.gallup.com/poll/171044/depression-rates-higher-among-long-term-unemployed.aspx

19. Maslach, Christina; Schaufeli, Wilmar B.; Leiter, Michael P. Annual Review of Psychology; 2001; 52, p397-422.

20. Stansfeld, Stephen A., et al. "Work characteristics predict psychiatric disorder: prospective results from the Whitehall II Study." *Occupational and environmental medicine* 56.5 (1999): 302-307.

21. Maslach, Christina; Schaufeli, Wilmar B.; Leiter, Michael P. Annual Review of Psychology; 2001; 52, p397-422.

PART III:
LIVING WITH DEPRESSION

CHAPTER 9

DESPAIR:
When Nothing Helps

with contribution by Larkin Kao, MD

Case: Matthew

An Interview with Rick and Kay Warren

Rick and Kay Warren are the founders of Saddleback Church in Lake Forest, California, and they are both well-known speakers and authors of several books, including the Purpose-Driven Life and Choose Joy. The youngest of their three children, Matthew, struggled with severe depression throughout his life, and Matthew finally took his own life in 2013. Since his death, they have launched a ministry to educate and equip the church to care for people struggling with mental illness. They graciously agreed to share their story.

JH: Can you share the story of your son? What was his journey like with depression?

KW: Matthew was our youngest child, and it was pretty clear from the beginning that he was different from his older brother and sister. He was a difficult and an unhappy baby. He would be constantly crying, and nothing you could do would change his mood. When he was seven, he would start coming home from school and say he was sad. I would ask, what happened? Did you have a fight with your friends? Did you get in trouble at school? And he said, nothing happened. I checked with his teacher, and nothing had happened. This would go on for days and weeks. He lost interest in playing video games, which is a big deal when you're seven. He changed. And it finally occurred to me to ask my children's pastor, could children be depressed? Because I didn't know. That was shocking, to think our little boy was more than sad, that he could be depressed.

We started with his pediatrician, who sent him to a counselor, and then within a year he had his first panic attack. Then he was diagnosed with ADHD. Then we started this progression of one mental illness label after another. By age 11 he was diagnosed with early onset bipolar disorder. They diagnosed him with this because he and I had been running through the house playing hide-and-go-seek, teasing, laughing. And then I couldn't find him. I finally found him in his closet and he was crying. I didn't know what to do with that.

The first time he told me that he wanted to die was Mother's Day. He'd had a hard day, and as I was tucking him in, he said, "Would you just kill me and put me out of my misery?" I was grateful it was dark so that he couldn't see the horror on my face. To hear these words coming out of my little boy's mouth, to hear that was what my little boy feeling inside.

It went on from there. In school he struggled. He had a sleep disorder—his body clock was backwards. He was awake at night and asleep during the day, which of course made school very hard. In high school he developed OCD, body dysmorphic disorder, where he was thin and fit and thought he was overweight. And then the last diagnosis he received was borderline personality disorder. His life was tortured, and underneath it all was a depression that rarely lifted. The depression showed itself first, and it was pervasive for his whole 27 years.

He went from diagnosis to diagnosis and none of it ever seemed to get better, nothing seemed to help, and nothing seemed to help for very long. In some ways, I'm amazed that he was able to live as long as he did.

JH: Was it a similar experience for you, Rick?

RW: Often our emotions would mirror what he was experiencing. When he had an emotion, we would feel it as well. If he was frustrated, we were frustrated for him. If he was fearful, we were fearful for him. If depressed, we were depressed for him. A parent of a child with mental illness will have a gamut of every possible emotion from frustration to despair. It was gut wrenching when it felt hopeless. How many times did we say, if there was a way we could take his pain, we would take it. Lord, put his depression, put his insecurities on me. I am older, I'm bigger and I can handle this. He's just a little boy.

It affects the whole family. His brother suffered. His sister suffered. We all suffered. Just as in the body of Christ, when one member of the family suffers, everyone else suffered. We were always trying to think of a way to pull him out. Every night when he would come home, either Kay or I would go into the swimming pool and try and distract him and play games. We would try and distract him from this pervasive depression that had taken over this little boy's mind.

He was such a wonderful kid—he was bright, creative, witty, loved God, tender with people—he had so many good qualities. Yet the depression could make him mean, the depression could make him angry. You would get angry, too, if you never felt good. Every day was a struggle. Kay and I thought how courageous he was, that he would keep going, when everything in his mind said to just end this.

If you are having thoughts of suicide, please contact the National Suicide Prevention Hotline at 1-800-273-8255 (1-800-273-TALK).

KW: I want to be clear, as he became an adult and as he became seriously ill, in many ways he became unrecognizable to us. Those qualities—kindness, tenderness—were still there on occasion. We would catch glimpses of who he was without the illness. But when he died, he was in a very bad place, thinking some scary thoughts, with thoughts of violence. He was so ill when he passed away.

RW: The week that he died, he had a couple good things happen in his life. But our minds can get so in a rut that he couldn't see it. You can be afraid of hope, when you've had so many let downs.

JH: Can you describe briefly what happened with Matthew's death?

KW: So for years, Matthew had talked about suicide, He'd made several attempts, he'd been hospitalized. So it was not a surprise to us that he died by suicide. It was just a surprise that it was that day.

We'd had dinner with him, he talked about how tired he was, he was feeling pressured by the expectations of a new job that he'd started. But he was looking forward to some things—a date coming up, he was working with a personal trainer, he was planning to upgrade his phone—he had future plans. But something that night snapped. That speaks to how with suicide there can be chronic suicidality, and yet there can be some event, or some trigger, that makes things unbearable. And evidently that's what happened. Something happened by the time he got home from our place. I was talking to him on the phone and then he abruptly cut off. I wasn't able to connect with him again. The next day we found out that he had died.

RW: People often call suicide a selfish thing. But it's not. Sometimes suicidal people think that it will be easier for the people they love if they're not around. But that is distorted thinking. They don't realize how devastating their death can be. They don't understand the long-term damage that it does to everyone who loves that person.

KW: If I've learned anything about suicide, it's that they know very little as to what happens inside the mind of someone who dies by suicide. There's a lot of speculation about it. All we know is that at the end of the day, there is distorted thinking and tremendous pain.

JH: Some people think of depression as people as something that's willful, a lack of faith, something where people just let themselves go in that direction. But it sounds like you all experienced clearly how depression can be a disease, and how there can be a clear biological basis for it.

KW: Talking about genetic predisposition, looking back through my family tree, I can trace depression back four generations. My great grandmother struggled with bouts of being "blue," they talked about her having one of her spells. Then in the next generation, my grandmother, they also talked about sadness, melancholy. And my mother. And I had a low level of depression. But I think Matthew had it the worst. So we're talking a very long line of a genetic predisposition for depression.

RW: When people say, why can't you just believe, have faith, think positive—the metaphor we use is that if you're a bird and you lose a wing, no matter how much positive thinking in the world you might have, you're still not going to fly. One thing we often do as Christians is underestimate the impact of the physical, the biological. Of course we are spiritual beings, of course we're emotional beings, but we're also spiritual beings who live in broken bodies. We live in a broken world with broken bodies and nothing works perfectly. Everyone has something—a broken back, a broken body, some get arthritis and some get diabetes. But we all have brokenness in our bodies. Physical problems require physical solutions. Emotional problems require emotional solutions. Spiritual problems require spiritual solutions. Mental illness is far more than just emotional or just emotional, or just physical. It's all the above. Because we are so complex, it's never just a simple answer.

KW: We're whole beings, and it requires whole being solutions and care.

JH: I think you've just summed up the entire book in those words. What kind of impact did it have on your faith, having your son struggle with depression? How did it change your views on God and understanding how He works?

KW: Matthew's mental illness became chronic. There were some periods of relief, but then he would slump backwards again. It really began to wear on us, particularly as the illness made him talk more and more about suicide. There's just so many times it felt like I was sitting on the edge of hell.

He would be threatening to kill himself, or telling me about how he was going to do it, how there was no meaning in life, how there's no God, how it's all a joke. It shook his faith, that he couldn't seem to get well. I remember one night in particular, three years before he died, I felt like I was in darkness. He was in darkness, I was in darkness. I didn't know how to get out of the darkness.

So I did a word study in the Bible looking for the word dark, darkness and night. And it was stunning to see how many verses, particularly in the Old Testament, when writers would say, "God, you've hidden yourself, the darkness is so deep, I can't find you." In Psalm 88 where it says, "Darkness is my only companion." It just resonated inside of me. This must be how Matthew must feel. Darkness that feels impenetrable. And I'm sliding towards that myself. God, where are you? God, why don't you help him?

And I came across Isaiah 45:3, where there is a prophecy about King Cyrus, and God says, "I will give you the treasures of darkness, riches in secret places, so you may know that I am the Lord Your God who calls you by name." That verse jumped off the page to me. Yes, I was in darkness, but God kept encouraging me that even in the darkness, there are treasures hidden here. There are riches in the darkness. You are going to do it, so that I will know that you are great, and that you are near, and you call me by name. There are so many places where God would provide a verse like that, or lyrics to a song, or a word someone would say, which would rekindle my hope that even in our darkness, God would be near us, and would be near Matthew.

So I created a hope box where I would put verses I would read at nighttime, when the darkness felt enveloping. And it helped me, both now and in the last years of his life, when he was worsening by the day. God continues to bring those little flashes of light and comfort that keep my faith steady.

I've tried to do a lot of reading and study and reflection about hope, particularly in the last years of his life and even more so after he died. Because at the end of the day, Matthew lost hope that things could be any different for him. Rick mentioned that sometimes hope can be dangerous. For people living with depression, there's a legitimate question, of how many times can I prop myself with hope believing that this is going to be different, that this treatment is going to make that difference, or this doctor is going to be the right one, or this approach, this is going to be the thing that changes me and makes me well, can make me better. Only to find that it doesn't, or that it doesn't last. So sometimes hope can erode. And when hope is finally gone, there is apathy, and a belief that nothing is ever going to change. That is a dangerous place. Hope is the last thing we lose.

After he died, I can honestly say my hope was crushed, because I had really believed that God would outright heal Matthew, or make it so that the depression was manageable, so that he could live a normal life, which is all that he really wanted, just to be normal.

And when that didn't happen, I had to start over. My hope fell through past the basement into a yawning black hole. I had to resurrect that hope in order to go on myself. So I don't think we can ever underestimate the value or the necessity of hope to live, but also to live again when you feel like your faith is ground into the dust.

JH: I really appreciate how raw and honest you all are, because it is not easy to talk about this. Because you hope that God will do something. You hope that He will heal, that He will bring goodness out of the rocks and the darkness in this life, and when that doesn't happen, what does that mean about God? What does that mean about your faith in God? What does it mean about the hope you can have in God?

RW: It is important to remember that this is earth, not heaven. When we expect it to be heaven, we're going to be sorely disappointed. The Bible tells us that heaven is perfect. No sorrow, no suffering, no sadness, no sickness, no depression, no doubt, no darkness, no despair. Heaven is perfect. That's why we are told to pray, "that your will be done on earth as it is in heaven." Because in heaven, God's will is done perfectly. None of that is true on earth. So when we expect earth to be heaven, we're going to be severely disappointed.

We're never going to be happy in this world, because it's a broken world. The more you are aware of what's going on in the world, the more you see the suffering. Being in ministry, we deal with people's suffering literally every day.

JH: What advice would you give to a family member on how to best care for and encourage someone with depression?

KW: You know, there's some really good books that have been helpful. Talking to Depression (by Claudia Strauss) was a good book for me to read, because it gave me some language of how to talk with Matthew. Because if you don't experience depression you just don't get it. Because the things that might help someone get out of a slightly blue mood are not necessarily effective for someone who has major depressive disorder and may make it worse.

Just don't be passive and put your head in the sand hoping that you can wake up one morning and your loved one's no longer depressed. Because that's not likely to happen. So do what you can do. Learn what can make it better. It's important for family members to get educated. There's a value in seeking medical help, spiritual, emotional help. It's the responsibility of loved ones to educate themselves about depression, take a class. Go to NAMI (National Alliance for the Mentally Ill), they have free family classes.

Learn how to protect your own heart, because studies show that people who live with depressed family members are more prone to depression themselves. Frederick Buechner, in his book Telling Secrets, talks about when his daughter had an eating disorder, and he was wearing himself out worrying about her, someone told him he needed to protect his own heart because a bleeding heart is of no use to anyone if it bleeds out. So those of us who are parents, spouses, siblings, roommates with someone with depression—you do have to take care of your own self because it's a long journey. We have to be ready for the long haul, and nurture ourselves to support them.

JH: What do you think we could be doing differently in the church?

KW: Supporting families is critical. But it also starts with a theology of mental illness, and a theology of sickness and illness, and theology of suffering. When we act as though, "to come to Jesus" means all our problems go away, then when depression strikes, or some other long-term illness or tragedy, then we're not prepared for it. We don't even know what to do with it. We believe the lie that this is heaven, when it is not. And so a correct and robust theology of suffering, of God's nearness to those with sickness, how Jesus responded to the sick with compassion. Jesus' first response to those who were ill was compassion, and then He touched them. We need to have a robust theology of suffering and mental illness, that mental illness is not a sin, mental illness is not about demons, a character weakness or a lack of faith. But it is an illness. Then we can treat them with the respect and kindness that they deserve. We need to make church a safe place to bring your whole self, and be a whole person, and know that you'll be met with care, with kindness, and with practical help.

RW: In the last few verses of Romans 8 where it says "nothing can separate you from the love of God," you can throw mental illness in there too. I might lose my mind, but God's not losing me. That's true of other things too—people with dementia may lose their minds, but they will never lose the love of God. And once our theology is correct, then you start removing the stigma.

Every stigma is caused by ignorance. People stigmatize and fear things they don't understand. So the church needs to remove the stigma simply by talking about mental illness, and doing conferences, giving messages, to bring it out into the open. What you'll find is that the more you bring it out in the open the more people become open. Everyone thinks they're the only one that thinks this way. Everyone needs to realize that we're all in the same boat, we all have our weaknesses. All this is an effect of the fall.

KW: Another thing I would add, is that one of the things the church can promise to people is to be with them, whether they are healed or not healed. We would never say to someone who has cancer, "well, if you get well, we will be here with you." We recognize some people do not get well, and we still make a commitment to walk with them to the very end. When it comes to mental illness, substance use—people often draw a line. Well, if you get better, then we will you can join us. But if you're not well, if you're not on your medication, then you can't come here anymore. And that absolutely breaks my heart. Because the body of Christ should be the one place that commits to be with you to the end.

Your physical family may not be able to do that. You may burn those bridges with mental illness or substance abuse. You may create havoc in your family where they can't sustain that relationship. But the body of Christ needs to be with you.

Persistent Darkness

Depression can be a devastating disease. Despite implementing as many strategies as possible—bodily, mental, spiritual, environmental—there are some who face the possibility that depression may never entirely lift. As Rick and Kay Warren describe, there are some for whom depression is a chronic illness. There may be brief periods when the clouds seem to part, where one can catch glimpses of who the person is when not afflicted by depression, but for the most part, the person lives in constant darkness. The analogy they drew to cancer is a good one. Although there are many cases of cancer that can be cured, there are also cases of cancer in which the risk of this is always present and can prove to be fatal. Both cancer and depression may go into *remission*, and be inactive for a while, but they can also *relapse* and come on in full force. Books on depression that suggest that all cases can be cured may be denying what is a reality for many people. If that is the case, where do you go from there?

One must cling onto hope and continue to fight against depression in faith. There may be times, however, when the battle seems to be tipping in favor of depression, and in those cases, there are some additional resources that may be of help.

In the Greco-Roman myth of Ulysses, the hero Ulysses sails with his crew all over the world to fulfill tasks and encounters various dangers and monsters. One of these encounters was with the Sirens, monsters whose heads were that of women and whose bodies were that of birds, whose irresistible songs would drive men mad, and lure them to shipwreck off the coast of their rocky island. When their travels were to lead them past the place of the Sirens, Ulysses instructed his crew to place wax in their ears, so they would be immune to the Sirens' song, and tie him to the ship's mast. He instructed them not to untie him, no matter what he said. As they sailed past, the Sirens song was so enticing that he begged his men to let him go, but they tied him tighter, and rowed more quickly, until they sailed past to safety.

When people experience severe relapses of depression, the call of depression can be like the Sirens, driving reason from the mind and causing one to consider self-destructive acts. At these times, people may need a higher level of support to keep them safe. In these situations, individuals may enroll in intensive outpatient programs (IOPs) or partial hospital programs (PHPs). For individuals who are suicidal or otherwise so depressed they cannot care for their own basic needs such as food and shelter, inpatient psychiatric hospitalization is needed. In this chapter we provide information on levels of psychiatric care, followed by a discussion of the deadly siren song of suicide.

Ulysses Contracts - Psychiatric Advance Directives

Severe depression often impairs one's decision-making ability, and in such cases, it can be extremely helpful to have a conversation when a person is well, about what they would want done if in crisis. Ulysses made a contract with his crew to bind him to the ship mast and prevent him from self-destruction. In cases where a person experiences repeated episodes of severe depression, it may be valuable to establish what is known as a Ulysses contract— or a psychiatric advance directive. A *psychiatric advance directive* is a legal document that describes a person's plan for when they experience a mental health crisis, and it lists their preferences for treatment, services and supports. It can also list individuals authorized to make treatment decisions on their behalf. This can help de-escalate a crisis, prevent a person from receiving treatment they would not otherwise desire and prevent forced treatment.[1] States permit healthcare advance directives for general medical care, and they are starting to adopt psychiatric advance directives as well. The areas that such directives can cover include medication types, hospital preferences, alternatives to hospitalization and de-escalation methods, as well as a way to identify people who can serve as their decision maker.[2] More information can be found at the National Resource Center for Psychiatric Advance Directives at www.nrc-pad.org.

Even if a full psychiatric advance directive is not implemented, it is valuable for a depressed person to have a discussion with their loved ones and their mental health team about what kind of plan and treatment to pursue when their depression worsens, so the plan of action is clear when the crises occur.

Levels of Care

Intensive Outpatient Programs and Partial Hospitalization Programs

Intensive outpatient programs (IOPs) and partial hospital programs (PHPs) are helpful options for individuals who need a "jumpstart" to outpatient treatment, whether they are new to mental healthcare or are continuing in care. These programs represent a step up in intensity from outpatient services, and they are designed to help those who do not meet the level of acute illness required for inpatient hospitalization. For individuals new to care, an IOP or PHP can be a useful path to establishing psychiatric care sooner than would be possible on most outpatient waiting lists (which can be several months long). Intensive outpatient programs typically meet each weekday for a few hours in the evening, designed to allow participants to continue with daily activities such as work outside of the home. These programs consist of group and individual therapy, along with the option of starting medication, with counsel from a psychiatrist. PHPs typically meet from approximately 9 a.m. to 3 p.m. on weekdays. These programs consist of elements similar to those in IOPs, with a slightly more intensive nature given the greater time commitment. Individuals typically participate in these programs for one to four weeks at a time, with personalized planning to determine how long they should stay in this level of care. For those who work full-time outside of the home, PHP participation typically requires time off from work. While many are hesitant to take time off, PHP participation tends to be a worthwhile investment, as the intervention allows the individual to continue working and otherwise functioning without the hindrance of severe depression.

Inpatient Hospitalization

In some situations, an IOP or PHP may not be sufficient to treat the distress a depressed individual is having. Imagine experiencing a severe depressive episode such that it feels nearly impossible to get out of bed and commute to a program each day. Consider an individual who is unsure if he can keep himself safe from attempting suicide each night at home after an IOP or PHP. For individuals in these and similar situations, psychiatric hospitalization is needed.

To many individuals, the idea of being psychiatrically hospitalized brings up negative connotations. In movies and television from decades past, the psychiatric hospital was often portrayed as a scary and even barbaric place, where individuals remained in locked wards for months or years. Present-day psychiatric hospitals in the U.S. are extremely different. Staff do not threaten patients, treatments are not forced and lengths of stay are often less than a week. With that said, the experience of psychiatric hospitalization, similar to that of medical hospitalization, is not easy or fun. This is primarily due to the severity of illness prompting hospitalization and the associated work needed to heal. Compared to medical hospitalization, psychiatric hospitalization has the additional feature of taking place on a locked unit. Understandably, few people want to be on a unit where part of their freedom is taken away. Another unique feature of psychiatric hospitalization is that patients often share rooms with other patients and have a great deal of interaction with other patients on the unit during mealtimes, free time and therapeutic activities. While this is intended to be therapeutic, as patients can learn from one another, this also means they may be exposed to other patients who are psychotic or emotionally unstable.

Recognizing these less desirable aspects of psychiatric hospitalization, for some it can be lifesaving. Many patients look back on hospitalization and note that although they did not want to be hospitalized, they are thankful for the help provided and understand that a lower level of care was not sufficient for them. One woman who was hospitalized on a psychiatric unit where I (LK) worked struggled with severe depression and prominent suicidal thoughts, to the point she attempted suicide several times on the unit. She wrote a letter to the staff at the time of discharge which read, "I am so thankful that you took care of me and saved my life, even when I really didn't want you to at the time."

While others may have only bad memories from a hospitalization, this is no reason to avoid hospitalization when it is needed for someone's safety. If an individual is concerned for the safety of himself or someone in his community, it is never wrong to go to an emergency room for evaluation so that a clinician can determine the need for psychiatric hospitalization. If a clinician deems an individual unsafe to be in the community, most states have laws that mandate psychiatric hospitalization in certain circumstances. While it is always the goal of clinicians to help people understand the recommendation for hospitalization, and to help them voluntarily agree to hospitalization, these laws exist to ensure safety for those who lack insight into their need for care, since depression can often impair judgement.

What to Expect During a Psychiatric Hospitalization
On the inpatient psychiatric unit, all patients are closely monitored in order to minimize risks to and from themselves and others. This may involve checks every 15 minutes by staff members or a staff member sitting with a patient at all times for patients at higher safety risk.

Upon arrival to the unit, most patients are observed for a period of time to ensure safety before they earn privileges to leave the unit on supervised walks or breaks. Visitors are typically allowed according to each unit's visiting hours and rules. To ensure the safety of all patients, personal belongings may be searched. Once items have been searched, patients are typically allowed to wear their own clothing.

While on the unit, patients receive a full medical and psychiatric evaluation, including a diagnostic interview with a psychiatrist, blood tests and other assessments as needed. This evaluation, along with continued assessment by staff throughout the hospitalization, ensures an accurate diagnosis is made. Clinicians then recommend interventions accordingly, including medications and/or behavioral or cognitive strategies to address each patient's unique struggles. Patients are also encouraged to participate in various therapy groups and recreational programs available on the unit daily. Participation in these activities can help optimize the therapeutic value of hospitalization.

In addition to speaking with psychiatrists, patients also have frequent contact with mental health counselors, nurses and social workers. Each of these professionals helps to monitor patient progress, and the entire treatment team meets often to discuss and adjust each patient's treatment plan. Most units have a chaplain available, and patients may also request to have their own priest, pastor or church elders visit.

A major advantage of hospitalization over outpatient care is that both medication adjustments and psychotherapy can be conducted in a more intensive manner, due to the more frequent contact with mental health professionals and the close oversight of staff at all hours. Medication changes can be made more rapidly, and serious side effects can be immediately detected. Other advantages include that the patient is kept safe (from harm inflicted either by self or others) due to staff monitoring, and that the patient can have a reprieve from outside factors that may have been contributing to depression or distracting from depression treatment. For patients who may need electroconvulsive therapy (ECT), the hospital is often an ideal place to prepare for and undergo treatments. For more information on ECT, please see Chapter 5.

Reasons for Hospitalization in Depression

Determining who needs hospitalization can be difficult and relies on assessment by a psychiatrist. This might be the individual's psychiatrist in the outpatient, IOP or PHP setting, or it might be an emergency room psychiatrist. Individuals who have difficulty caring for themselves or keeping themselves safe outside of the hospital should seek emergent evaluation. For those who sense a similar situation in someone they know, it is recommended to speak with that individual, tell him or her about your concern and see if he/she is open to help in coming in for an evaluation. If the individual refuses, but there is still concern, it is recommended to call 911. While it feels bad to do this when a loved one is stating he or she does not want care, this action could save a life. Lack of insight into one's illness or its severity, and lack of desire for help, can be prominent features of depression. It is much better to have someone upset over having been brought in for evaluation, than to look back on tragedy and regret having not intervened. Further guidance on what to do in the situation of feeling suicidal or learning of someone else's suicidal thoughts is included later in this chapter.

Inability to Care for Oneself

A depressed individual may need to be hospitalized due to problems caring for oneself. For example, one may be so depressed that he or she does not get out of bed for days on end or stops eating to the point of malnutrition or severe weight loss. Other people may develop distorted views of reality along with their depression that may cause them to become suicidal, homicidal or develop obsessional thoughts or behaviors that interfere with basic functioning. They are often unaware of their need for help, or they may be unmotivated and/or physically incapacitated as a result of their depression, requiring friends or family members to seek medical attention on their behalf. Depending on how long a patient has been without adequate food or drink, or what other unsafe conditions may be present, medical stabilization prior to psychiatric stabilization may be needed. For example, if an individual has been not shifting position in bed leading to bed sores or has been walking in cold weather with insufficient clothing leading to frostbite, he or she might be medically hospitalized prior to transfer to the psychiatric unit.

Suicidality

Suicidality is the most common reason for hospitalization for a depressed person. While some patients are psychiatrically hospitalized after they have expressed a plan for suicide or have attempted suicide, one should not wait for symptoms to become this severe before seeking help. The remainder of this chapter is devoted to this important topic.

Suicide

Do Christians consider suicide?

Death by suicide is rising in the United States. Suicide is now the 10th leading cause of death in the U.S. In 2017, there were an estimated 1.4 million suicide attempts in the U.S., with

47,173 individuals dying by suicide; this averages to 129 deaths by suicide per day.[3] In 2017, 4.3 percent of the population (not specific to depressed individuals) had suicidal thoughts in the last year.[4] While a variety of life situations and mental illnesses can contribute to suicidality, depression is recognized as one of the most common conditions. Half of suicides are impulsive, many (nearly one-quarter) considering it only five minutes before the suicide.[5,6]

In September 2019, evangelical churches were shaken to learn of the suicide of Jarrid Wilson, an associate pastor at Harvest Christian Fellowship. He had been a public advocate to decrease mental illness stigma in the church and had founded Anthem of Hope to support Christians struggling with mental illness.[7] He was open about his own struggles with depression. The day he took his own life, he tweeted, "Loving Jesus doesn't always cure suicidal thoughts. Loving Jesus doesn't always cure depression…But that doesn't mean Jesus doesn't offer us companionship and comfort. He ALWAYS does that."[8,9] His death highlighted the reality of believers struggling with mental illness and, in particular, the urgency of helping pastors, who experience almost double the rate of depression compared to the general population and may find it particularly difficult to seek help because of fear that others will believe they are unfit for ministry.[10]

Though it has been shown that religious involvement can protect against both suicidality and depression, this does not reduce the risk to zero.[11,12] We have given examples of prominent Christians who have struggled with depression, including William Cowper, Charles Spurgeon and Abraham Lincoln. The Bible includes various accounts of believers who express transient suicidal thoughts, including Moses (Numbers 11:15), Elijah (1 Kings 19:4) and Job (Job 7:16). Importantly, God does not appear to punish these individuals for their thoughts; instead, their suffering appears to draw each man closer to God as he prays for comfort.

Is it possible a person, even a devout Christian, who is struggling with depression might consider suicide? The answer is yes. It is highly likely he or she has thought about death or *considered* suicide, even if he or she might never act on these thoughts.

What causes suicidal thoughts?
Suicide seems particularly terrible to most of us because it contradicts our normal human drive to live. If you have watched any nature program on television and see, for example, how few of the tadpoles that are born actually make it to adulthood, you can see how many forces—hungry fish, predator birds, weather, scarcity of food—conspire against life, and how surviving itself should be prized. What would cause someone to try to take their own life?

Dr. Kay Redfield Jamison, a psychologist and researcher, has written extensively both clinically and personally about her struggles with suicide and bipolar disorder. In her book *Night Falls Fast: Understanding Suicide,* she writes, "When people are suicidal, their thinking is paralyzed, their options appear spare or nonexistent, their mood is despairing, and hopelessness permeates their entire mental domain. The future cannot be separated from the present, and the present is painful beyond solace. 'This is my last experiment,' wrote a young chemist in his suicide note. 'If there is any eternal torment worse than mine I'll have to be shown."[13]

Those with suicidal thoughts often feel trapped. Their thinking has become so poisoned that life seems like a living death, a dead end with no future possibility. When suicidal ideation occurs, one has begun to entertain the idea that death appears to be freedom. Inherent in all living beings is the desire to live; one can only become suicidal when death appears to be life, more than life itself.

When it comes to the general factors leading to suicide, it seems there are usually several commonalities, as Kay Jamison writes, "The causes of suicide lie, for the most part, in an individual's predisposing temperament and genetic vulnerabilities; in severe psychiatric illness; and in acute psychological stress. Addressing only one of these causes at the expense of others is unlikely to be enough to keep suicide at bay."[14]

Suicidal thoughts occur usually in the meeting of these three forces. As we saw in the Warren's description of their son Matthew's death, a person with biological vulnerability who develops severe depression may cope with this for a long time. However, one's ability to cope becomes severely tested when a person faces a sudden increase in life stress, making them vulnerable to suicide. This may be a loss of job, diagnosis of an incurable disease, a breakup, a public shaming, etc. It is at this time when those who are depressed are at high risk and need to be monitored closely. Substance use may also further impair a person's reasoning abilities and decrease their ability to control impulsive thoughts about suicide.

Self Harm

Sometimes people who are depressed engage in self harm behavior, such as cutting themselves, hitting themselves, burning themselves, or some other means of causing themselves pain. Signs that someone may be self-harming include scars, bruises, scratches, wearing long sleeves or pants, or having sharp objects on hand.

Sometimes these are done with suicidal intent, but more often self harm behavior is done for other reasons, such as an looking for some kind of release from their emotion, or self-punishment. Usually it is due to lack of better ways to manage their negative emotions. It is important to develop better coping strategies, such as talking to someone one trusts, physical or expressive activities such as exercise, art, or music. We strongly recommend addressing the underlying emotions by seeking help from a therapist or counselor.

What do I do if I am struggling with suicidal thoughts?

1. Remove yourself from danger. Eliminate your access to any dangerous means, so if you sink into those hopeless feelings, any attempt you make impulsively is less likely to be fatal. Remove them from the house and give them to someone trustworthy for safe keeping.

2. This includes medication that may be taken in sufficient amounts to seriously harm yourself.

3. Seek help. If you are concerned about your own safety, have a friend take you to an emergency room or call 911. Call a suicide prevention hotline such as the National Suicide Prevention Hotline (1-800-273-8255). Often just telling somebody else how you are feeling can help decrease the weight of the feelings.

4. Remember that depression can distort your thinking. You may feel like you are a burden on others, and you may easily delude yourself thinking that other people's lives might be better without you. But that is not true. Suicide causes lifelong devastation for those left in its aftermath, and it increases the risk of depression and suicide in those you may love the most.

5. If external pressures are causing you to consider suicide, consider stepping back, whether that means taking a leave from a stressful job or ending a destructive relationship, even if it risks angering or disappointing others. No job or relationship is worth your life.

6. Remember that death is not a solution. Depression can cause tunnel vision and impair your ability to see the big picture, think logically or come up with other solutions. Often people turn to suicide when they feel trapped and convince themselves there is no other way out. Remember, suicide leads to death that is neither rest nor comfort. Death like this is the Christian's enemy (1 Corinthians 15:26, 54-56).

7. Hold onto hope. No matter what depths of pain or circumstance you are experiencing, you have a sovereign God who created you (Psalm 139), and He has a purpose for you and your life (Jeremiah 29:11), though the reasons may be unclear when you are in the throes of depression. Getting out of bed each day may be hard. Each step may forward may be hard. Remember, though, to hold onto the fact that there will ultimately be hope and redemption and relief.

How can I tell if a friend or loved one is at risk of suicide?

One of the most important ways to help a friend who may be at risk of suicide is simply to start a conversation on the topic. If someone has shared that he or she feels very depressed, or shows other risk factors associated with suicide such as those listed in Table 1, it is recommended to ask directly whether he or she has thought of suicide. If the answer is yes, more information needs to be gathered. While some fear that asking these questions will plant the idea of suicide, this has not been shown to be the case. More likely, the individual will feel cared for and less alone in the struggle. A few potential ways to enter this conversation are listed below:

> "When someone is very depressed, it is common to feel they would be better off dead. Has that ever crossed your mind?"

> "It sounds to me like you are feeling overwhelmed, almost desperate to end your pain. For some people, this leads to thoughts of suicide. Has that ever been the case for you?"

Most people who are not considering suicide will immediately say, "No. I'm not considering that." Alternatively, if someone responds with silence or affirmation, there is reason for concern. While the conversation will differ for each circumstance, below are a few points to keep in mind as the conversation continues:

> Sharing about suicide is difficult. A good place to begin in response to hearing that someone is suicidal is to thank him or her for sharing. Express compassion and acknowledge the vulnerable nature of the discussion.

> If there is some openness to dialogue, try to discover what is happening in the individual's life that makes suicide seem the only way out. This can help the individual feel heard and know that the listener is not afraid of suffering, but instead would like to join the individual in walking through his or her struggles.

> It is important to validate how the person feels, rather than trying to convince him or her to feel cheerful or grateful. Similarly, telling someone that suicide is cowardly or selfish is not typically helpful in moments of struggle, and it may be harmful.

> It is often helpful to explicitly share one's worry for the individual's safety, in a way that conveys care. For example, it may help to explain to the individual that he or she would be missed from this world by the community. Similarly, one might convey that others have hope for the individual's life and believe God has plans for him or her to flourish (see Jeremiah 29:11; 1 Peter 1:2), even if the depressed individual cannot sense that hope or those plans during a time of pain. Overall the listener should convey the feeling that

the depressed individual's life is worth living, and that the world is better off with him or her alive.

Beyond these points of compassion, once someone has shared suicidal thoughts, it is important to ask whether that person has a plan to harm themselves, what the details of the plan are and whether he or she has already taken some action. The following is a sample conversation starter that conveys empathy and also moves toward information-gathering:

> "I want you to know that I consider it a privilege that you've given me this glimpse into your heart. Thank you for trusting me that much. Because I want to honor that trust, I need to know how serious you are. I, for one, would really miss you if something like this happened. Have you ever thought about how you might end your life? Have you taken any steps toward that plan?"

Through this conversation, one can determine whether to bring the individual to the nearest emergency room or call 911 (if risk appears high), or, if risk appears lower, to instead begin with other measures. The latter might include calling the individual's outpatient treatment team to inform them of the situation. It may also be helpful to take steps to optimize the individual's safety at home. This might include helping the individual remove potentially dangerous objects from the environment (guns, knives, ropes, unnecessary medications), and ensuring the depressed individual has regular visits or other contact with supports such as friends, family or church staff. Some find it helpful to make a list of five to 10 people to call when they are having a tough time.

We conclude this discussion with the reminder that *any persistent thoughts or talk of suicide must be taken seriously.* If someone speaks of suicide, even jokingly, it is critical to ask more questions. If in any doubt about what should be done, call 911 or go to the nearest emergency room. As discussed earlier in this chapter, it is the task of a clinician to perform a full safety assessment, and it is better to have an individual be upset with you over seeking help than to look back on tragedy.

To educate yourself more about suicide, please visit:

1. American Association of Suicidology (www.suicidology.org)

2. American Foundation for Suicide Prevention (www.asfp.org)

3. National Insutitue of Mental Health Suicide Research Consortium (www.nimh.nih.gov/research/suicide.htm)

4. Suicide Prevention Advocacy Network (www.spanusa.org)

Suicide Risk Factors

This table describes some common warning signs of suicidality. These risk factors do not carry equal weight. For example, the final three items on this list are more specific to suicide risk and should raise concern even in the absence of other overt signs of suicidality or depression.

> Expressions of helplessness or hopelessness

> Extreme withdrawal from friends, family and usual activities

> Talking about "ending it all"

> Lack of concern with the future

> Self-destructive, reckless or impulsive behaviors

> Sudden changes in mood—unexplained cheerfulness or suddenly diminished depression

> Access to firearms

> Increasing use of alcohol or drugs

> Recent loss of social supports or dearth of social supports

> Poor self-care (not taking medications, not eating or showering)

> Previous suicide attempts

> Family history of completed suicide

> Saying goodbyes to people, making amends, closing bank accounts, selling possessions

> Presence of any sort of goodbye message

> Referring to everyday objects as weapons

What can the church do?

In addition to those acute situations where suicide risk is present, there are many important steps the church can take. Here are four ways the church can help create an environment to diminish stigma, encourage suffering individuals to reach out for help as needed, equip the community to care for suicidal individuals and grieving families, and ultimately reduce suicide risk.

1. **Pray.** As always, all actions should be accompanied by prayer, as it is God who is able to heal.ievers, like anyone else, may be prone to consider suicide when faced with emotional distress. When discussing suicide, it is prudent to include resources for help, including a suicide hotline as well as ways to be in touch with church staff.

2. **Use appropriate language.** The way suicide is discussed is critical. It is important to speak frankly about suicide when it occurs, as avoiding mention of the cause of death can enhance shame and stigma. Alternatively, excessive focus on the means of death can risk glamorizing or sensationalizing the event. Both the American Association of Suicidology and the American Foundation for Suicide Prevention encourage the avoidance of certain terms and phrasing that can increase stigma. First, the phrase "committed suicide" should be avoided and replaced with descriptions of someone "dying by suicide" or "ending his life." This shift in emphasis frames suicide as a tragic, fatal outcome of a disease, rather than a crime. It is advisable to not speak about completed suicides as "successful," or of suicide attempts not ending in death as having "failed." When possible, individuals should avoid sharing details of how someone may have attempted or completed suicide, as such sharing can contribute to glamorizing the attempt while also leading to "copycat" suicides or suicide contagions.

3. **Be cautious when speaking about the eternal repercussions of suicide.** Should a community member die by suicide, it is important to provide support to those who are grieving. Many individuals have stories of church communities effectively shunning them after a family member has died by suicide, or of pastors focusing on suicide being a sin that cannot be absolved. One can imagine how such comments can negatively affect the bereaved. Nobody ends their life unless they are seriously ill, so ill they are not in their right mind and therefore not responsible for their actions. Even the Catholic church, which for centuries had depicted suicide as the unpardonable crime, has recently softened its approach to suicide, acknowledging that those who die by suicide are almost always mentally ill and not culpable.

The question of whether suicide is an unforgiveable sin is controversial. Most Christians agree suicide is a sin due to the murderous action involved with ending any life (Exodus 20:13; Matthew 19:18; Romans 13:9). Some argue suicide is an unpardonable sin and precludes entry to heaven. For some, the rationale for this view is that as ending one's life is a sin that leaves no time for repentance (due to death following immediately after the suicidal behavior). This argument makes various presumptions that many Christians would refute. First, this argument presumes that people must identify and repent of each sin before it can be forgiven, which is a view not all Christians share. Second, for those who do place high value on repenting of specific sins in order to receive forgiveness, the idea of suicide being unforgivable may become problematic when noting that few people speak in a similar manner about the many other sins we are all accountable for at our deathbed (such as lust, greed, envy, bitterness, contempt), or about the many sins one might enact throughout life but not fully repent of before death. In an article written for the Gospel Coalition, Sam Storms notes that "common sense reveals that many, if not most, of us will die with sins of which we have not repented."[15] Practically speaking, it is also impossible to know if an individual repented of ending his or her life in the moments between a suicidal action and actual death. Even if this period of time is brief by worldly standards, we know God is not constrained by such concepts of time (2 Peter 3:8). Regardless of the timing, presence or critical nature of specific repentance, Kay Warren further highlights some of the problems with naming suicide as unpardonable, noting this view undermines Jesus's teachings that nothing can take a believer from His hands (John 10:27-30; Romans 8:38-39).[16]

As Christian psychiatrists, it is our perspective that God's forgiveness extends even to the sin of suicide. The Scriptures describe Jesus dying on the cross for *all* of humanity's sin. While suicide is a tragedy, it would be undermining Christ to consider suicide a sin outside the purview of God's grace and forgiveness, particularly when the act was performed by someone with a mental illness (depression or severe suffering) that interferes with their ability to weigh evidence and make competent decisions. We urge readers to examine their own beliefs on the nature of suicide in light of Jesus Christ, with encouragement for all to show love to those who are grieving.

4. **Pray.** As always, all actions should be accompanied by prayer, as it is God who is able to heal. Pray with the person about the hard situations they are struggling with. Cry out to God for deliverance and mercy. Pray for God to restore joy in the hearts of those considering suicide. Pray for the Holy Spirit to intercede so individuals considering suicide will sense their worth, identity and purpose through Christ. Pray for communities grieving after suicide deaths to forgive the deceased and to heal. Pray for the Holy Spirit to give you words to speak to those who are suffering.

Living in the Dark

Whether through outpatient services, an IOP or PHP or an inpatient psychiatric hospitalization, helpful resources are available. If an individual feels so much pain that a desire to end one's precious and God-given life arises, help should be sought immediately to prevent potentially fatal outcomes.

Depression is a hard battle to fight. It is hard because it infects our mind and spirit, and it impairs our reason, our will and our emotion. It is hard because there is still a lot of stigma out there, particularly in the church.

But even if we find ourselves living in perpetual night, even if our reason flees and our will wavers, we can have confidence that God's love will never leave us and He will be present with us, even in the dark.

> "Where shall I go from your Spirit?
> Or where shall I flee from your presence?
> If I ascend to heaven, you are there!
> If I make my bed in Sheol, you are there!
> If I take the wings of the morning
> and dwell in the uttermost parts of the sea,
> even there your hand shall lead me,
> and your right hand shall hold me.
> If I say, 'Surely the darkness shall cover me,
> and the light about me be night,'
> even the darkness is not dark to you;
> the night is bright as the day,
> for darkness is as light with you"
> (Psalm 139:7-12, ESV).

Endnotes

1. Swanson, Jeffrey W., et al. "Psychiatric advance directives and reduction of coercive crisis interventions." *Journal of Mental Health* 17.3 (2008): 255-267.

2. Srebnik, Debra S., et al. "The content and clinical utility of psychiatric advance directives." *Psychiatric Services* 56.5 (2005): 592-598.

3. American Foundation for Suicide Prevention. (2019). "Suicide Statistics." Retrieved from https://afsp.org/about-suicide/suicide-statistics/.

4. National Institutes of Mental Health. (2019). "Suicide." Retrieved from https://www.nimh.nih.gov/health/statistics/suicide.shtml.

5. Lim, M., Lee, S., & Park, J. (2016). Differences between Impulsive and Non-Impulsive Suicide Attempts among Individuals Treated in Emergency Rooms of South Korea. *Psychiatry Investigation*, 13(4):389-396.

6. Simon, O.R., Swann, A.C., Powell, K.E., Potter, L.B., Kresnow, M.J., & O'Carroll, P.W. (2001). Characteristics of impulsive suicide attempts and attempters. *Suicide and Life Threatening Behavior*, 32(1), 49-59.

7. anthemofhope.org

8. Stone, Roxanne, et al. "Pastor and Mental Health Advocate Jarrid Wilson Dies by Suicide" *Christianity Today*. September 10, 2019

9. Schnell, Lindsay. "Suicide of prominent pastor Jarrid Wilson forces church leaders to confront mental health." *USA Today*. September 14, 2019

10. Proeschold-Bell, R.J., Miles, A., Toth, M. et al. Using Effort-Reward Imbalance Theory to Understand High Rates of Depression and Anxiety Among Clergy. *J Primary Prevent* 34, 439–453 (2013). https://doi.org/10.1007/s10935-013-0321-4

11. VanderWeele, T. J., Li, S., Tsai, A. C., & Kawachi, I. (2016). Association between religious service attendance and lower suicide rates among US women. *JAMA Psychiatry*, 73(8), 845-851.

12. Koenig, H. G. (2016). Association of religious involvement and suicide. *JAMA Psychiatry*, 73(8), 775-776.

13. Jamison, Kay Redfield. *Night Falls Fast: Understanding Suicide*. New York, NY: Random House, 1999

14. Jamison, Kay Redfield. *Night Falls Fast: Understanding Suicide*. New York, NY: Random House, 1999

15. Storms, S. (2015, June 17). "Is Suicide the Unpardonable Sin?" *The Gospel Coalition*. Retrieved from https://www.thegospelcoalition.org/article/is-suicide-the-unpardonable-sin/.

16. Blair, L. (2015, September 10). "Kay Warren Says Suicide Doesn't Condemn Believers to Hell; Says She Prayed 'Audacious Prayers' Before Son Took His Life." *Christian Post*. Retrieved from https://www.christianpost.com/news/kay-warren-says-suicide-doesnt-condemn-believers-to-hell-says-she-prayed-audacious-prayers-before-son-took-his-life-145019/.

CHAPTER 10

LOVE:
The Crucial Role of Family, Friends, and the Church

Depression affects more than just an individual. No matter how estranged a person might be, he or she always exists within a network of relationships—with spouse, parents, children, siblings, friends, co-workers, church members, neighbors, etc. Whatever relationships a person may have, those relationships are always affected by depression. This can be painful for the depressed person to acknowledge. A spouse may feel guilty, rejected, discouraged, frustrated or angry. Family members may feel embarrassed, even ashamed. Friends may feel manipulated, confused or alienated. Fellow church members may wish to help but feel immobilized because they do not know what to do or say.

But a person's community is an important source of strength in the fight against depression. In the last chapter, Rick and Kay Warren shared their heartbreaking journey with their son Matthew during his depression.

"Often our emotions would mirror what he was experiencing," Rick Warren said. "When he had an emotion, we would feel it as well...A parent of a child with mental illness will have a gamut of every possible emotion from frustration to despair. It was gut wrenching when it felt hopeless. How many times did we say, if there was a way we could take his pain, we would take it. Lord, put his depression, put his insecurities on me. I am older, I'm bigger and I can handle this. He's just a little boy."

It was a painful journey for them. Nevertheless, what is clear throughout their story was how much love they had for their son, as well as the important role they had in helping him fight the depression as long as he did. They listened to him and were present with him through his pain, his anger, his doubts and his hopelessness. They taught themselves about depression and suicide; they took him to doctors and therapists and hospitals; they sought all treatment options. They tried to distract him from the pain; they helped him find a job; they had meals with him. The times when he was not able to hold onto hope, they held onto hope for him. They loved their son, and they fought his depression with him.

As we discussed in Chapter 8, we were not designed by God to be alone. We were made to be in relationship with one another, and we were made to function in community. Supportive relationships are vital to healing from depression, but people may not know how best to help those who are depressed. We provide some strategies in this chapter as to how friends, family and churches can best care for those who are depressed.

The Burden of Love

The everyday burden of loving someone with depression can be heavy. The book *What to Do When Someone You Love Is Depressed* by Mitch and Susan Golant describes the experience of having a loved one with depression:

> "When someone you love is depressed
> …you feel lost, afraid, confused.
> …you long for the person who was.
> …you don't recognize who he or she has become.
> …you feel shut out.
> …you feel angry and frustrated.
> …you feel drained.
> …you are desperate for a way to connect.
> …you feel guilty and alone.
> …you will do anything to help."[1]

Feelings of frustration and helplessness are common. This may be due to feelings of responsibility for the person's depression. It may be due to frustration if the person refuses to seek help. Or as the months and years wear on, it may be due to feelings of fear that the depression may be here to stay and this is what life is going to look like.

It can be helpful for friends and family members to realize that when a family member has depression, the role you take becomes that of a caregiver. The burden on caregivers can be just as great as if you had a family member with cancer. Just as with cancer, there can be frequent appointments to doctors and therapists, with a whole new world of specialists and treatment options to learn about. Just as with cancer, there is a change in lifestyle—interruptions in work either for the depressed or the family member, medical and therapy visits and sometimes hospitalizations which can result in financial strain, and adjustments in expectations. Just as with cancer, there can be uncertainty of prognosis—of how long this will last, of how severe this is going to be and whether ultimately this is going to be terminal. Just as with cancer, there is a toll on caregivers—the worry, the giving, the exhaustion, the isolation.

However, unlike cancer, there is much less understanding and much less sympathy toward depression. And one reason for this is the problem with the diagnosis of "depression." As we described in Chapters 2 and 3, "depression" is used to describe a large spectrum of problems and causes. It can be used to describe the experience of just feeling down and unmotivated, it can be used to describe grief after a loss or it can be used to describe a clearly biological disease. But all of these different problems, with different causes and prognosis, fall under the label of "depression." As a consequence, everyone has had the experience of feeling "blue" at one point or other, and they may assume that a person with depression is experiencing what they did. They may be frustrated that the person with depression does not just "pull themselves together." Without a better understanding of depression and its biological basis, stigma will persist.

Another difference is that while cancer attacks only part of the body, depression attacks the whole person. (This occurs in an even greater degree in cognitive disorders such as dementia). And that can be a painful journey. Rick and Kay Warren describe how their son Matthew became unrecognizable to them as the depression continued and the years wore on. It was hard to find the son they knew underneath the depression. People with depression usually lose interest in all the things that used to animate them, can be irritable and angry or can be withdrawn and shut people out. They no longer seem like the person you loved, and the relationship may feel increasingly one-way, rather than a mutual giving relationship. Times like this that can test a spouse's commitment to fulfill their marriage vow, "for better or for worse, in sickness and in health."

Depression can do real damage to relationships. Research has shown that children are impacted by a parent's depression, and this is often associated with an increased risk of the child developing depression and acting out. Spouses are at increased risk for becoming depressed. Depression increases conflict in marriages, and this has an effect on children too. When one member of the family suffers, everyone suffers.[2]

Things to Keep in Mind

There are a few important principles to keep in mind.

1. *You're not responsible for how they feel.*

The connection between relationships and depression is complicated. As we discussed, conflict in relationships can contribute to depression (Chapter 3), but a supportive relationship can be helpful in recovering from depression (Chapter 8). In addition, there is also the possibility that due to the distorted thinking of depression, the depressed person might blame their depression on their loved one even when they are not at fault. Or the depression itself may cause conflict within the marriage. Communication breakdowns are common with depression. If these issues are present, it would be wise to seek the help of a family or couples therapist in order to detangle what exactly is going on.

However, in many cases, family members take on too much responsibility for how the depressed individual is feeling. Family members might always feel like they are walking on eggshells around the depressed individual, for fear of saying or doing something "that would make them bite your head off and make it impossible to discuss anything in a rational way," as psychologists Laura Rosen and Xavier Amador write in their practical and helpful book, *When Someone You Love Is Depressed: How to Help Your Loved One Without Losing Yourself*.[3] However, walking on eggshells tends to be destructive to relationships in the long run. If friends and family do not feel they can be honest, this can lead to frustration and resentment. It can be very helpful to educate yourself on understanding depression, on helpful language to use when speaking with those who are depressed and on establishing guidelines for constructive communication. (See Rosen and Amador's book, Chapters 7 and 8).

2. *You're not responsible for curing their depression.*

Family and friends may blame themselves for the depressed person's inability to get better. Parents may feel it is their duty to rescue their children. Children may blame themselves—if they were better at meeting their parent's needs, perhaps the parent would not be depressed. Men in particular may feel an obligation to fix problems. When people feel a need to fix the depression, they may give a lot of advice, which may be ignored or rejected. This leads to feelings of frustration or helplessness.

Family and friends should help the depressed person obtain and stick with treatment, particularly since many depressed people are resistant to seeking help. But they are not responsible for the results—that is outside their control.

3. *Try to distinguish between the person and their depression.*

Learn about the symptoms of depression and, in particular, the depressed person's pattern of depression. This can help you keep in mind the difference between the person and their disease. Living with someone who is depressed is hard, and it is extremely normal to feel frustrated, exhausted or fed up. It can be helpful to try to separate the disease from the person and think of it as being fed up with the depression, rather than being fed up with the person.

4. *Being depressed does not take away a person's responsibility for their actions and words or entitle them to bad behavior.*

Depression increases the vulnerability to sin, but a person is still responsible for their actions. A family member can be loving and supportive to an individual who is depressed, while still maintaining clear limits on behavior. Rules for respectful communication and behavior apply in relationships with a depressed person just as they would in any other relationship. Verbal abuse, name calling, put-downs, mockery and threats should not be tolerated. Irresponsible behavior, such as substance use, destruction of property, gambling or reckless behavior may be a sign that a person's depression is worsening. In addition, behavior that causes worry or is provocative should also be discussed, such as not answering the phone for long periods of time or making dishonest statements intended to increase anxiety or increase guilt in loved ones.

Specific Suggestions on How to Help

Learn

Learn all you can about depression and how it affects people. Read books. Attend support groups. Learn how you can come alongside your loved one in their fight against depression. As Kay Warren stated in the previous chapter, "Just don't be passive and put your head in the sand, hoping that you can wake up one morning and your loved one's no longer depressed. Because that's not likely to happen."

Our suggestions for books are ones we have mentioned in this chapter:

> *Talking to Depression* by Claudia Strauss

> *When Someone You Love is Depressed: How to Help Your Loved One without Losing Yourself* by Claudia Rosen and Xavier Amador

> *What to Do When Someone You Love is Depressed* by Mitch Golant and Susan Golant

Listen

It is difficult for someone who has never been depressed to fully understand what the experience of depression is like. Ask the depressed person to describe what their experience is like, and then listen.

Effective listening is not as passive as most people think. It requires work to track with the person who is talking. Many depressed people find it difficult to put their feelings into words, as this requires concentration and articulation as well as emotional energy, which they may lack. Some people who are depressed become eerily quiet. Friends and family, being unused to silence, may end up filling the uncomfortable conversation gaps with meaningless chatter, which may confirm in the mind of the depressed person that the speaker truly does not understand or care to understand.

To listen effectively, you will have to stifle your desire to try to fix what you think is broken. The problem with this approach is that most of the time, friends and family may not realize they were simply answering their own questions and not the real questions the depressed person is struggling with. To be helpful, one must have listened long enough to truly understand the speaker, before one has earned the right to speak.

If you are going to help someone who is depressed, you must also be open to hearing whatever surfaces, even if it is uncomfortable or frightening. In the previous chapter, Kay Warren describes her horror the first time she heard about her school-aged son's desire for death. In order to heal from depression, a person must be able to be honest with the dark thoughts and questions that have been brewing in their minds. In order to have faith, they must be able to voice their true feelings about God. Many people who are depressed feel like they are not allowed to have a voice. Many are convinced no one will let them say what they need to say, so they experience frustration and anger or guilt and shame. But God never condemns honest questions; He only condemns dishonesty and hypocrisy (Matthew 23). As we described in Chapter 7, God can take our anger, our complaints, our doubts and our fears. God is far greater than any of those.

Be Patient

The word "longsuffering," mentioned as a fruit of the Spirit in Galatians 5, carries particular relevance here. Longsuffering means patiently enduring lasting offense or hardship.[4] When dealing with someone with depression, numerous things may try one's patience, such as changes in mood and plans, irritability and sometimes meanness, tears and despair. When talking with someone who is depressed, try not to take their comments personally or react defensively. If you can, try to step back and reflect that it may be the depression talking. As noted above, depression does not take away the person's responsibility for their actions and words, nor does it entitle them to bad behavior. However, there is a role for longsuffering love, which may mean overlooking faults, forgiving sins and bearing with weakness.

Encourage

There are various ways family and friends can encourage depressed persons. With depression, you may need to be gently intrusive with your love. Richard Baxter is helpful with his advice, "Intrude into their space and interrupt their ruminations. Rouse them from such musings with loving and unwavering insistence. Don't allow them to spend too much time alone…

Be especially careful not to let them be idle, but press or entice them into some pleasant activity that may entail physical as well as mental action."[5]

Here are some suggestions:

1. Offer to take your loved one to the doctor's or therapist's office. You should plan to remain in the waiting room during the visit, unless they request you be present.

2. Telephone your loved one regularly to ask how they are doing, or schedule a regular coffee together. Knowing you care enough to call will be an encouragement to the depressed person, a reminder that others do love them and are there for them, whether or not they can return that love at this time.

3. Help them stay healthy. Go on regular walks together. Take them to the grocery store to make sure they are not neglecting their diet.

4. Go with them to church. Make sure they are under the care of a pastor who preaches the gospel of grace and is also comfortable dealing with depression. Take them to a community group or prayer meeting.

5. Attend a support group together. One way to encourage your depressed friend to get out, get help and find community is to find a good depression support group and invite your loved one to attend it with you. Groups like this are becoming more common and are often sponsored by churches. It can be intimidating to attend a group alone and is much easier with a companion.

6. Try to distract them from their negative thoughts. Try to engage them in activities they have previously enjoyed, such as painting, exercise or music. Find out what the person's favorite movie is and make a movie night. Or schedule watching Monday night football or a TV show together.

7. If possible, encourage them to engage in the lives of others by volunteering, participating in community activities and meeting with other people.

Monitor

People who are depressed may need help in taking their medication on time and at the right dose. They may need help in keeping doctors' appointments—both help remembering to go and help getting there. This is the most monitoring that mild to moderately depressed people usually need.

If your loved one is severely depressed, however, they may need observation to ensure they eat their meals and do not harm themselves. If the medication they take makes them feel sleepy, they may need to be monitored if they are driving or operating any dangerous equipment. Care should be taken when allowing severely depressed people to drive since their reaction times and concentration may be off.

A few monitoring suggestions:

1. If you cannot be with the depressed loved one in person, call or text him or her frequently to check in. It can be helpful, with the depressed person's permission, to arrange for coworkers, friends or roommates to monitor the depressed person and contact you or the mental health team if the person displays signs of worsening.

2. Pick up their medications for them. Get a weekly pill box for them, and then help them fill the box in order to keep track of the medication. Help them set up daily alarms or phone apps to remind them to take their medication.

3. Talk to your loved one about suicide. Talking about suicide does not increase the risk they will act on this; instead, talking about it is usually a source of relief. See Chapter 9 for guidance about this conversation. All talk of suicide must be taken seriously, even if it is mentioned offhand or jokingly.

4. If a person has moderate or severe thoughts about suicide or self-harm, lock up dangerous medications and dispense them in small quantities to reduce the risk of overdosing. Remove any dangerous items from the house, such as guns, knives, ropes and razors.

Establish Clear Expectations

You are on the same team together to fight depression, and anyone who has played team sports understands the importance of clear communication. Without communicating clearly about expectations on both sides, frustration, guilt and exhaustion can develop. It is important to agree upon mutual expectations. It may be helpful to have the help of a social worker, counselor or pastor present during this discussion.

Reasonable expectations one can suggest with someone who is depressed:

1. The depressed person will make every reasonable effort to get better.

2. The depressed person will seek help, be evaluated and follow the treatment plan, whether the plan is to take medication or see a counselor on a regular basis or both.

3. The depressed person will do their best to take care of their daily functions, such as getting out of bed, dressing themselves, showering regularly, eating meals, etc.

4. The depressed person will refrain from physical or verbal abuse or reckless behavior such as substance abuse.

5. The depressed person will be honest with you if their depression worsens and they develop thoughts of harming themselves.

6. The depressed person will respect the family members' decisions and actions to maintain their safety. This includes removing any dangerous items from the house, contacting the doctor to admit the person to the hospital, if this becomes necessary, or calling 911.

Some reasonable expectations a depressed person can have of their family members:

1. Family members will do their best to support a depressed person in obtaining help, whether it is transportation or finding financial resources including applying for government aid or health insurance.

2. Family members will monitor the depressed person, check in with them and make sure they are staying healthy, taking their medications and following with treatment.

3. Family members will help the depressed person obtain emergency care in case they are not able to stay safe or care for themselves by contacting their doctor or counselor, taking them to the emergency room or calling 911.

4. Family members should not engage in physical or verbal abuse, and they should refrain from reckless behavior such as substance abuse.

5. If family members start to show signs of stress and depression themselves, they will seek care for themselves as well.

Family members and depressed individuals should both show mutual respect for one another. Emotional or physical abuse should not be tolerated in either direction. Family members should not dominate or control the depressed person's life or make all decisions for him or her. A balance must be achieved that respects the depressed person's autonomy and independence, while also seeking his or her improvement and safety. Consider writing a Ulysses Contract (psychiatric advance directive) as we described in Chapter 9 to establish a plan together on what to do in times of crisis.

Enlist Allies

Due to the complex dynamics of depression, it is easy to feel exhausted, rejected, inadequate, helpless, unloved and unappreciated when you are the primary caregiver. Depressed people may not have sufficient energy or emotional reserve to show much appreciation for what others do for them. In order to avoid burnout yourself, you should enlist other sources of support for the depressed person, including other family members, friends, a pastor and church members. Try to put the depressed person in touch with a fellow sufferer of the same gender who has experienced and emerged from depression.

Keep Yourself Healthy

As much as possible, try to maintain your personal routine during your loved one's depression. For example, if you currently participate in a social or athletic activity on a regular basis, you should do everything possible to continue to do so. Make sure to maintain your own friendships outside of the relationship with your loved one. All of these things will help you maintain a rhythm and a sense of yourself, be a source of personal support and prevent burnout.

Friends and family can better cope with the stress of living with a depressed person by developing a regular exercise regime. You can accomplish this at home with home equipment or with workout videos if you have difficulty finding time outside the home. Even a leisurely walk on a regular basis can help, particularly if it is with a close friend in whom you can confide.

It is easy to become all-consumed with taking care of the needs of a depressed person. For Christians in particular, it can be hard to take care of your own needs out of fear of being selfish. In their helpful chapter on "Is it fair to ask for what you need?" Rosen and Amador offer these helpful suggestions:

> ⟩ "Talk about your needs constructively…Convey that you want to resolve your dilemma together."

> ⟩ "Look for ways in which [the depressed person] can help you…In fact, the more your depressed loved one can feel that she is useful and less of a burden, the better off she will feel."

> ⟩ "Don't be afraid to disappoint your loved one occasionally. No one is capable of meeting every need another person has."[6]

Time away from the depressed person is necessary so that a caregiver can be refreshed in order to fully able to meet the depressed person's needs when with him or her again. If you are concerned about leaving the depressed person alone because of safety issues, then arrange for a friend or other family member to spend time with him or her while you are away. However, it is important to keep in mind that if the depressed person is at the point of requiring this level of constant monitoring for safety's sake, then it is time to consider hospitalization.

A Special Case: When Your Depressed Love One Is a Child or Teenager

Adolescent depression is becoming increasingly common. One in six teenagers (18 percent) report being depressed, and the rate is even higher in those who report bullying, substance use or physical symptoms.[7] Without treatment, an episode of major depression in adolescence will last about eight months. Within two years, 40 percent will have another episode of depression, and within five years, 72 percent will do so.[8] What is particularly frightening about depression during adolescence is the skyrocketing rate of suicide. It is estimated that one in four teenagers have considered suicide, and suicide is currently the second most common cause of death among teenagers.[9] Depression in children and adolescents needs to be taken extremely seriously, and treatment needs to be sought.

Depression is not an easy diagnosis in children and adolescents. Depressed children and adolescents don't always complain of sadness or depressed mood. Instead, they may complain of physical symptoms such as headache, stomach upset or fatigue. They may be irritable, complain of boredom, lose interest in their usual activities or have academic or behavioral problems at school. It is essential, as in all cases of depression, that medical illness be ruled out as the first step in the evaluation process, since the symptoms may represent other treatable medical conditions.

For children and adolescents, the first mode of treatment should be counseling or therapy. We strongly recommend this be with a professional who is specifically trained in dealing with this age group, since the therapy with this population can be vastly different from that in adults. Most children and adolescents are typically not seeking treatment themselves, and they may be difficult to engage in treatment. It may take trying several therapists to find one whom a child trusts and with whom they can open up. Otherwise treatment may become week after week of a child sitting sullen and silent in a therapist's office. Nevertheless, it is important for parents to take their children's depression seriously and continue to pursue treatment.

If therapy is not helpful and a child is experiencing severe mood problems, is harming themselves or is expressing thoughts of suicide, medication should be seriously considered.

However, we strongly recommend seeking care from a child psychiatrist and not from a pediatrician, due to the complexity of diagnosis in children. Depression can be the initial presentation of other illnesses, such as bipolar disorder, schizophrenia or substance use, and this needs to be carefully ruled out. Just as with adults, if safety is an issue, a higher level of support such as hospitalization in a children's psychiatric unit may need to be pursued.

Case: Janelle

Janelle was almost seventeen when she told us her story. She just remembered being unhappy most of her life. Her mother had suffered for years from a very painful, extremely rare medical condition. As a result, for most of the time Janelle was growing up, her mother's time and energies were more or less consumed by her illness. In addition, their family was very active in the only evangelical church in their little town in New Hampshire. Her father was a church leader who set a high standard not only for himself, but also for his children.

Things started to get out of control in her first year of high school. Besides struggling with all the adjustments to high school life, including trying out for various athletic teams, Janelle also struggled with guilt that she couldn't help her mother. She found a listening ear and the camaraderie she needed not with the kids in the church's youth group, but with another group of kids that helped her drown her sadness in alcohol. By the end of her freshman year, she was drinking more and drinking alone.

By the start of her sophomore year, Janelle became more consumed with dulling her pain and less about what anyone, including her parents, might think. She got caught smoking marijuana and was kicked off the volleyball team. Her parents made it clear they were very disappointed and expected her to straighten up and stay away from the kids who were bad influences.

By then, however, bad influences were only part of Janelle's increasingly complex problem. She was depressed, without knowing what to call it. "Part of it," she explained, "was that I just didn't really care about consequences. I wasn't looking past the next day because I couldn't see myself living more than another day. I was literally living day by day. There was no 'long term,' so if someone said, 'Do this,' or, 'Don't do this or else,' it didn't mean anything to me."

"What really sent me over the edge was that once, after a party, my parents really got upset. They came down really hard on me. I felt like a complete failure, especially compared to my dad who is a successful kind of person, hardworking and all. I just knew I wasn't ever going to amount to anything…that my whole life was one big mistake. I felt pretty hopeless," she said.

"When I started slitting my wrists," she said, "one of my coaches noticed and asked me about it. I just made something up every time. But finally, I told him what was going on, and of course he told my parents, who were absolutely shocked. I had already been to counseling, which didn't help much. The counselor would ask me if I was depressed, but I was in total denial, so I said 'no.' I mean, I didn't want to be a crazy person or anything. But I finally suggested to my parents that I probably needed medication."

Admitting the truth was Janelle's first step toward recovery, but her situation got worse before it got better. Her doctor put her on a low dose of medication—low enough that it didn't really help much. Grounded and threatened with being kicked off the track team, Janelle felt isolated and cut off. Every day she came home from school with nothing to do.

Gradually over time, Janelle developed a plan. It started with an idea: "I'm no good. I'll never amount to anything. I'm a problem to everyone, just taking up space, so I should just do the world a favor and take myself out of here." Next, her depressed mind formulated specific steps to take: "Most girls take the easy way out—pills. But I want people to remember me not as a weak person but as a strong person. I'll use a gun."

Once she had a plan, she wrote a note to her friends and family apologizing for everything, apologizing for being in the way, apologizing for just being. So this was her way to make things easier on everyone, to make the world a better place.

"Then when I was calling one of my friends to basically say goodbye, my dad heard me talking," she said. "He came downstairs and asked who I was talking to, and then he found the note and the whole thing blew up. It's weird, but when I was on the phone, it was as though I stepped out of myself and saw what I was doing, and I just knew that I needed help. That was really the first time I realized how really messed up I was. Even though I knew I needed help, I didn't want anyone to help me. I wanted to do it myself. Strange as it sounds, that's the way I was thinking."

"Another strange thing," Janelle added, "is that my parents didn't freak out; they were just totally shocked. I don't think they knew what to do. So they didn't do anything for three days, which still frustrates me. Then they took me to my doctor, saying that I needed a medication adjustment. I needed more than that, though, which he could tell by the deep gashes and scars on my arms. So he made arrangements for me to see a therapist in a city about an hour away."

Janelle didn't know that she was about to be admitted to a psychiatric ward. Her parents didn't tell her, most likely because they were afraid she would fight their plan.

"At first I was really upset about it," Janelle recalls. "I was confused. I thought they didn't care, that they were just dumping me. But it was probably the best thing for me. They didn't know what to do, but I'm glad they did something. I'd rather have them dump me and feel abandoned than to be dead."

Janelle stayed in that psychiatric ward for one very long week. "I was supposed to be there for three days," she says, "but I was really honest with them, because I didn't want to leave unless I was better. When they asked me if I was suicidal, I would say 'yes.' I wasn't going to lie just to get out. But when I saw kids coming in overnight or for a day or two, I started to think that I would never get out of there."

Overwhelmed with a sense of hopelessness, she removed the small razor from her pencil sharpener and slit her wrists again. "Then they took me more seriously," she recalls, "and the doctor changed my medication and gave me a higher dose, and my perspective started to change. I didn't like being there, but I was scared to leave. At least in there I didn't have to constantly fight myself, because I knew that even if I wanted to kill myself, they wouldn't let me. So in a weird way it took that fear away. Also, being in the group sessions was good for me because I could see that my feelings weren't weird since other people had them too. In fact, some of them were more messed up than me."

Janelle remains under a physician's care and sees a therapist from time to time. She believes that the combination of both is important. "You need to be on the right amount of the right medication," she said, "and you have to find a therapist you really like. The one I see now is the fifth one I've seen in the past year. I couldn't stand the others, because I knew they were just going through the motions. If I don't think that someone cares about what I'm saying, I am not willing to talk to him or her. The one I have now lets me know that she cares about me as a person, not just as another appointment. That has really made a big difference in helping me find my way through a lot of things I used to find confusing."

When we asked Janelle what her parents did that was helpful, she said: "I'm glad they finally did something, that they finally took me seriously and realized I need professional help. When I get really depressed I'm impulsive, and that was interpreted as rebellion.

When we had a family session at the hospital, for the first time they saw my depression, as my dad says, 'eyeball to eyeball,' for what it was—not rebellion, but depression."

Some teens (and adults) are not as fortunate as Janelle, and they become lost in the wasteland of their depression because they have no guide to help them find a way out. We asked Janelle what other parents could do for their own kids in a similar situation.

"Well, first of all," Janelle said, "let them know they are loved and respected, even if you're extremely worried about what kind of crazy thing they might do next. They aren't insane, you know; they're just crying out for help. So they need to know that your love for them hasn't changed just because they're depressed."

"A second thing parents could do if their kids are really serious about hurting themselves," she continued, "is admit them to the hospital. It's an extreme decision, and they may hate you for a while. At first I thought my parents hated me to put me in there. But then I realized that if they really hated me, they would have let me do what I wanted to do, and I'd be gone. So gradually I realized I really needed to be in the hospital where I could get help. In the end—maybe after a long time—they'll thank you."

"Also, there is a fine line between correcting a kid and always criticizing what they do," she said. "Parents can correct them when they're wrong and punish them and stuff like that, but parents need to choose their battles wisely, because if you're on your kids all the time, they'll eventually get the idea that they do everything wrong.

"One other thing," she added. "Parents should not expect the person to be just fine overnight. Don't get frustrated with them if they fall back a couple of times. Overcoming depression can take a long time. I know that after I was at the hospital I went backward and cut myself twice, but I haven't done it since then. Sometimes it's two steps forward, one step back."

The Role of the Church in Depression

We have mentioned throughout this book that the church has an important role to play in caring for members who struggle with depression. In many churches, misconceptions about depression persist, which result in stigma (see Chapter 4). Yet even churches that don't have stigma against depression find it hard to engage in this conversation. Why is this? We propose that one of the reasons why the church is so bad at dealing with depression is because many in the church do not know how to deal with suffering.

Two theological truths are fundamental to a discussion about depression. The first is that due to the fall, life involves suffering and pain. The second is that a loving God is in control. We can by faith affirm that both things are true, even if we don't understand how that is possible. To move through and beyond depression, a depressed person must fully grasp both truths. Our churches are quite good at acknowledging the second truth, and they sing loudly of the love of God, but they are often silent when it comes to acknowledging the first truth, that suffering is inherent to life.

In *Hurting with God*, Glenn Pemberton writes: "How can churches help believers maintain their faith and relationship with God while they are hurting—not just until they get better or until the crisis is over, but when the storm continues or leaves irreparable damage in its wake? And if my story is in fact our story, and I am convinced it is, then our churches are filled with believers who are hurting, to one degree or another, whether visible or unseen. Some come every Sunday clinging to a thread of hope that somehow the church will be the body of Christ that supports them, offers a word of hope, and helps them find a way to walk through the storm with God instead of without God."[10]

Depression is where faith crashes up against the brokenness of this world. And if churches deny the brokenness and go on saying the victorious Christian life is immune to suffering, then we will lose our relevance in this world. If our churches do not equip people with the answers to suffering, people will leave the faith. They will turn to Buddhism, to philosophy, to existentialism, to self-actualization or to hedonism. They will turn to therapy and medication, which do not themselves provide the answers to the question, "Why do we suffer?"

The irony is that Christianity, of all the religions and philosophies of the world, is uniquely equipped to engage the problem of suffering. As Tim Keller points out, "Only Christianity, of all the world's major religions, teaches that God came to earth in Jesus Christ and became subject to suffering and death himself."[11]

Hindus view suffering as a punishment for crimes committed in this or a previous lifetime. Buddhists view suffering as evidence that we are overly attached to impermanent things, and that the answer is detachment. According to an atheistic point of view, suffering is a product of random chance, and meaning must be made in the face of meaninglessness. In all of these, suffering is a condition that must be avoided. But at the heart of Christianity is a suffering Savior, who died an unjust death because He loved the world. At the heart of Christianity is the paradox that joy can be found in the midst of suffering (1 Peter 4:13). Christianity alone holds that there is value and meaning to suffering, and this allows us to move with compassion toward those who suffer.

Depression can be one of those windows of opportunity in a person's life when the gospel can come alive. Those with depression know themselves to be sick, trapped in their own prisons, aware of their own powerlessness. They see the world for the vanity that it is (Ecclesiastes 1:1-11). This represents a particular opportunity for family, friends and the church to encourage them and speak the gospel of grace into their lives. For Jesus' call is for them—He came to call not the well but the sick, not the righteous but the sinners (Mark 2:17).

Here are some suggestions for how the church can better care for those with depression:

1. Talk about a theology of suffering.

As Kay Warren suggested in her interview in the previous chapter, *"When we act as though, 'to come to Jesus' means all our problems go away, then when depression strikes, or some other long-term illness or tragedy, then we're not prepared for it. We don't even know what to do with it. We believe the lie that this is heaven, when it is not."*

The Bible promises that we as Christians will go through trials and tribulations. If that is the case, then churches need to prepare their members to deal with suffering. Why does God allow suffering? How do we walk through the valley of the shadow? What is our hope? Lament can be an important tool for helping people deal with these questions. As Mark Vroegop writes in *Dark Clouds, Deep Mercy*, "Lament is the language of a people who believe in God's sovereignty but live in a world with tragedy."[12]

2. Talk about personal weakness and sin.

Paul talks openly about being the worst of sinners (1 Timothy 1:15) and boasts that in his weaknesses God would be more glorified (2 Corinthians 12:9). Yet numerous pastors and church leaders feel pressure to pretend they have it all together. Perhaps this has to do with a too-small view of the gospel, which sees it as Good News only for the unbeliever, as a one-time prayer of acceptance. No, the gospel grows richer and greater as we grow in our faith. As we grow more like Christ, we see more of our sin and our need for God.

3. Talk about mental illness.

Decrease stigma by increasing understanding. What does our faith say about illness, and mental illness, and disability?

Educate the church about depression and mental illness. Address the stigma in the church about depression being a lack of faith, or evidence of sin in the believer's life. Explore the examples in Scripture of depression: Job, Elijah, Jeremiah, Psalms and Lamentations. What is our theology about diseases and broken bodies? What is our hope for restoration in the redemption of our bodies (Romans 8:22-25)?

4. Keep a list of local mental health professionals whom you trust.

Develop a list of mental health professionals, such as counselors, therapists and psychiatrists, whom you can refer members of your congregation to when they need help.

5. Be the hands and feet of God to them.

Ask how you can help. Check on those who are depressed. Visit them. Bring meals. Help with transportation if that is a need. Invite them to join in activities and participate in prayer meetings, small groups and ministry opportunities. Help them find their role in the body of Christ.

6. Be the love of God to them.

Be present with them. Bear with them in their weaknesses. Pray for them and with them. Listen to them. Be present with them. Never cease preaching the reality of the gospel to them and our hope for redemption.

The Greatest Commandment

Love is the hardest, and it is the greatest thing we can do as human beings (Matthew 22:36-40). The love described in 1 Corinthians 13 is not what we see depicted in movies and love songs, when the object of one's love is beautiful and glorious. "Love is patient, love is kind…" (1 Corinthians 4, NASB). Love only needs to be patient when the object of one's love is frustrating. Love only needs to be kind when the object of one's love is irritating. The love described in 1 Corinthians 13 is a tough love that loves even when the object is un-lovely. This is love we are called to have for one another—depressed individuals, their friends, their family and their churches.

> "Love is patient and kind; love does not envy or boast; it is not arrogant or rude. It does not insist on its own way; it is not irritable or resentful; it does not rejoice at wrongdoing, but rejoices with the truth. Love bears all things, believes all things, hopes all things, endures all things. Love never ends…For now we see in a mirror dimly, but then face to face. Now I know in part; then I shall know fully, even as I have been fully known. So now faith, hope, and love abide, these three; but the greatest of these is love" (1 Corinthians 13:4-13, ESV).

Endnotes

1. Golant, Mitch, and Golant, Susan K.. What To Do When Someone You Love Is Depressed: A Practical, Compassionate, and Helpful Guide for Caregivers. United States, Henry Holt and Company, 1998.

2. L. Burke "The impact of maternal depression on familial relationships, International Review of Psychiatry, 2003: 15:3, 243-255.

3. Rosen, Laura, and Amador, Xavier. When Someone You Love is Depressed. United States, Free Press, 2016.

4. Merriam-Webster dictionary, https://www.merriam-webster.com/dictionary/long-suffering

5. Lundy and Packer, p160

6. Rosen and Amador, p142-143.

7. Saluja, Gitanjali, et al. "Prevalence of and risk factors for depressive symptoms among young adolescents." Archives of pediatrics & adolescent medicine 158.8 (2004): 760-765.

8. David A. Brent and Boris Birmaher, "Adolescent Depression," New England Journal of Medicine 347, no. 9. 29 August 2002: 667-71.

9. Centers for Disease Control and Prevention (CDC) Data & Statistics Fatal Injury Report for 2017

10. Pemberton, Glenn. Hurting With God: Learning to Lament with the Psalms. Abilene Christian University Press, 2012.

11. Keller, Timothy. Walking with God through Pain and Suffering (p. 121). Penguin Publishing Group. Kindle Edition.

12. Vroegop, Mark. Dark Clouds, Deep Mercy: Discovering the Grace of Lament. United States, Crossway, 2019.

CHAPTER 11

FAITH:
Acknowledging Depression's Gifts

"If we are faithless, he remains faithful…"

—2 Timothy 2:13 (ESV)

Internationally known hand surgeon Dr. Paul Brand wrote a book with Philip Yancey called *Pain: The Gift Nobody Wants*, which was subsequently renamed *The Gift of Pain*. Through his pioneering surgical work with leprosy patients in India, he observed how important physical pain is for our survival. This may seem counterintuitive to our sensibilities, for who wouldn't want a pain-free life? Leprosy attacks the nerves, so people with leprosy lose their ability to sense pain in their extremities. Consequently, they end up repeatedly injuring their feet and hands, to the point where they lose fingers or toes or even a hand or foot, causing the disfigurement for which leprosy is known. Most of them, given the choice, would wish to recover their ability to experience pain. The sensation of pain plays an important role in the body by signaling danger—perhaps a fire or a sharp rock—and protecting the body from harm. Brand writes, "Pain is not the enemy, but the loyal scout announcing the enemy...I now regard pain as one of the most remarkable design features of the human body, and if I could choose one gift for my leprosy patients, it would be the gift of pain."[1]

If indeed we believe God has designed all things for a purpose, in the same way, there may be a beneficial role for depression as well. We want to be careful here. When someone is in the midst of depression, it is little comfort to think of how depression could be useful. As Proverbs states, "Whoever sings songs to a heavy heart is like one who takes off a garment on a cold day, and like vinegar on soda" (Proverbs 25:20, ESV). It is only in hindsight, when depression is long past, that we might be able to see God's purposes for depression. It is also possible we may never receive any explanation for our suffering, and it is also possible these purposes may be only evident from God's perspective and not from our finite vantage point.

What does it mean to walk with faith through the trial that is depression? Hebrews 11:1 describes faith as "…the assurance of things hoped for, the conviction of things not seen" (ESV). Or as Phillip Yancey paraphrases it, "Faith means believing in advance what will only make sense in reverse."[2] Faith means perseverance in seeking deliverance from the depression by bodily, mental, spiritual and environmental means. Faith means believing who God says we are—His chosen ones, holy and beloved children (Colossians 3:12). Faith means believing that God is who He says He is—both sovereign and good, and that He will fulfill every word of His promises (Matthew 5:18). And faith also means a childlike resting in our Father's will and timing, as well as trusting that He is doing something with the depression.

"Not only that, but we rejoice in our sufferings, knowing that suffering produces endurance, and endurance produces character, and character produces hope" (Romans 5:3, ESV).

With God, there is no meaningless suffering. Depression, though certainly the gift that nobody wants, can be a way we grow. Here are some of the ways that may help you see how God can use depression.

Honesty

Depression confronts us with ourselves. It forces us to drop our pretenses and exposes us at our weakest and most vulnerable. When we are trapped in our prisons of dark thoughts and despair, depression confronts us with the brokenness of our minds and the brokenness of our bodies. When we see our own unworthiness and inability to get ourselves together, depression confronts us with our spiritual brokenness too. When depression involves grief after a loss, we are confronted with the fragility of human life and relationships, how little we can depend on things of the world, how fragile our plans are and the emptiness of what the world offers—all vanity of vanities, as Ecclesiastes emphasizes. Depression can bring us to an honest reckoning with ourselves.

It is a well known that teenagers often attempt risky or reckless things because they think they are invincible. But this sense of invincibility actually extends to the rest of the human population as well. The phenomenon known as the optimism bias is where most people predict the future to be better than it actually ends up being. In general, humans have a bias towards overestimating the likelihood of positive future events and underestimating the likelihood of negative future events.[3] Some interesting research suggests that people with depression are actually more realistic in their predictions about the future. People with mild depression have been shown to have the most accurate ability to predict the likelihood of positive or negative events happening in the future. However, those with more severe depression tended to have a pessimism bias and predict that the future will be worse than it actually ends up being.[4,5]

What depression gets right is how everything in the world falls short of how it should be. Depressed individuals are more acutely aware of the existence of sin, brokenness and evil than the rest of us. The world is not safe. Bad things happen. People hurt you. We are all sinful, and we all deserve death. However, this pessimism receives its answer in God. As pastor Jack Miller has said, "Cheer up! You're a worse sinner than you ever dared imagine, and you're more loved than you ever dared hope."[6] God's love and promise of redemption is the answer to our honest assessment of the brokenness in ourselves and the world.

Focus

Some researchers hypothesize that depression may serve a purpose by allowing people with depression to focus and solve complex social problems. This hypothesis is based on several observations. People with depression tend to ruminate, meaning they think about the same thing over and over. By decreasing their interest in other things and other people, depression conserves a person's energies and focuses them inward on solving the problem facing them.[7] Depression pushes us to think over and over on a problem until we can get resolution. However, if we try to run away from the problem and avoid dealing with it, the depression simply continues. What is God trying to bring to your attention?

Refinement of Our Hearts

Just as fire is used to refine gold and burn away the dross, God uses trials to refine our faith (1 Peter 1:6). One of depression's greatest lessons is that it helps us to see what we actually value. Things that once seemed crucial are suddenly shown to be trivial at best, while other things that may have been taken for granted are seen for their real value. Depression may serve a purpose in detaching us from the world and forcing us to reexamine our priorities.

1 John 2:15-17 exhorts us: "Do not love this world nor the things it offers you, for when you love the world, you do not have the love of the Father in you. For the world offers only a craving for physical pleasure, a craving for everything we see, and pride in our achievements and possessions. These are not from the Father, but are from this world. And this world is fading away, along with everything that people crave. But anyone who does what pleases God will live forever" (NLT).

Is our misplaced love the source of our depression? Is it looking for joy and fulfillment in things that don't satisfy? Depression may open our eyes to see how far off course we may have gotten and be an opportunity to turn our ships around and re-chart our course for what actually matters.

Compassion

"Blessed be the God and Father of our Lord Jesus Christ, the Father of mercies and God of all comfort, who comforts us in all our affliction, so that we may be able to comfort those who are in any affliction, with the comfort with which we ourselves are comforted by God. For as we share abundantly in Christ's sufferings, so through Christ we share abundantly in comfort too" (2 Corinthians 1:3-5, ESV).

When we walk through suffering, we discover what it means to be comforted by God. We also learn to have more compassion for others who are suffering, as well as how to comfort them. People who have been through depression tend to be less judgmental and more compassionate toward other people's suffering.

All human beings have an amazing ability to experience empathy for one another, which is the result of fascinating cells in the brain known as *mirror neurons*. These neurons fire both when we perform an action and when we observe the action being performed by someone else. Imaging studies of the brain show we can actually feel what is happening to someone else.

Research suggests that those who are more empathetic as children may be more prone to depression later in life. Although people with depression have the same level of empathy as other people, they are more sensitive to other people's distress. Typically, empathizing with someone else's distress moves people to action. However, those with depression tend to blame themselves for other people's pain, even when it is not their fault.[8] People with depression tend to experience too much empathy-based guilt and withdraw from others. The antidote is suggested by 2 Corinthians 1:3-5. Instead of withdrawing within ourselves, we need to take our distress and our guilt to God and receive His comfort and forgiveness. And having received this comfort, we move outward to comfort others.

Grace

Grace has a simple definition: "unmerited favor." Yet the full implications of this are staggering.

As Tim Keller explains:

> "We can be fully accepted and counted legally righteous in God's sight through faith in Christ, solely by free grace. To understand and grasp this is to finally know freedom from the crushing burden of proving yourself—to society, family, other people, or even to yourself. It means freedom from fear of the future, from any anxiety about your eternal destiny. It is the most liberating idea possible and it ultimately enables you to face all suffering, knowing that because of the cross, God is absolutely for you and that because of the resurrection, everything will be all right in the end."[9]

Of all the gifts depression might bring, the gift of grace is the greatest. When depression has humbled us, and when the world is no longer attractive, we are exactly where we need to be to hear the call of Jesus. Grace invites us to come just as we are.

> "But God, being rich in mercy, because of the great love with which he loved us, even when we were dead in our trespasses, made us alive together with Christ—by grace you have been saved—and raised us up with him and seated us with him in the heavenly places in Christ Jesus, so that in the coming ages he might show the immeasurable riches of his grace in kindness toward us in Christ Jesus. For by grace you have been saved through faith. And this is not your own doing; it is the gift of God, not a result of works,

so that no one may boast. For we are his workmanship, created in Christ Jesus for good works, which God prepared beforehand, that we should walk in them" (Ephesians 2:4-10, ESV).

Growth

Suffering is more tolerable when we know there is an end in sight, and when we know there is a reward for our pain. Childbirth, for example, is a pain tolerated by many women because they know there will be an end to the suffering, as well as the reward of holding a child in their arms at the end. Depression, too, can be tolerable, for although we do not know when it will come to an end, we can trust some good can come from it. We can follow the example of Jesus, "…who for the joy that was set before him endured the cross, despising the shame, and is seated at the right hand of the throne of God" (Hebrews 12:2, ESV). Jesus endured the agony of the cross, knowing the redemption of the world was beyond the pain.

In God's promise to Israel in Joel, we find a particularly powerful metaphor for God's promise of goodness for us that will outweigh our times of sorrow:

> I will restore to you the years that the swarming locust has eaten, the hopper, the destroyer, and the cutter, my great army, which I sent among you. You shall eat in plenty and be satisfied, and praise the name of the Lord your God, who has dealt wondrously with you. And my people shall never again be put to shame" (Joel 2:25-26, ESV).

Depression feels so much like those years that the locusts have eaten. Times that should have been bounty reduced to famine, months and years of life that seemed like an utter waste. But God's purposes never cease to be at work even in the winters of our lives.

Studies have found that those who find meaning and purpose in their negative emotions are less likely to develop negative consequences to their health.[10] We can gain strength from our hardships, growth from our suffering.

Having walked through the valley of the shadow of death with our Shepherd at our side (Psalm 23), we discover that we are no longer afraid of the dark.

Endnotes

1. Yancey, Philip, and Brand, Paul W.. The Gift of Pain: Why We Hurt & what We Can Do about it. United States, Zondervan Publ., 1997.)

2. Philip Yancey, Disappointment with God: Three Questions No One Asks Aloud

3. Sharot, Tali. "The optimism bias." Current biology 21.23 (2011): R941-R945.

4. Strunk, Daniel R., Howard Lopez, and Robert J. DeRubeis. "Depressive symptoms are associated with unrealistic negative predictions of future life events." Behaviour research and therapy 44.6 (2006): 861-882.

5. Moore, Michael T., and David M. Fresco. "Depressive realism: A meta-analytic review." Clinical psychology review 32.6 (2012): 496-509.

6. Tchividjian, Tullian (2010). Surprised by Grace: God's Relentless Pursuit of Rebels. Crossway. p. 44.

7. Andrews, Paul W., and J. Anderson Thomson Jr. "The bright side of being blue: depression as an adaptation for analyzing complex problems." Psychological review 116.3 (2009): 620.

8. O'Connor, Lynn E., et al. "Empathy and depression: the moral system on overdrive." Empathy in mental illness (2007): 49-75.

9. Keller, Timothy. Walking with God through Pain and Suffering (p. 49). Penguin Publishing Group. Kindle Edition.

10. Luong, Gloria, et al. "When bad moods may not be so bad: Valuing negative affect is associated with weakened affect–health links." *Emotion* 16.3 (2016): 387

CHAPTER 12

HOPE:
Looking to Redemption

All people, when faced with depression, are looking for hope. They seek hope for relief from their suffering. They seek a treatment that will cure. But beyond that, they also seek hope that there is meaning for what they are going through, hope that they have a purpose and hope that there is some reason to keep on living.

Jewish psychiatrist Viktor Frankl was imprisoned in the Nazi concentration camps and wrote about his experience as a therapist for fellow prisoners in *Man's Search for Meaning*. He describes how he and some of his fellow prisoners were able to endure the horrors they faced, while others' spirits broke under the pressure. "Everything can be taken from a man but one thing," Frankl wrote, "the last of the human freedoms—to choose one's attitude in any given set of circumstances, to choose one's own way."[1]

Frankl observed that if a person lived for their own personal happiness, when faced with suffering in which no happiness was possible, they quickly turned to suicide. Those who could find meaning, whether in religious beliefs, an obligation to live for someone waiting for them or to complete a life's work, were able to find the inner strength to endure the suffering. "Everyone has his own specific vocation or mission in life; everyone must carry out a concrete assignment that demands fulfillment. Therein he cannot be replaced, nor can his life be repeated, thus, everyone's task is unique as his specific opportunity to implement it," he wrote. He urged people to find the particular meaning for their individual life, the task that only they were able to do to serve other people, no matter how small, how menial or how hidden it might be.

What Frankl is saying here gets close to real hope in the face of suffering. We do not have to be prisoners to our circumstances. We can choose how we respond. But what is missing from his assessment of hope is the person and promises of God. We each have meaning and a purpose for our lives, a God-given task to do, and it is for this reason that we continue to live even when we suffer (Philippians 1:19-26).

Our culture so prizes happiness that we have made "pursuit of happiness" a fundamental right of each human being. But for many, life is hard, and happiness may be out of reach. When happiness is our goal, we believe we require a set of circumstances in order to achieve it. If that circumstance is taken from us, we react in anger or despair. As Paul Brand observes, "happiness tends to recede from those who pursue it. Ever elusive, it appears at unexpected moments, as a by-product rather than a product."[2] Happiness is elusive when it is a goal in and of itself. We can, however, take as our example Jesus, who for the joy set before him endured the pain of the cross (Hebrews 12:2). Only when our hope is in God's sovereign plan can we rejoice even in our suffering (Romans 5:2-5).

Our Hope in God

The word "hope" has two meanings. It can mean "to want something to happen or be true." In that sense, the word hope does not instill much confidence. For example, if someone says, "I hope the weather's nice," or "I hope I get the promotion," the result is uncertain. Whether what is hoped for will actually happen depends on the trustworthiness of the person making the promise, as well as their ability to make it come to pass. The second, more archaic meaning of the word hope is "trust, to expect confidently."[3] God is both trustworthy and able to make His word come to pass. He alone is deserving of our hope.

The name of this book is taken from Psalm 42, and it seems fitting to visit the first part of the Psalm which we omitted from the first chapter:

> "As a deer pants for flowing streams,
>   so pants my soul for you, O God.
>
> My soul thirsts for God, for the living God.
>   When shall I come and appear before God?
>
> My tears have been my food day and night,
>   while they say to me all the day long,
>   'Where is your God?'
>
> These things I remember, as I pour out my soul:
>   how I would go with the throng
>   and lead them in procession to the house of God
>   with glad shouts and songs of praise,
>   a multitude keeping festival...
>
> Why are you cast down, O my soul,
>   and why are you in turmoil within me?
>   Hope in God; for I shall again praise him,
>   my salvation and my God" (Psalm 42:1-6a, ESV).

In this book, we have sought to understand depression, we have discussed strategies for handling depression and we have offered perspectives on living with depression. At the end of the day, however, the answer to our depression is our hope in God. The Psalmist here feels abandoned, but he remembers the feeling of deep fellowship when he worshipped with the multitudes in the presence of God. The Psalmist's only drink is now his own tears, but he remembers the delight of quenching his thirst from the flowing streams of God's presence. His soul is downcast and in turmoil. "Hope in God," he exhorts himself. Joy and delight in the Lord is waiting for him on the other side of his suffering.

We all pray for deliverance from depression. Some find that the dark clouds part, and they find themselves living in the sun again. For others, however, God allows them to continue to face the tribulation of depression, just as Paul was never delivered from his thorn in the flesh (2 Corinthians 12:7).

Charles Spurgeon understood this difficulty of walking by faith in the darkness of never-ending night:

> "[Yet] some of the best of God's people frequently walk in darkness…wrapped in a sevenfold gloom at times, and to them neither sun, nor moon, nor stars appear. Some whom I greatly love and esteem, who are, in my judgment, among the very choicest of God's people, nevertheless, travel most of the way to heaven by night. They do not rejoice in the light of God's countenance, though they trust in the shadow of his wings. They are on the way to eternal light, and yet they walk in darkness…."[4]

Those who are depressed hold the promises of future joy, but they may not experience the fullness of this joy during their time on earth (as none of us may). Our hope is not in relief from depression, because that is uncertain. Our hope is not in medications or strategies or therapies. But our hope is in God, that He is who He says He is.

This is the hope of Jeremiah, the weeping prophet, who saw his share of sorrow in life:

> "I am the man who has seen affliction by the rod of his wrath. He has driven me away and made me walk in darkness rather than light…He drew his bow and made me the target for his arrows. He pierced my heart with arrows from his quiver. I became the laughingstock of all my people; they mock me in song all day long. He has filled me with bitter herbs and sated me with gall. He has broken my teeth with gravel; he has trampled me in the dust. I have been deprived of peace; I have forgotten what prosperity is. So I say, 'My splendor is gone and all that I had hoped from the Lord.' I remember my affliction and my wandering, the bitterness and the gall. I well remember them, and my soul is downcast within me. Yet this I call to mind and therefore I have hope: Because of the Lord's great love we are not consumed, for his compassions never fail. They are new every morning; great is your faithfulness" (Lamentations 3:1-2, 12-23, NIV 1984).

Though our circumstances change, God is steadfast in His love, His compassion and His faithfulness.

Strangers in a Strange Land

Depression reminds us that the earth is not our home, a truth we too often forget. Remembering this brought Jan comfort in her depression:

> "Before my depression, if anyone had asked me then what joy was, I would probably have said something like, 'Joy in the Lord is being happy all the time because of our salvation. We should even be happy when bad things are happening, since it says in James to count it all joy when you suffer various trials.'

> "Of course, my convictions about this made me feel quite guilty, because when things were difficult I was either sad, depressed, hurt, frustrated or angry. Then I would think: 'But I'm a Christian—Christians shouldn't feel like this.' And in my deepest thoughts, I couldn't quite fathom how to be happy or filled with joy if things were really going bad.

> "When I went through a deep depression after a friend was killed in a car wreck, I just couldn't imagine ever feeling good again about anything ever. I lost all hope and seemed to be sinking deeper every day. It was like I was enveloped with a huge black fog, and I couldn't possibly find my way out, much less find any hope or care if I even lived anymore. My only source of hope and joy then was my longing for heaven and to be with God. I prayed and prayed for God to take me home, but of course He chose not to. Maybe this doesn't sound very joyful or hopeful, but really and truly, a Christian's only real hope is not in this sin-infested world but in the world to come.

> "One mistake I made, I believe, was assuming that joy and happiness are the same thing. Now that I am for the most part depression-free, I can see how my trials have changed my outlook and my attitude. I am not the happy, carefree person I once was. Sure, I have happy moments, and I don't live my life with a scowl on my face all the time, but even if I am not as happy with my life as I wish I could be, there are two things that do fill me with joy and hope: (1) I find joy in being able to reach out to others who have suffered in the same way as I have and to help them in their struggle in some way. (I could never do that as effectively had I not gone through my own struggles.) (2) I find joy in my continued hope for eternal life where all tears and sadness will be gone.

> "I tell my 12-year-old son, 'This life is like a vacation. We get all ready for it and go on the vacation. We have good times and even bad times on the vacation, and then when it's over, we get to go home.' Our ultimate hope and joy will be when we finally get 'home.'"

This last point is what drove the heroes of faith on, through the storms and through the dark night, through terrible persecution, even to death, as Hebrews 11:13-16 explains: "All these people were still living by faith when they died. They did not receive the things promised; they only saw them and welcomed them from a distance. And they admitted that they were aliens and strangers on earth. People who say such things show that they are looking for a country of their own. If they had been thinking of the country they had left, they would have had opportunity to return. Instead, they were longing for a better country—a heavenly one. Therefore God is not ashamed to be called their God, for he has prepared a city for them" (NIV 1984).

This truth—that we are only aliens and strangers, sojourners on this earth, and that our true home is yet to come—has tremendous power to provide hope. Our citizenship is ultimately not of any of the countries here on earth. Paul reminds us that "…our citizenship is in heaven. And we eagerly await a Savior from there, the Lord Jesus Christ" (Philippians 3:20, NIV 1984).

The Hope of Redemption

In *The Problem of Pain*, C.S. Lewis makes this observation:

> "'I reckon,' said St Paul, 'that the sufferings of this present time are not worthy to be compared with the glory that shall be revealed in us.' (Romans 8) If this is so, a book on suffering which says nothing of heaven, is leaving out almost the whole of one side of the account. Scripture and tradition habitually put the joys of heaven into the scale against the sufferings of earth, and no solution of the problem of pain which does not do so can be called a Christian one."[5]

The less we have here on earth, the more we long for heaven. For those who have the happiness and pleasure in life here on earth, talk of heaven has no charm. For as Lewis states, "It is safe to tell the pure in heart that they shall see God, for only the pure in heart want to."

The passage Lewis references is Romans 8:18-25:

> "For I consider that the sufferings of this present time are not worth comparing with the glory that is to be revealed to us. For the creation waits with eager longing for the revealing of the sons of God. For the creation was subjected to futility, not willingly, but because of him who subjected it, in hope that the creation itself will be set free from its bondage to corruption and obtain the freedom of the glory of the children of God. For we know that the whole creation has been groaning together in the pains of childbirth

until now. And not only the creation, but we ourselves, who have the firstfruits of the Spirit, groan inwardly as we wait eagerly for adoption as sons, the redemption of our bodies. For in this hope we were saved. Now hope that is seen is not hope. For who hopes for what he sees? But if we hope for what we do not see, we wait for it with patience" (ESV).

As those who inhabit broken bodies in a broken world, we long for the redemption of all creation. For those of us who struggle with mental illness, with chronic medical problems, with mental and physical disabilities, with the slow breakdown of old age or with dementia, this promise of the redemption of our bodies is particularly precious. We will one day inhabit bodies that are not broken but will function as they were intended. All creation is not simply moving toward entropy (i.e., decline into disorder, as the second law of thermodynamics states). All creation is moving in the direction of redemption, and the pains we feel here on earth are like the pains of childbirth, until God perfects His creation. All the suffering we have undergone will pale in insignificance compared to the glory that will be.

A discussion of heaven would be incomplete without the passage from Revelation that paints a glorious vision of our hope:

> "Then I saw a new heaven and a new earth, for the first heaven and the first earth had passed away, and the sea was no more. And I saw the holy city, new Jerusalem, coming down out of heaven from God, prepared as a bride adorned for her husband. And I heard a loud voice from the throne saying, 'Behold, the dwelling place of God is with man. He will dwell with them, and they will be his people, and God himself will be with them as their God. He will wipe away every tear from their eyes, and death shall be no more, neither shall there be mourning, nor crying, nor pain anymore, for the former things have passed away.' And he who was seated on the throne said, 'Behold, I am making all things new'…" (Revelation 21:1-5, ESV).

How painfully we do long for heaven! How we long to see the church in all its splendor and glory, as she awaits the wedding to her bridegroom Jesus. How we long not to just know the presence of God but to be able to see and feel His presence dwelling with us. How we long to truly know that we belong to God and He belongs to us. How we long for that day when there will be neither tears, nor death, nor grief, nor pain.

And in the meantime, while we wait for His kingdom to come and His will to be done, we encourage each other: "Wait for the Lord; be strong, and let your heart take courage; wait for the Lord!" (Psalm 27:14, ESV).

Endnotes

1. Frankl, Viktor Emil. Man's Search for Meaning. United Kingdom, Beacon Press, 2006. p75.

2. Brand and Yancey. *The Gift of Pain*. p291.

3. Merriam Webster Dictionary, https://www.merriam-webster.com/dictionary/hope)

4. CH Spurgeon, Sermons, vol 18. (New York: Funk and Wagnalls, n.d.), 351-521

5. CS Lewis, The Problem of Pain

Appendix: Suggested Reading

Depression

Eswine, Zach. *Spurgeon's Sorrows: Realistic Hope for Those Who Suffer from Depression.* Fearn, UK: Christian Focus Publications, 2015.

Lundy, Michael and JI Packer. *Depression, Anxiety, and the Christian Life: Practical Wisdom from Richard Baxter.* Wheaton, IL: Crossway, 2018.

Welch, Edward. *Depression: Looking Up From the Stubborn Darkness.* Greensboro, NC: New Growth Press, 2011

Bipolar Disorder/Memoir

Greene-McCreight, Kathryn. *Darkness Is My Only Companion.* Grand Rapids, MI: Brazos Press, 2015.

Biography / Memoir

Dravecky, Jan. *A Joy I'd Never Known.* Grand Rapids: Zondervan, 1996.

Koenig, Harold G. *The Healing Connection.* Nashville: Word, 2000.

Tada, Joni Eareckson. *Joni: An Unforgettable Story.* Grand Rapids, MI: Zondervan, 2001.

Thurman, Debbie. *From Depression to Wholeness.* Monroe, Va.: Cedar House, 2000.

Walsh, Sheila. *Honestly.* Grand Rapids: Zondervan, 1996.

Cognitive Behavioral Therapy Self Help

Gillihan, Seth. *Cognitive Behavioral Therapy Made Simple.* Emeryville, CA: Althea, 2018.

Burns, David. *The Feeling Good Handbook.* New York, NY: Penguin, 1999.

Suffering and the Problem of Evil

Biebel, David. *If God Is So Good, Why Do I Hurt So Bad?* Grand Rapids: Revell, 1995

Clarkson, Margaret. *Grace Grows Best in Winter.* Grand Rapids, MI: Zondervan, 1984.

Keller, Timothy. *Walking with God Through Pain and Suffering.* New York, NY: Penguin, 2013.

Kreeft, Peter. *Making Sense out of Suffering.* Ann Arbor: Servant, 1986.

Lewis, C. S. *The Problem of Pain.* New York, NY: Harper Collins, 1996.

Nouwen, Henri. *The Wounded Healer*. New York: Doubleday, 1979.

Powlison, David. *God's Grace in Your Suffering*. Wheaton, IL: Crossway, 2018.

Schaefer, Edith. *Affliction: A Compassionate Look at the Reality of Pain and Suffering*. Old Tappan, N.J.: Revell, 1978.

Tada, Joni Eareckson, and Steve Estes. *When God Weeps: Why Our Sufferings Matter to the Almighty*. Grand Rapids: Zondervan, 1996.

Yancey, Phillip. *Where is God When it Hurts?* Grand Rapids, MI: Zondervan, 2002.

Lament

Pemberton, Glenn. Hurting *With God: Learning to Lament with the Psalms*. Abiliene, TX: ACU Press, 2012.

Vroegop, Mark. *Dark Clouds Deep Mercy: Discovering the Grace of Lament*. Wheaton, IL: Crossway, 2019.

Family Members and Friends

Strauss, Claudia. *Talking to Depression: Simple Ways to Connect When Someone In Your Life is Depressed*. New York, NY: Penguin, 2004.

Rosen, Claudia, and Xavier Amador. *When Someone You Love is Depressed: How to Help Your Loved One without Losing Yourself*. New York, NY: Fireside, 2016.

Golant, Mitch and Susan Golant. *What To Do When Someone You Love is Depressed*. New York, NY: Holt, 2007.

Biebel, David B. *How to Help a Heartbroken Friend*. Grand Rapids: Revell, 1993.

Graham, Ruth Bell. *Prodigals and Those Who Love Them*. Grand Rapids: Baker, 1999.

Mental Health Clinicians

Pearce, Michelle. *Cognitive Behavioral Therapy for Christians with Depression: A Practical Tool Based Primer*. West Conshohocken, PA: Templeton Press, 2016.

Tan, Siang-Yang. *Counseling and Psychotherapy: A Christian Perspective*. Grand Rapids, MI: Baker Academic, 2011.

Yalom, Irvin. *The Gift of Therapy*. New York: Harper, 2017.

Author Bios

Jennifer Huang Harris, MD

Dr. Jennifer Huang Harris is a board certified outpatient psychiatrist at the Brigham and Women's Hospital in Boston, Massachusetts and an instructor in psychiatry at Harvard Medical School. After graduating from Stanford University, she studied how Christianity informs psychiatry in a post-graduate fellowship with the Trinity Forum Academy. She subsequently earned her medical degree at the University of Texas Southwestern and was trained in psychiatry at both the University of Texas Southwestern and Cambridge Health Alliance/Harvard Medical School. She has written and taught on the subjects of trauma, spirituality, cross-cultural issues, psychiatric nosology and ethics, psychotherapy and medical education. She lives in Boston with her husband and three children.

Harold G. Koenig, MD, MHSc

Dr. Koenig completed his undergraduate education at Stanford University, medical school at the University of California San Francisco and geriatric medicine, psychiatry and biostatistics training (MHSc) at Duke University. He is Professor of Psychiatry and Behavioral Sciences and Associate Professor of Medicine at Duke, and he is an Adjunct Professor in the Department of Medicine at King Abdulaziz University, Jeddah, Saudi Arabia, and the School of Public Health at Ningxia Medical University, Yinchuan, China. He directs Duke University's Center for Spirituality, Theology and Health (https://spiritualityandhealth. duke.edu/) and has done so since its origins in 1998. Dr. Koenig has written more than 500 scientific peer-reviewed academic publications, nearly 100 book chapters and more than 50 books. He has also given testimony before the U.S. Senate, the U.S. House of Representatives and the current White House Administration on the health benefits of religious faith. In 2012, he received the Oskar Pfister Award from the American Psychiatric Association, and he is the lead author of the Handbook of Religion and Health, 3rd edition (2021, forthcoming, with Harvard University professors Tyler VanderWeele and John R. Peteet).

John R. Peteet, MD

After receiving his medical degree at Columbia University, Dr. Peteet completed a medical internship at University of North Carolina in Chapel Hill, a residency in psychiatry at the Massachusetts Mental Health Center and a fellowship at the Peter Bent Brigham Hospital in Boston. For more than 40 years, he has been a psychiatrist at Brigham and Women's Hospital and Dana-Farber Cancer Institute, where he is an Associate Professor of Psychiatry at Harvard Medical School. A Distinguished Life Fellow of the American Psychiatric Association and 2020 recipient of the Oskar Pfister Award, he has received several teaching awards and published numerous papers in the areas of psychosocial oncology, addiction and the clinical interface between spirituality/religion and psychiatry. He has authored or co-edited nine books, including Doing the Right Thing: An Approach to Moral Issues in Mental Health Treatment, Depression and the Soul and The Soul of Medicine: Spiritual Perspectives and Clinical Practice. He has served as president of the American Psychiatric Association's Caucus on Religion, Spirituality and Psychiatry.

Larkin E. Kao, MD

Dr. Kao is a consultation-liaison psychiatrist at the VA Boston Healthcare System and Assistant Professor of Psychiatry at Boston University School of Medicine. She completed medical school at the University of California San Francisco School of Medicine, residency in adult psychiatry at Boston University Medical Center and fellowship in consultation-liaison psychiatry at Brigham and Women's Hospital. She serves as site director for Boston University School of Medicine clerkship students and psychiatry residents rotating on the consultation-liaison psychiatry service at VA Boston. Her current scholarly work focuses on the connections between psychiatry and spirituality/religion.

Index

CPSIA information can be obtained
at www.ICGtesting.com
Printed in the USA
JSHW011500010720
6435JS00003B/6